# Sports Law in Macedonia

# Sports Law in Macedonia

**Goce Naumovski**
**Marija Ignjatović**
**Dimtri Chapkanov**
**Goran Stanković**

This book was originally published as a monograph in the International Encyclopaedia of Laws/Sports Law.

Founding Editor: Roger Blanpain
General Editor: Frank Hendrickx
Volume Editor: Michele Colucci

Wolters Kluwer

*Published by:*
Kluwer Law International B.V.
PO Box 316
2400 AH Alphen aan den Rijn
The Netherlands
E-mail: lrs-sales@wolterskluwer.com
Website: www.wolterskluwer.com/en/solutions/kluwerlawinternational

*Sold and distributed by:*
Wolters Kluwer Legal & Regulatory U.S.
920 Links Avenue
Landisville, PA 17538
United States of America
E-mail: customer.service@wolterskluwer.com



ISBN 978-94-035-2846-5

e-Book: ISBN 978-94-035-2966-0
web-PDF: ISBN 978-94-035-2976-9

# The Authors

Dr. Goce Naumovski holds an L.L.B., LL.M. and Ph.D. in Legal Sciences from the SS. Cyril and Methodius University in Skopje and a Ph.D. in Private Law from the University of Strasbourg. He is a professor at the Faculty of Law "Iustinianus Primus" of the SS. Cyril and Methodius University in Skopje, Macedonia, where he has been teaching Sports Law, Roman Law, Trademark Law and Information Technology Law. In 2009, he was a visiting scholar at the Kernochan Center for Law, Media, and the Arts at Columbia University in New York. Professor Naumovski was co-chair of the Double Degree LL.M./DU program of Intellectual Property Law, jointly organized by the SS. Cyril and Methodius University and the University of Strasbourg, with participation of professors from the European Intellectual Property Institutes Network (EIPIN). He is a member of the *Lex Sportiva* Sports Law Association, the International Association for the Advancement of Teaching and Research in Intellectual Property (ATRIP), the Argumentum Research Association, etc. He regularly participates in several international professional and scientific conferences and realizes study stays, including WIPO/WTO Colloquium for Teachers of Intellectual Property; Commercial Law Development Program/Intellectual Property Program of the US Patent and Trademark Office; at the Center for International Intellectual Property Studies (CEIPI), University of Strasbourg, France; at the University "Macedonia" in Thessaloniki, Greece; Sofia University St. Kliment Ohridski and others.

He is the author or co-author of over eighty scientific and professional papers, many of which are in the field of sports law. Dr. Naumovski is fluent in English, Greek, French, Croatian, Serbian, Bulgarian, Albanian and Latin.

## The Authors

Prof. Dr. Marija Ignjatović was born in 1974 in Niš, Republic of Serbia. She graduated in 1989 from the Faculty of Law, University of Niš. She received her Master's in 2005 at the Faculty of Law "Justinijan Prvi" of the University "sv. Kiril i Metodij," in Skopje, Republic of Northern Macedonia. She received her Ph.D. in 2009 at the Faculty of Law "Justinijan Prvi" of the University "sv. Kiril i Metodij," in Skopje, Republic of Northern Macedonia. She has published a large number of scientific and professional papers. She has participated in numerous scientific and professional conferences of national and international importance in the country and abroad. She is the vice president of the Balkan Association for Roman Law and Roman Legal Tradition (SIR). She is a member of the World Association of Historians of the Laws of the Antiquity (SHIDA). She is the vice president of the Supervisory Board of the Science Fund of the Republic of Serbia. She is a member of the *Lex Sportiva* Sports Association (Macedonia). She is a visiting professor at the state law faculties in Skopje, Republic of Northern Macedonia, Sofia, Republic of Bulgaria, and Parma, Republic of Italy. She is a full professor at the Faculty of Law, University of Niš, Republic of Serbia.

Dr. Dimitri Chapkanov is both lawyer and psychologist and currently works at the SS. Cyril and Methodius University in Skopje. Dr. Chapkanov is president of the Macedonian Sports Law Association *Lex Sportiva.*

He holds a Ph.D. in Legal Sciences, LL.M. and DU (Strasbourg) in Intellectual Property, M.A. and B.A. in Psychology and L.L.B. in Law (SS. Cyril and Methodius University). He is the author of thirty scientific and professional papers, mainly in the field of sports law and information technology law. Dimitri has participated in numerous sports law projects on topics that included relations of sports with games of chance, broadcasting of sports events, legal psychology, and reforms of higher education. He is fluent in Greek and English.

Goran Stanković graduated from the Faculty of Law, Security and Management in Niš "Konstantin Veliki." He received his master's degree in 2020 from the Faculty of Law at "Justinijan Prvi" University "sv. Kirili Metodij" in Skopje, Republic of Northern Macedonia. He is a member of the *Lex Sportiva* Sports Law Association (Macedonia). He is a member of the Management Board of the Association of Sports Journalists of Serbia and a long-term president of the Sports Organization "Sports Journalist." He is a professional sports journalist with twenty-five years of experience as an editor, journalist, and presenter in local, regional and state media (TV5 Niš, TV Copernicus, Public Service Radio Television of Serbia, List "Sport," TV Zona Plus). He is also the author of a large number of television shows, documentaries and publications in the field of sports journalism and sports law (TV shows "Sports Zone," "Sports of Southeast Serbia," "Local Sports Idols," publications "Sports in Serbia" of the Association of Sports Journalists of Serbia, "Sports Bulletin of the Sports Association of Niš "). He is the holder of the award of the best sports journalist in the city of Niš for 2020.

**The Authors**

# Table of Contents

# List of Abbreviations

| | |
|---|---|
| MPC | Macedonian Paralympic Committee |
| NFSRDM-MPC | The National Federation for Sports and Recreation of the Disabled of Macedonia-Macedonian Paralympic Committee |
| FFM | Football Federation of Macedonia |
| RFM | Handball Federation of Macedonia |
| IHF | International Handball Federation |
| EHF | European Handball Federation |
| ECTS | European Credit Transfer System |
| RFA | Regional Football Associations |
| MFA | Municipal Football Associations |
| IFAB | International Football Association Board |
| CAS | Court of Sport Arbitration |
| IOC | International Olympic Committee |
| FIFA | Fédération Internationale de Football Association |
| UEFA | Union of European Football Associations |
| KFSM | Basketball Federation of North Macedonia |

## List of Abbreviations

# General Introduction

## Chapter 1. General Background

### §1. Philosophical, Societal, and Legal Aspects of Sport

*1.* The issue of regulation of sports and sports activities in contemporary society is more important than ever. The reasons for these tendencies lie in several spheres. The presence of negative situations in the sports fields, as well as the actualization of dilemmas concerning athletes and sports organizations, are the core of this issue.

*2.* Each legal system regulates the care for sports in principle in the constitution of the country, while specific laws on sports are being enacted for the purpose of detailed regulation of its practice. Also, the process of European integration requires certain activities of countries aspiring for membership in the Union in the area of harmonization of the legislation that treats sport as an activity. In this constellation, sports law, according to its merits, obtains a place in the legal system and in legal practice.[1]

*3.* In a broader philosophical sense, sport is considered one of the phenomena related to "homo ludens" (man, the player), a concept developed by Huizinga, in which sport has an expressively significant compensatory phenomenon of great significance to modern society that has penetrated numerous areas.[2] Furthermore, competition in skills, strength and endurance has an important place in each culture.[3]

*4.* In order to be able to talk about the roles and significance of sport in the legal context, the question of the origin and meaning of the term sport itself necessarily arises as a preliminary question.

*5.* The term "sport," as a generic term, has a wide modern practical use and is generally accepted in modern speech, and has its origin in Latin (*disportō*, āre,[4] or

1. G. Naumovski, *The Importance of Certain Roman Law Solutions for Contemporary Sports Law*, 2nd FIEP Congress, Proceedings, Vrnjacka Banja, 2004, pp. 481–486.
2. J. Huizinga, Homo Ludens: A Study of the Play-Element in Culture, Angelico Press, 2016.
3. *Ibid.*
4. Du Cange, et al., Glossarium mediae et infimae latinitatis, éd. augm., Niort: L. Favre, 1883–1887, t. 3, col. 141a.

deportō, āre[5] which could be translated as "to carry away"), with an emphasis on leisure, play. The medieval Latin term disportare was used in archaic Italian as "to have fun" or "to entertain." The Old French *deporter, -ourter; desporter (amuser, réjouir),*[6] as well as the Middle English term "sporten (to divert),"[7] are also considered etymological pillars of the contemporary term "sport." The term "sport" is being accepted and is in regular worldwide use to this day.

*6.* Sport is a multidisciplinary activity for the study of which numerous scientific fields are interested (medicine, biology, psychology, sociology, law, as well as many other natural and social-humanistic sciences and scientific disciplines), and due to its importance for society, the state itself.

*7.* Although attempts to provide a definition of sport are challenging, one of the most comprehensive definition is given by Coakley, who describe sports as "competitive activities that involve vigorous physical exertion or the use of relatively complex physical skills by individuals whose participation is motivated by a combination of intrinsic and extrinsic factors."[8]

*8.* Further definitions of sport label it as "free physical human activity oriented towards development of psychophysical abilities."[9] In this manner, sport can be viewed as: (1) top sport (sport with the aim of realizing top competitive results); (2) school sport (characterized in a class of physical education in schools, aiming at the development of children and youth); and (3) sport for everyone (recreation, which is defined as "an area that comprises engaging in sports activities for relaxation and recreation, refining health or improving personal outcomes in all segments of the population").[10] Awareness of the significance of sport for human health subsidizes the global acceptance and application of health advancement policies that accentuate sport and its vital role in protecting human health.[11]

*9.* Since antiquity, people have contested in numerous sports, and the victors have acquired the position of heroes. In the Middle Ages, beneath the severe impact of religion and the realization that earthly life is temporary and that actual life begins afterward, the physical death sport was frequently considered a course, ruthless and harsh physical activity. In contemporary culture, the traditional concept that sport signifies educational societal phenomenon merged with game, whose objective is the physical and spiritual enhancement of character, augments with including new dimensions.

---

5. E. Forcellini, Totius Latinitatis Lexicon, Tomus Secundus, p. 73.
6. F.Godefroy, Dictionnaire de l'ancienne langue française et de tous ses dialectes du IXe au XVe siècle, Tome deuxième, Casteillon-Dyvis, F. Vieweg, Paris, 1883, p. 517, 634.
7. S. Gardiner, J. O'Leary, R. Welch, S. Boyers, U. Naidoo, Sports Law, Routledge, 2012, p. 13.
8. J. Coakley, Sport in Society: Issues and Controversies, Mosbey. 1994, p. 21.
9. B. Nešić, Sportsko pravo, Sportska akademija, Beograd, 2020, 70.
10. *See* Branimir Nešić, supra, 71–72.
11. B. Jorgić, M. Aleksandrović, F. Mirić, H. Čolović, L. Dimitrijević, Holistički pristup adaptiranoj fitičkoj aktivnostim, Fakultet sporta i fizičkog vaspitanja Univerziteta u Nišu, Niš, 2020, 8.

*10.* Hence, contemporary sport is a flexible notion that elaborates more on the athlete than on the sport itself. Consequently, from the aspect of sportspersons, sport is a rigid competition for conquest or for a record and from the point of view of a coach, it is a way of living. Sport fans are attracted to sport events due to the uncertainty of the outcome of the contest between opponents, whereas sociologists and social psychologists understand sport as a means of meeting the needs during the sport battle. Contemporary sport also faces challenges, such as use of illicit substances, match-fixing, athletes' status abuse for personal enrichment, etc. Therefore, the chore of contemporary society is to prevent and defeat harmful doings as much as possible and to return all constructive features to sports as a planned activity. A significant tool for accomplishing this objective is the standards of sports law.

*11.* At the same time, the name *L*ex Sportiva can often be heard for these rules. There is a special danger in the case of identifying the term lex sports with the term sports law, insisting on its autonomous and supranational character. In this way, attention is diverted from the norms of national legislation and the norms of international public law, which in recent years have become increasingly important in regulating social relations in sports.[12]

12. See, M Galactic, Lex sportiva – Origin and Meaning of the Term, Themes, XXXIX, edition 2, Niš, 2015, 559–577.

# Chapter 2. Specificity of Sports Law

## §1. Sports Law as a Branch of Law and Academic Field of Legal Science

*12.* Having in mind the above features, legal regulation of sports has imposed the requirement to develop a special branch of law—sports law,[13] which is more and more becoming attractive to the academic community in general, and legal theory in particular, especially for the purpose to determine the place of sports law in the legal system and legal practice.

*13.* In this context, sports law is in specific relations with the following legal disciplines: civil law (property issues of sports in general and the property of sports fields as well), commercial law and company law (management of sports clubs), intellectual property law (both industrial property law and copyright and related rights, especially in terms of broadcasting rights); labor law (transfer and movement of athletes); criminal law (particularly regarding acts committed at sports events and doping); public international law, private international law, etc.

*14.* The basic dilemma of legal academics that emerges from the above circumstances is whether sports law is a branch of public or private law, i.e., whether, given the broad social influence and public function of sport, sports law is a branch of public law,[14] or it pertains to the private law area, due to the importance of sports law rules that derive from the individual interest.[15] According to a third opinion, sports law is a legal discipline sui generis (in itself, independent), which aims to emphasize its multidisciplinary approach, which has a goal to indicate the equal influence of public and private law in the development of sports law as a separate branch of law. This concept affirms sports law as an exclusive field of law, equally targeting both public and private law, a concept that is also reflected in legal science.

*15.* Modern legal theory summarizes these approaches in a twofold definition that reiterates the legitimacy of sports law as a separate branch, i.e., a collection of rules that (1) regulate sports activities; and (2) establish their organization.[16]

*16.* One of the basic assumptions for the aspiration of sports law to become a well-established field of legal science is the fostering of application of a wide spectrum of specific methods and techniques for scientific research for the purpose of

---

13. In contemporary science, there is a dilemma which of the two terms Sports law or Law in sports is more appropriate. The first term is generally used by legal science, while the second is present in sports sciences.
14. Naumovski G. (2004).The Importance of Certain Roman Law Solutions for Contemporary Sports Law, 2nd FIEP Congress, Proceedings, Vrnjacka Banja, 2004, p. 482.
15. It seems that the assertions deriving from the individual interest criterion given the private law definition has a theoretical foundation in the public and private law distinction provided in legal theory: Publicum ius est quod ad statum rei Romanae spectat, privatum quod ad singulorum utilitatem pertinet (Inst, 1.1.1, 2)
16. F. Buy, J. Marmayou, D. Poracchia, F. Rizzo, Droit du Sport, LGDJ, Lextenso edition, 2015, p. 34.

acquiring new scientific knowledge and verification of various hypotheses related to the subject of sports law research. Similar to sport management, sports law research, besides the historical and normative method, should include application of quantitative statistical methods, particularly empirical jurisprudence, which would lead to novel impartial findings.

## §2. The Notion of *Lex Sportiva*

*17.* There are several meanings of *lex sportiva* in contemporary sports law science. As noted by Djudrjevic, Micovic and Vukovic,[17] some authors consider *lex sportiva* as legal order created by international organizations on a contractual basis, i.e., a legitimacy emerging from the subordination of national federations, being in that way a global sports law with the characteristic of a private system which is confirmed by the existence of a global forum—the Court of Sport Arbitration (CAS).[18] Other conceptions outline that *lex sportiva* consists of several pillars: (1) the rules of the international federations as transnational supplementary system; (2) the decisions of the CAS and the World Anti-doping Agency that provide harmonization of the standards in different sports, including the procedural equity, the right of precise information, the protection from misuse and unjust decision of sport federation, etc.[19]

*18.* Panagiotopoulos provides a wider definition, outlining *lex sportiva* as "legal order that incorporates state-adopted law and the law adopted by the national and international bodies representing organized sport," being in this way "non-national law which claims for oneself direct and preferential application with national sports legal orders and the par excellence law in sports life."[20]

*19.* Due to the significance of international arbitration, certain scholars consider *lex sportiva* as the ultimate vehicle for independent and worldwide sports law that encompasses federations regulations, customs and general principles.[21]

*20.* Similarly to the benefit of applying the *lex mercatoria* concept and its advantages in the foundation of other new legal branches, *lex sportiva* is a vital determinant of contemporary sports law.[22] This feature is also present in Macedonian sports law.

---

17. N. Djurdjevic, M, Micovic, Z, Vukovic, 2014, Ugovori u Sportu, Pravni fakultet Univerziteta u Kragujevcu, 2014, p. 34.
18. *Ibid.*
19. *Ibid.*, p. 35
20. D. Panagiotopoulos, Sports Law, Lex Sportiva & Lex Olympica, Biblioedit, Athens, 2017, p. 105.
21. F. Buy, J.M. Marmayou, D. Poracchia, F. Rizzo, Droit du Sport, LGDJ, 2015, 38.
22. *Ibid.*

## §3. Historical Aspects of Regulation of Sports Activities

*21.* The evaluation of historical legal sources can play a considerable role in confirmation, improvement and advancement of sports law as a new legal discipline. This role has numerous elements. For instance, the significance of usage of the historical method in the research of legal phenomena related to sports activities is very significant, having in mind the character of historical legal science.

*22.* Coming to conclusions for contemporary sports law requires research of a variety of legal and social-economic circumstances through history (the laws of antiquity, as well as medieval law and modern history law). As noted above, one of the current problems is also the determination of the place of sports law as a new discipline in the private law system.

*23.* An example of the importance of sport activities and dance and their regulation for contemporary Macedonian culture, i.e., its continuity since antiquity until today, is the Maenad, a small bronze statue representing a dancer-follower of Dionysus, dating from 530-520 BC discovered in the center of Tetovo in 1933. Many scholars[23] believe that its representation in dancing position resembles the contemporary 2/4 time signature folk dance "Tresenica" from the Mariovo region.

*24.* The analysis of available literature indicates that historical science has not sufficiently treated the regulation of sport activities in Macedonia in antiquity, particularly regarding Upper Macedonia, which reaffirms the challenge to address these issues in subsequent research.

*25.* Due to the Roman conquest of Macedonia, after the end of the third Roman-Macedonian war in 168 BC, given the fact that Macedonia became a formal Roman province in 146 BC, it could be concluded that Roman law was introduced in Macedonia.[24] Under Roman rule, Macedonia was divided into two provinces: Macedonia Prima and Macedonia Salutaris/Macedonia Secunda.

*26.* In the Roman provinces of Macedonia, organized games (especially gladiators' fights), as well as fights with wild beasts (venationes), were present in the theater of Stobi, especially in the first century with the enhanced colonization of Roman veterans.[25] Furthermore, evidence of sport activities is found in the ancient city of Scupi (today's Skopje), particularly those dating from the time of Diocletian

---

23. *See*: Dimova, K. (1978). Za tancot na Tetovskata Menada [On the Dance of the Maenad of Tetovo. In Macedonian]. Prilozi za istorijata na fizičkata kultura na Makedonija, Komitet za fizička kultura na SRM, 4, pp. 109–112.
24. For these and other notions on history of private law in Macedonia, see: Naumovski, G. (2004). The Concept of Societas in Justinina's Legislation, Proceedings of the International Symposium "Contemporary Law, Legal Science and Justinians Codification," Faculty of Law Skopje, Skopje and Ohrid, 2004, pp. 515–523.
25. *See*: Stanimirovic D. (1976), Svedoštva za gladijatorski borbi vo antickiot grad Stobi [Testimonies for Gladiators' Fight in the Ancient City of Stobi. In Macedonian]. Prilozi za istorijata na fizičkata kultura na Makedonija, Komitet za fizička kultura na SRM, 2, pp. 107–114.

as well as later when Scupi became the seat of the bishopric.[26] Swimming, games with large and small balls (similar to contemporary tennis), as well as jumping, running, throwing sports, and wrestling, were everyday activities in the thermae, palestrae and esplanades.[27] Of particular interest are also historical sources regarding the sport activities and rules of work (particularly oil supply) of the gymnasium in Styberra on the Erigon River (near today's Prilep).[28]

*27.* The roman proverb "*Mens sana in corpore sano* (a sound mind in a sound body)"[29] is the best proof of the status of physical activities in ancient Roman society. Among the most important sport games were: *expulsium ludere* (a type of today's handball), *trigon* (similar to baseball or softball), *harpastum* (that looked a bit like American football), *pila* (passing a ball to a player who was in the middle, trying to catch it). From individual sports, wrestling was the main sport. However, part of the so-called manifestations of "panem et circenses (bread and games)," besides the games of the gladiators, were the chariot races, being held at "Circus Maximus (the Great Circle)" in the city of Rome. The status of gladiators was very specific since they were persons to which a special civic penalty-*capitis deminutio maxima* was imposed, i.e., they were deprived of their freedom and citizenship). Identification of these persons with free persons that practice sports is impossible, not only from the aspect of *ius quod ad personas pertinet* (the law that refers to persons) but due to the absence of a humanistic dimension of the fight.[30]

*28.* This is a sufficient reason to analyze Roman law sources that regulate sport activities. Furthermore, the role of Roman law is crucial in a general sports law context too since Roman law is a systematic basis of contemporary private law, particularly in the states that belong to the so-called roman-German legal family.[31]

*29.* The importance of roman casuistic is also interesting since it has formed different solutions for numerous situations (in)directly related to sport activities. Most of these solutions, without serious difficulties, could be today fitted in national legislatures. The narrow connection of these solutions with the philosophical principles gives the opportunity to affirm the principles in order to prevent the abuse of sports in any way.

---

26. *See*: Stanimirovic D. (1977), Aktivnostite na fizičkata kultura vo rimskite termi so poseben osvrt na tie vo antičkiot grad Skupi [Activities of Physical Culture in Roman Thermae with special reference to those of the Ancient City of Scupi. In Macedonian]. Skopje, Prilozi za istorijata na fizičkata kultura na Makedonija, Komitet za fizička kultura na SRM, 3, pp. 103–114.
27. *Ibid.*
28. *See*: Stanimirovic D. (1975). Gimnazium vo antickiot grad Stibera [The Gymnasium in the Ancient City of Styberra. In Macedonian]. Prilozi za istorijata na fizičkata kultura na Makedonija, Komitet za fizička kultura na SRM, 1, pp. 93–112.
29. Juvenal, 10.356.
30. Naumovski G. (2004).*The Importance of Certain Roman Law Solutions for Contemporary Sports Law*, 2nd FIEP Congress, Proceedings, Vrnjacka Banja, 2004, p. 482.
31. Naumovski, G., Akimovska, P.M., Naumovski V., (2011), *Roman Law and The Foundations Of Contemporary Sports law: The Approach Of Justinian's Legislation*, Research in Kinesiology, 39(2), pp. 197–200.

*30.* Certain sports law scientists within the context of Roman law examine the concept of "certaminia" (contest, fight, rivalry, clash) presented by Gualazzini.[32] According to this concept, normative solutions of Roman law regulate the contests globally in the texts of the laws, while there is a so-called ordo certaminis, as a specific bylaw for each type of sport contest. "Ordo certaminis" contains the rights and obligations of the contestants and the organizers.[33]

*31.* Up until now, Roman law scholars have rarely treated the issue of legal provisions concerning status of athletes and other issues of sports in Ancient Rome in all three periods of development of roman state and law.[34] Yet, through the prism of several Roman law sources, one can come to certain facts about the status of athletes and the rules that did (not) apply at the sport fields. The analysis of these solutions might be a contribution toward improvement of the legal solutions for sports in our time.

*32.* In the context of cultural and legal heritage is the emergence on the historical scene of the Byzantine Emperor Justinian I (482-565), born as Petrus Sabbatius, in Tauresium (nowadays the village of Taor near the capital city of Skopje), known for his legislation (later known as Corpus Iuris Civilis), one of the greatest achievements for the foundation of contemporary legal science, especially in the area of private law.

*33.* The analysis of Justinian's legislation shows that in the frames of legislation activities of the emperors, which were characteristic of the post-classical Roman law, a suitable place was found for the issues of law in sports. Generally, two types of solutions were made: First, solutions that refer to rules of sport games and their effects on everyday life, and second, solutions concerning status of athletes in roman society. Sources of Roman law have connected both groups of solutions with outstanding art and technique.[35]

*34.* In this context, the main characteristic of its Digest is the presentation of specific cases, as examined by classical jurisprudence. In this way, the aim of the Digest is successful application as well as harmonization of these institutes, which means successful realization of interests of all persons.[36] One of the best examples of this tendency is the rule for reparatio damni in the circumstances of sport contests or

---

32. Povil, A.C, and Paloma, J.C.B. (1998). *Origin of Sports Law. Fundamental Principles of Sports Law. Law in Sport. Tempus Joint European Project*, Lectures and Summaries of the Intensive Course. Sofia: National Sports Academy.
33. *Ibid.*
34. Amelotti, M., (1955). Laposizione degli atleti di fronte al diritto Romano, Studia et Documenta Historiae etIuris, 32, pp. 123–156.
35. Naumovski, G., Akimovska, P.M., Naumovski V., 2011, *Roman Law and The Foundations Of Contemporary Sports law: The Approach Of Justinian's Legislation*, Research in Kinesiology, 39(2), pp. 197–200.
36. Ankum, H., (1995). Societas Omnium Bonorum and Dos in Classical Roman Law. Israel Law Review, 29(1–2), pp. 105–129.

games. In one of the provisions of the Digest, an accent is made on the ways to discharge from liability an athlete (a wrestler or a boxer) who has killed his opponent in a public fight[37] This case deals with exemption from the rules for claim of damages (reparatio damni), as determined by Lex Aquilia de damno.[38]

*35.* Certain provisions of the Digest deal with cases of deaths and injury as a consequence of sport contests in a very detailed way. For instance, it was anticipated that if during a ball game, the ball falls on the hand of a barber who is shaving a slave at that moment, if the razor cuts the throat of the slave, according to Lex Aquilia, the barber will be responsible for negligence (*negligentia*), since, to a certain degree, he is responsible for performing his business in a place where usually a ball is played, although there is partial responsibility of the shaved, since he has accepted to be shaved at such dangerous place.[39,40]

*36.* In the matter of whether sport contests could be a source of obligations, the issue of award-winning is prescribed for only specific sport disciplines. Awards were anticipated only if the aim of the game was demonstration of courage. These games were considered as allowed "games for money (*pecunuim ludere*).[41] In all other cases, playing for money was forbidden. The Digest provided the possibility for a loan to an athlete, but the athlete was obliged to return the loan (with appropriate interest) only if he won.[42] In other words, placing such condition as an element of the contract points out the high quality of roman athletes.[43] The fact that mechanisms for financial aid exist shows the roots of the contracts for sponsorship that exist today.[44]

*37.* Athletes enjoyed favorable positions and distinctions in Roman society. Roman statutory law contains several provisions that prove this assertion. Athletes

---

37. D.9.2.7, 4.
38. Lex Aquilia de damno is a source of old Roman law (enacted in 287 B.C.) for the purpose of regulation of compensation of damages, i.e., obligations deriving from torts. However, in the specific case, the death or the injury should have been done without intention and only because of "reasons of courage and glory." This provision had exclusive validity for persons that had the right to participate in such contests (persons that had at least status libertatis), but it also used to be applied for an injured son, if he was under patria potestas, although he was not a person sui iuris. Lex Aquilia de damno was applied, which means that the injurer was responsible for the damage, if the injured was wounded during his withdrawal from the fight. Such legal frame would allow the Roman judge to determine the truth and the degree of guilt of one of the fighters and by that to solve the matter (*Ibid*).
39. D. 9.2.11, pr.
40. Naumovski, G., Akimovska, P.M., Naumovski V., 2011, *Roman Law and The Foundations Of Contemporary Sports law: The Approach Of Justinian's Legislation*, Research in Kinesiology, 39(2), pp. 197–200.
41. D. 11. 5. 2. 1
42. D. 22.2.5.
43. Pleket, H.W. (2001). *Greek sport and Greek athletes*. The International Sports Law Journal, (5/6), 4–5.
44. Naumovski, G., Akimovska, P.M., Naumovski V., 2011, Roman Law and The Foundations Of Contemporary Sports law: The Approach Of Justinian's Legislation, Research in Kinesiology, 39(2), pp. 197–200.

were exempted from the duty to be guardians if they were crowned in the so-called sacred games (D.27, 1, 6, 13). Practically, it was one type of *excusationes voluntariae*, reasons that enabled persons capable of tutelage (guardianship) if they were holders of "free professions" to avoid the obligation on their demand.[45]

*38.* The Justinian's Code (Codex) reaffirms the fundamental solutions presented in the Digest, at the same time explaining the clear and precise position of state regulations on sport activities and related issues. From nomo-technical feature, one must not neglect the importance of the fourth book of the Codex, where a separate titulus (fifty-fourth) is dedicated to the athletes, also named "De Athletis (On Athletes)."[46] This provision contains the rule for exemption of athletes from all civic duties, which is an extension of the previously mentioned rule of the Digest concerning guardianship.[47] The main condition for application of the rule was, however, the fact that the athlete should have won (been crowned) in at least three formal contests during his life. At least one of those crowns should have been won in Rome or in the territory of Ancient Greece. This clear condition derived from the systematization of contests in ancient Rome. Concerning this issue, Pleket states that this provision, similar to the provision in the Digest, is related to the hierarchy of games, i.e., the existence of four types of "sacred, crown" games: Olympic, Nemean, Pythian and Isthmian Games, mentioned in Justinian's legislation and fully recognized in the world at that time.[48]

*39.* Drawing a parallel between the philosophical dimensions of law and sports is one of the outcomes of the evaluation of principles and considerations about these two social phenomena in the ancient and contemporary world. In the field of Roman law, one of the central points is the principles of classical Roman law that had a character opposite to the previous *ius civile antiquum* (that was strict and formal law). The prevailing principle of classical Roman law was the so-called *quod bonum et aequum est* (Good and equitable.), and in that context, the definition of law was "art of good and equal (*ars boni et aequi*)."[49] In this period also, the reaffirmation of philosophy of law was present by sublimation of Greek philosophy and by proclamation that moral, law and equity derive from human nature.[50]

*40.* However, in the field of sports law, several principles have been systemized. A.C. Povil and J.C.B. Paloma outline the following principles: (1) fair play that contains honesty and loyalty of athletes, accordance and acceptance of all arbitrary

45. *Ibid.*
46. C. J. 10, 54, 0, 0.
47. C. J. 10, 54, 1, 0.
48. Pleket, H.W. (2001). Greek sport and Greek athletes. The International Sports Law Journal, (5/6), 4–5.
49. D. 1,1,1,1.
50. Naumovski, G., Akimovska, P.M., Naumovski V. (2011). Roman Law and The Foundations of Contemporary Sports law: The Approach of Justinian's Legislation, Research in Kinesiology, 39(2), pp. 197–200.
C. J. 10, 54, 0, 0.

decisions without reactions, respect of the opponent and exemption of the possibility to win by any means; (2) equality of contestants and conditions (prohibition of use of illegal methods and substances); (3) prevention of discrimination on racial, political, gender and other reasons; (4) organizational autonomy of sports structures in relation to the state; and (5) unique sport federations, i.e., adoption of the principle one state-one federation.[51] The first three principles have deep philosophical dimensions, which, with no doubt, could be easily connected with the "*quod bonum et aequum*" principle of Roman law. Good faith, honesty and equity as characteristics of each athlete, coach, manager of sport clubs and each individual that participates in sport practice is a conditio sine qua non for realization of social aim of the sport activities. Maybe the best proof for the eternal validity of equity in each sphere, including law and sports, is Ulpian's maxim: "*Iuris praecepta sunt haec: honeste vivere, alteram non laedere, suum cuique tribuere*" (the following are the precepts of the Law: to live honestly, not to injure another, and to give to each one that which belongs to him).[52,53]

*41.* Byzantine law, as a continuation of Roman law, has reaffirmed the above regulations. Sports is a phenomenon of great significance in the Byzantine Empire, having in mind the rivalry between the "Blues" and the "Green" fractions (that were the leading two powers in the quadrigae, besides the Reds and the Whites). As noted by Schrodt,[54] when it comes to sports, particularly chariot racing and other competitions, "Byzantine circus fractions were more than mere sporting associations," and "they represented the political, religions, economic and social divisions of the population of Constantinople creating "an urban militia that played an important role in the city's history." This tendency has been widely accepted around the territory of the empire, having a result of their institutionalization as part of the state administration, dominated by Blues and Greens, resulting in the disappearance of the Reads and Whites.[55] Venationes continued to exist, but other sports appeared, such as the tyzkanion, a variant of Persian tschougan (predecessor of modern polo).[56]

*42.* Regarding the regulation of sport activities in Byzantine, two other issues are of importance: (1) the 399 decree of Theodosius I (Theodosius the Great) stating that: "*Just as We have already abolished profane rites by a salutary law, so We do not allow the festal assemblies of citizens and the common pleasure of all to be abolished. Hence We decree that, according to ancient custom, amusements shall be furnished to the people, but without any sacrifice or any accursed superstition, and they shall be allowed to attend festal banquets, whenever public desires so demand*

51. Povil, A.C, and Paloma, J.C.B. (1998). Origin of Sports Law. Fundamental Principles of Sports Law. Law in Sport. Tempus Joint European Project, Lectures and Summaries of the Intensive Course. Sofia: National Sports Academy.
52. D. 1, 1, 10, 1.
53. Naumovski, G., Akimovska, P.M., Naumovski V. (2011). Roman Law and The Foundations Of Contemporary Sports law: The Approach Of Justinian's Legislation, Research in Kinesiology, 39(2), pp. 197–200.
54. Schriodt, B. (1981). Sports of the Byzantine Empire. Journal of Sport History, 8(3), p. 41.
55. *Ibid.*, pp. 48–49.
56. *Ibid.*, pp. 52–53.

(CTh.16.10.17.)";[57,58] and (2) the issue of whether there is any decree forbidding the Olympic games, which remains a challenge for modern historians, having in mind the approach of Theodosian Code (438) under the rule of Theodosius II; the prohibition of pagan practices and the considerations that the last Olympic Games were held in 405 or 433.[59]

*43.* During the Ottoman Rule in Macedonia, folk (pehlivan) oil wrestling became a widely practiced sport. Other sport popular sport activities included rock throwing (from the shoulder) (frlanje na kamen od ramo vaulting (over seven real horses), long jump, shooting competitions, horse riding, etc. Most of these activities and their regulation are documented in Macedonian historiography. For example, Gjurchin Kokale, one of the prominent figures among the Mijaks, a Macedonian ethnographic group, in his autobiography, provides us valuable details on the organization and regulation of sport activities.[60] Furthermore, sport activities and competitions were organized within the Macedonian Revolutionary Organization, such as running, relay running, jumping for distance, wrestling, horse racing, stick fighting, shooting, etc.[61]

*44.* According to Pop-Gjorcev, the first football ball was brought to Bitola in 1891, while the football competitions were organized in the physical education courses in Bitola schools.[62] Until 1919, football clubs were established in Skopje, Prilep, Veles and Tetovo.[63] In this period, other sport competitions, such as horse racing and athletic competitions also started to flourish.[64]

---

57. Pharr, C. (1952): *The Theodosian Code and Novels and the Sirmondian Constitutions: A Translation with Commentary, Glossary and Bibliography*, Princeton University Press.
58. The Latin text reads (CTh.16.10.17): De paganis, sacrificiis et templis: Ut profanos ritus iam salubri lege submovimus, ita festos conventus civium et communem omnium laetitiam non patimur submoveri. Unde absque ullo sacrificio atque ulla superstitione damnabili exhiberi populo voluptates secundum veterem consuetudinem, iniri etiam festa convivia, si quando exigunt publica vota, decernimus. Imperatoris Theodosii Codex, Liber Sextus Decimus (Text submitted by Dr. Alexandr Koptev), available at: https://droitromain.univ-grenoble-alpes.fr/Constitutiones/CTh16.html#10, Accessed: May 1, 2022.
59. Schriodt, B. (1981). Sports of the Byzantine Empire. Journal of Sport History, 8(3), pp. 54–55.
60. *See*: Kuševski V. (1983). The Existence of Folk-Forms of Body Exercises and Competition among the Miacs according to Djurchin Cocale's Autobiography [Za prisustvoto I neguvanjeto na narodni formi na telesni vežbanja i natprevaruvanja srede Mijacite sportd Avtobiografijata na Gjurchin Kokale (1775–1863). In Macedonian]. Prilozi za istorijata na fizičkata kultura na Makedonija, Fakultet t za fizička kultura Skopje, 1, pp. 67–79.
61. Konstantinov D. (1978). Sport and Military Exercises of the Members of the Armed Forces of the Internal Macedonian Revolutionary Organization of the Ilinden Period (1903) [Sportski i voeni vezbi na pripadnicite na oruzenite sili od Vnatrešnata makedonska revolucionerna organizacija od ilindenskata epopeja (1903). In Macedonian]. Prilozi za istorijata na fizičkata kultura na Makedonija, Republički Komitet za Fizička Kultura Skopje, 4, pp. 67–79.
62. Pop-Gjorchev B. (1975). The Appearance and Development of Football in Macedonia until the First World War. [Pojava i razvitok na fudbalot vo Makedonija do Prvata svetska vojna. In Macedonian]. Komitet za Fizička Kultura Skopje, 1 pp. 83–86.
63. *Ibid.*
64. *See*: Stanimirovic D. (1975). Elements and Appearance of Modern Sports in Macedonian until World War I. [Elementi i pojavi na modernite sportovi vo Makedonija do Prvata svetska vojna. In Macedonian]. Komitet za Fizička Kultura Skopje, 1 pp. 73–82.

*45.* During the Yugoslav kingdom, a crucial factor was the appearance of the so-called Sokol gymnastics movement. According to Stanimirovic,[65] societies in the following cities we reorganized: Kumanovo (1909), Skopje (1910), Tetovo (1910) and Kriva Palanka (1912). After the wars (1912–1918), the activity of the societies was renewed, and new ones were established. Since 1930, this movement has also expanded in Kumanovo, Prilep, Gostivar, Kocani, Kicevo, Radovish, Kratovo, Berovo, Bitola, Debar, and other cities, as well as in the villages: Miravci, Negorci, Smokvica, Pirava, Rostuse and others. In certain places (Veles, Strumica, etc.), the active members regularly practiced with treadmills, simple row exercises, marching, etc.; they also had activities from athletics, and in more developed societies, to a lesser extent, from archery, cycling, basketball, volleyball, skiing, etc. The Sokol organization maintained close ties with all state authorities, the military, and schools.[66] The organization's statute had to be granted approval of the Ministry of Interior, while the rules also included "elections, desired profile, establishing of a quorum, extraordinary and emergency meetings, finance management, audit and disciplinary proceedings through the established Court of Honor."[67] Of particular importance for this period is the 1932 Law on Mandatory Physical Education that contained regulations "on organizational setting and sports rules/programs for Sokol clubs and umbrella organizations with the Ministry for Physical Education acting in an executive manner."[68]

*46.* After World War II, in 1945, the Presidium of the first legislative body of the contemporary Macedonian State, the Anti-fascist Assembly for National Liberation of Macedonia (ASNOM), enacted a Decree on the Establishment of an Interim Sports Board of Macedonia.[69] According to Article 2 of the Decree, under the competence of the board is the realization of the organization of all sport branches in the entire territory of Macedonia. The board included representatives of the Committee on Education, the Headquarters of the People's Liberation Army of Yugoslavia and Partisan Squads of Yugoslavia (NOV and POJ) for Macedonia, the (Unique National Liberation Front) ENOF, the Anti-fascist Women's Front (AFŽ), the National Liberation Youth Union of Macedonia (NOMSM) and the Action committee of the trade unions in Macedonia. The later act was obrogated by another decree that was promulgated by the Macedonian government in 1945—the Decree on Establishment of Initiative Sports Committee for Macedonia.[70] This decree stipulates that the movable and immovable property, such as the premises and other objects related to sport activities previously owned by the sport societies before and during World War II, are transferred to the newly established committee for the purpose of reorganization and advancement of sports in Macedonia. At the same time,

65. D. Stanimirovic, Sokolstvo u Vardarskoj Makedoniji-Nastanak i razvoj (Doktorska disertacija), Zagreb,
66. *Ibid.*
67. Begović, M. 2021. Sports Law in Montenegro: Origins and Contemporary Development. Entertainment and Sports Law Journal, 19: 1, pp. 1–8.
68. *Ibid.*
69. Rešenie za obrazuvanje na vremenen fizkulturen odobor za Makedonija (Official Gazette 1/1945).
70. Uredba za obrazuvanje na inicijativen fiskulturen odbor za Makedonija (Official Gazette, 9/1945).

the decree grants competence to the Ministry of Education to enact regulations, drafts, plans and management decisions for sports in Macedonia, following relevant proposals by the Sport Committee.

*47.* Begovic[71] notes several aspects of development of the regulation of sport activities during the period of the Yugoslav federation (in which Macedonia was one of the six constituent republics): (1) the provisions of the 1974 Constitution of Yugoslavia that recognized the citizens' rights to nurture and develop their persons, presupposing an increased need for play, recreation and other similar activities; (2) the 1976 Law on Physical Culture and Self-Management Communities of Interest/ samoupravni interesni zaednici-SIZ; (3) the 1976 Law on Associated Labour; (4) the 1979 Resolution on the Yugoslav Assembly on the Free Exchange of Labour in Social Activities (1979). In this context, of particular importance in 1975 is the Social Agreement on position, rewards and remuneration of top athletes was adopted by the Yugoslav Association for Physical Culture—Savez fizičke culture Jugoslavije that has introduced three sorts of athletes (merit, international and state class), as well as duties for the state and sport organizations to provide medical care and insurance policy, social security, pension plan and remuneration for athletes.[72]

*48.* In the second half of the twentieth century, many prominent Macedonian lawyers were either active as athletes and/or participated in the management of sports activities. Examples include the professors of the Law Faculty in Skopje, Nikola Matovski (handball) and Todor Pelivanov (athletics), the famous attorney Panta Polenak (activist of the "Vardar" sport society, president of the volleyball federation and secretary of the physical culture union and organizer of "mass games" and organizer of numerous water polo, boxing, gymnastics and other sports),[73] Vlado Buchkovski (handball) and others. Within the activities of the Federation of Sports Pedagogues of Macedonia, the kinesiology professors Tihomir Popovski, Slavko Matovski and Aleksandar Naumovski have outlined the need for analysis of societal and legal aspects of sports in several events and works, including in the "Fizicka Kultura" scientific journal that was first published in 1973.[74]

*49.* With the Macedonian independence on September 8, 1991, and with the enactment of the Constitution of the Republic of Macedonia on November 17, 1991, sport is a constitutional category, especially since the Republic is obliged to stimulate and assist sports (Article 47), providing participation of citizens (directly or through their representatives) in the units of local self-government in the decision-making on issues related to sports (Article 115).[75] This provided a legal framework for further development of sports law primary and secondary legislation elaborated below.

---

71. *Ibid.*
72. *Ibid.*
73. Encyclopaedia Macedonica, Macedonian Academy of Arts and Sciences, Skopje, 2009, p. 1772.
74. The current "Research in Kinesiology (RIK)" scientific journal is a continuation "Fizicka kultura" that was first published in 1973. RIK regularly publishes articles on sports-related sciences, including sports law. Available at: https://fsprm.mk/rik/.
75. Official Gazette, No. 1/92, 31/98, 91/01, 84/03, 107/05, 3/09, 49/11, 6/19, 36/19.

*50.* Due to the increasing demand for enhancing professional training of the legal and sport management community, the first Macedonian Sports Law Association, *Lex Sportiva*, was established on February 16, 2010. The founders of the association were Goce Naumovski, Blagoja Pandovski, Dimitri Chapkanov, Dimitar Apasiev, and Dime Milevski. Sports law was first introduced at Macedonian universities as a course of the LL.M. studies curricula in 2011 at the Justinian I Law Faculty of the SS. Cyril and Methodius University in Skopje, taught by professors Goce Naumovski and Borče Davitkovski.

## Chapter 3. Concept and Sources of Macedonian Sports Law

*51.* The essentials of regulations of sports and sports activities today in Macedonia are progressively imposed as a pillar of contemporary law. This feature is provoked by the occurrence of a great amount of "negative phenomena" in sports (including corruption in sports) and synergies to diminish them. Even more, the European integration process imposes challenges on Macedonia as a candidate country to take measures in order to harmonize regulations in the field of sports law with the appropriate EU legislation.

*52.* In Macedonia, sport, in the sense of the Law on Sport (LS), is an activity that covers all forms of sports activities of athletes of all ages, as well as sports—recreational activities of citizens.[76]

*53.* Sports law is one of the newer branches of the Macedonian legal system, which, due to its complexity, is characterized by mixed legal features. It includes basic principles and specific normas that belong to different areas of constitutional, civil, criminal, administrative and other classical branches of law. Combining different legal segments into a single entity within sports law becomes a separate legal branch reflecting the response of legal science to challenges imposed by sports. Sport has become a highly profitable business activity in Macedonia, as well as in other societies of modern times. In this regard, numerous questions were raised that equally affect the domain of public and private law (there was a need for new types of contractual and commercial agreements, for specific regulation of criminal and material responsibility, etc.).

*54.* Macedonia has adopted an interventionist approach to regulating the rules of conduct in sport, considering the importance of sport for the development of society and its individuals. Such a codified approach has certain technical advantages because it is easier to find and interpret not only legal norms but also political ones because, in this way, it sends a clear message that the state shows appropriate attention to the position of sport in its legal system.

*55.* These segments of sports law have a significant place in the regulation of sports, and the analysis of their role in regulating social relations in sports is essential for a proper understanding of sports law in the Republic of Macedonia.

*56.* The basic sources of Macedonian sports law are: the Constitution, the LS and ratified international conventions and agreements.

*57.* The Macedonian constitution (Constitution),[77] as an act of the highest legal force that regulates the basic and most important relations in the state, indirectly

76. Law on Sports, Article 2, Official Gazette, 29/02, 66/04, 196/2004, 83/05, 81/08, 18/11, 51/11, 18/11, 174/11, 64/12, 148/13, 187/13, 42/14, 138/14, 177/14, 72/15, 153/15, 06/16, 55/16, 61/16, 106/16, 190/16, 52/19, 98/19, 244/19.
77. Official Gazette, No. 1/92, 31/98, 91/01, 84/03, 107/05, 3/09, 49/11, 6/19, 36/19.

regulates relations in the field of sports. As noted above, the Constitution contains several provisions of importance for sports and recreation. The Republic of Macedonia stimulates and assists technical education and sport. (Article 47).

*58.* The most important legal source that contains legal norms that regulate national sport and its basic elements is the LS. The need to regulate by law a part of the matter of sports law ascends from the circumstance that the Macedonian constitution is a general framework, while the LS regulates the issues specifically. LS regulates the major quantity of rules of comportment in sports but, at the same time, formally confirms the traditional practice of state recognition of sports autonomy. The law recognizes the implementation of sports rules by national federations and the Macedonian Olympic Committee (MOC). It includes the possibility of resolving disputes in the field of sport and entrusting them to sports arbitrations. Also, the Law accepts the existing pyramidal organizational structure in the field of sports and adds to it certain organizational forms in order to improve social relations that are not regulated by international sports organizations and are of interest to the Republic of Macedonia. It is necessary to emphasize here that in addition to a number of legal norms related to the autonomy of sports and sports organizations, the Law also provides for the restriction of autonomy, which indicates that the Republic of Macedonia has opted for an interventionist model. Macedonian legislation also includes the Law on Law on Prevention of Violence and Inappropriate Conduct at Sports Contests as one of the major sport law sources.

*59.* On the Basis of ratified international conventions and documents important for the field of sports in the Republic of Macedonia, the Law on Ratification of the Anti-Doping Convention and the Law on Ratification of the European Convention for Prevention of Violence and Misconduct at Sports Events, Especially Football Matches.[78]

78. Republic of Macedonia is a party to the Anti-Doping Convention and the European Convention for the Prevention of Violence and Misconduct at Sports Events, Especially Football matches through succession on Mar. 3, 1994: Law on Ratification of International Convention against Doping in Sport Law (Official Gazette 104/08).

# Part I. Organization of Sport in Macedonia

## Chapter 1. General Issues

*60.* The Law on Sports (hereinafter "LS")[79] regulates the conditions and way of performing sports activity for the public interest of the sport under the authority of the Republic of Macedonia the municipalities, the municipalities in the City of Skopje and the City of Skopje, the management of sports facilities owned by the Republic of Macedonia, the municipalities, the municipalities in the City of Skopje and the City of Skopje, as well as other issues of importance to sport. In this regard, sport means an activity that covers all forms of sports for athletes of all ages, as well as sports and recreational activities for citizens. (Law on Sports, Article 2).[80]

*61.* LS defines the public interest in the following way:

- encouraging the sports activities of children and youth within the national sports federations;
- organizing and conducting sports training and competitions for training athletes to achieve top sports results;
- encouraging the realization of the programs of the sports federations of the Republic;
- encouraging and assisting the organization of sports events and manifestations;
- maintenance and functioning of the existing and planning and construction of sports facilities of public interest for the Republic;
- healthcare, pension and disability insurance, compensation for accident consequences and risks, for categorized athletes in accordance with this and other laws;
- encouraging and assisting the publishing activity in sports; and
- construction and maintenance of a sports information network (Law on Sports, Article 22).

*62.* In order to fulfill the public interest in the field of sports, the Government of the Republic of Macedonia (RM) brings an Annual Program proposed by the state

79. Official Journal of the Republic of Macedonia n. 29/2002, 66/2004, 81/2008, 18/11 И 64/2012.
80. For detailed analysis of the Regulation of Sport Activities in Macedonia, *See*: Akmovska-Maletic, I., Naumovski, G., Chapkanov, D.: Analysis of the Regulation Of Sport as Activity of Public Interest nn the European Union and in the Macedonian Legislation, Research in Kinesiology, 2017, Vol. 45, No. 1, pp. 72–77.

administration body responsible for the affairs of the sport. The state administration body in charge of the sports determines criteria for the allocation of the Program funds and allocates the funds to the beneficiaries. Also, this body controls the earmarked use of the funds and may stop or reclaim the allocated funds if it determines that they are used inappropriately.

*63.* In accordance with the Law on Sports, the municipalities, the municipalities within the City of Skopje and the City of Skopje also have authority in the field of sports.

*64.* Sport is a large system of social activities that requires a very elaborate management mechanism. From the point of view of legal competence, the competence in the field of sports is divided between the Republic of Macedonia and the municipalities. A distinction is also made between legal jurisdiction within the governmental and nongovernmental sectors.

*65.* Sports management in the Republic of Macedonia is performed by government institutions, the National Olympic Committee, and sports associations.

*66.* The government sector includes:

(1) Agency of Youth and Sports (AMC) is at the top of the hierarchical pyramid of the sports system as the main bearer of its definition, monitoring, and financing.
(2) The Council for Sports is a coordinating expert body that ensures the implementation of the strategy for the development of sports while respecting the principles of sports autonomy. This body represents a kind of link between the governmental and nongovernmental sectors in the field of sports.

*67.* The nongovernmental sector encompasses:

(1) MOC, which is organized at the national level, is in accordance with the rules of the International Olympic Committee (IOC). The body has an obligation to affirm the values of the IOC, affirm the values of Olympism, organize the preparation of Olympians for the Olympic Games, etc.
(2) The Macedonian Paralympic Committee (MPC) is a national body that aims to promote the sport of persons with disabilities and provide conditions for the participation of the Macedonian Paralympic team in the Winter and Summer Paralympic Games.
(3) The Association Macedonian Sport Federations (AMSF) is a territorial sports federation for the territory of the state (nongovernmental, nonpartisan and nonprofit sports institution). It unites branch sports federations and lower-level associations (city, municipal, provincial). It is in charge of affirming universal sports values and monitoring the development of sports.

(4) National branch federations are the uppermost system of association in the suitable division of sport. They are recognized with the goal of evolving a particular sports branch, sports activities, harmonizing the activities of their members, representing national sports, achieving top sports results, professional work and encouraging the organization of sports competitions. National branch sports federations are obliged to improve the conditions for the development of sports in accordance with the appropriate training and competition programs.[81]

(5) Sport Associations can be sport clubs, i.e., trade company that performs sports activity (LS, Article 6), or a legal entity registered as a sports association, that can also establish a limited liability company or a joint-stock company for performing sports activity to achieve its goals, interests and activities, as well as for financing its functions determined by the statute (LS, Article 6).

## §1. Government Institutions in the System of Sports Organization in the Republic of Macedonia

### I. Agency Youth and Sports of the Republic of Macedonia

*68.* When it comes to the state administration body responsible for the affairs of the sport, in accordance with the organizational structure of public administration in the RM, it is provided that, among other independent state administration bodies, the Agency for Youth and Sport is founded as a legal person. So, the Agency for Youth and Sport was established as a state administration body responsible for monitoring sports and sport and recreational activities in the field of sports, monitoring the development of professional sport and performing other duties specified by law. In accordance with the Law, the Agency establishes a professional advisory body – a Sports Council from among prominent professional, scientific, and other pronounced workers in the field of sports. The Sports Council: participates in the preparation of the Program for the development of the sport; gives opinions on the criteria for the allocation of the funds, the standards and the other acts brought by the head of the state administration body responsible for the affairs of the sport and performs other works set forth in this Law, as delegated by the head of the state administration body responsible for the affairs of the sport at least once a year.

*69.* The AMC of the Republic of Macedonia is at the top of the hierarchy of the sports management system in the Republic of Macedonia.

*70.* The Agency determines the fulfillment of the working conditions of the National Sports Federation of the Republic of Macedonia by issuing an opinion.

*71.* This range of competencies of the Agency, especially from the aspect of financing, clearly shows its key role in the system of sports development.

---

81. This approach is typical in comparative sports law theory. *See*: Branimir Nešić, Franja Fratrić, Osnove organizacije sporta, Edukons, Sremska Kamenica, 2013, 170.

*A. Organization of the Agency*

*72.* To perform the tasks within its competence, the Agency has several sectors: Sports Sector, Youth Sector, Sector for Capital Investments and Sport Premises, Legal and Financial Issues Sector, Sector for Human Resources and Support of the Director, as well as Sports Inspectorate (Division for Inspection in Sports) and Internal Audit Division. The agency is managed by Director and Deputy Director.

*73.* The structure of the different divisions is graphically presented on the chart below:

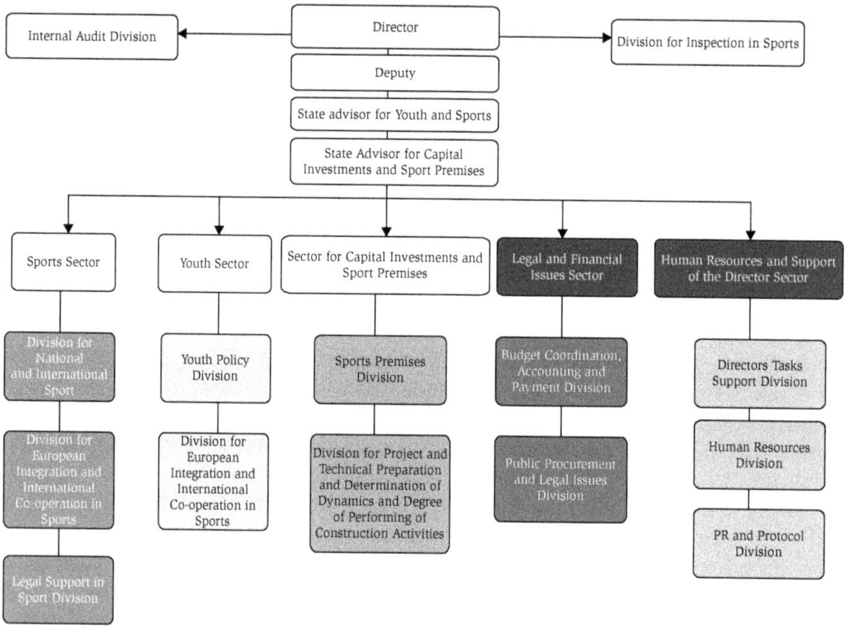


*Source*: Agency of Youth and Sport official web page[82]

*74.* From the aspect of sports law, the work of the Sports Sector is especially important. Namely, concerning its competencies, the Sports Sector:

- monitors, analyszes and processes issues related to the system and organization of sports and international cooperation in the field of sports and proposes measures for their promotion and development;
- monitors the situation in the associations and other entities that perform sports activity;

82. https://ams.gov.mk/en/home.

- monitors the condition of the professional staff in the sports associations and proposes measures for their improvement;
- monitors the network of associations in the field of sports and the system of competitions and proposes measures for promotion, development and professional development;
- follows special sports programs with talented students;
- monitors the sports activities of students and citizens;
- prepares a program for development of sports in the Republic of Macedonia;
- monitors the realization of international sports events and manifestations;
- proposes, plans and encourages international cooperation in the field of sports;
- monitors the activities of the Council of Europe in the field of sports development and undertakes measures for implementation of conventions and other international documents in the field of sports accepted by the Republic of Macedonia;
- proposes and prepares criteria for acquiring the status, rank, rights and obligations of top amateur athletes;
- proposes and prepares standards for health control of the participants in sports and recreational activities;
- proposes and prepares measures and criteria for financing the activity, the sports of the children, the youth and the sports-recreational activity of the citizens and the top sport and monitors their implementation;
- plans the programs necessary for the realization of the activity;
- proposes and prepares programs for international cooperation in the field of sports and monitors their implementation;
- gives opinions on programs for international cooperation that are prepared and proposed by other bodies and institutions;
- monitors the activities of the sports associations in the field of sports of the citizens of the Republic of Macedonia who live and reside abroad;
- proposes and prepares documents for bilateral and multilateral cooperation in the field of sports and monitors their implementation;
- performs the professional and administrative-technical work of the Sports Council;
- monitors and supports the publishing activity in the field of sports;
- prepares analyses, elaborations, reviews, information, reports and other materials in the field of sports; and
- collects reports.

*75.* The Division for National Sports, as an organizational unit within the Sector Sport, in its scope of work includes the following activities and works:

- monitors, studies and processes issues related to the system and organization of sports at the national level in the Republic of Macedonia;
- takes care of the implementation of the laws and other regulations in the field of sports at national level in the Republic of Macedonia;
- monitors the network of associations in the field of sports and the system of competitions and proposes measures for promotion, development and professional development;

– follows special sports programs with talented students;
– monitors the sports activities of students and citizens;
– participates in the preparation of the Program for development of sports in the Republic of Macedonia;
– proposes and prepares criteria for acquiring the status, rank, rights and obligations of top amateur athletes;
– proposes and prepares standards for health control of the participants in sports and recreational activities;
– proposes and prepares criteria for financing the activity, the sports of the children, the youth and the sports-recreational activity of the citizens and the top sport and monitors their implementation;
– plans the programs necessary for the realization of the activity;
– monitors and supports the publishing activity in the field of sports;
– prepares analyses, elaborations, reviews, information, reports and other materials in the field of sports; and
– collects reports.

*76.* The Division for European Integration and International Cooperation in Sports realizes the following activities:

– monitors, studies and processes issues related to international cooperation in the field of sports and proposes measures for their promotion and development;
– takes care of the implementation of the laws and other regulations in the field of sports at national level in the Republic of Macedonia;
– participates in the preparation of the Program for development of sports in the Republic of Macedonia;
– proposes, plans and encourages international cooperation in the field of sports;
– monitors the activities of the Council of Europe in the field of sports development and undertakes measures for implementation of conventions and other international documents in the field of sports accepted by the Republic of Macedonia;
– monitors the realization of the international sports events and manifestations that were held in the family or in which representatives from the country participate;
– proposes and prepares programs for international cooperation in the field of sports and monitors their implementation;
– gives opinions on programs for international cooperation that are prepared and proposed by other bodies and institutions;
– monitors the activities of the sports associations in the field of sports of the citizens of the Republic of Macedonia who live and reside abroad;
– proposes and prepares documents for bilateral and multilateral cooperation in the field of sports and monitors their implementation;
– prepares analyses, elaborations, reviews, information, reports and other materials in the field of international cooperation in sports; and
– collects reports.

*77.* The Department for Inspection Supervision in Sports, as an organizational unit within the Sector of Sports, in its scope of work:

- performs inspection supervision over the operation of sports clubs in the Republic of Macedonia;
- performs inspection supervision over the operation of National Sports Federations and other sports associations in the Republic of Macedonia;
- performs inspection supervision over the operation of other entities that perform sports activity as well as professional sports workers in the Republic of Macedonia;
- monitors the situation in sports clubs, National Sports Federations, other sports associations and other entities that perform sports activity;
- supervises the fulfillment of the conditions for performing sports activities;
- prepares analyses, elaborations, reviews, information, reports and other materials.

*78.* The organization, the manner of work, as well as the form and content of the acts prepared and adopted by the Department for Inspection in Sports, with a special Rulebook, shall be prescribed by the Director of the Agency for Youth and Sports.

### *B. Approval of Performing Sport Activities*

*79.* The Department for Registration of entities that perform sports activity, as an organizational unit within the Sports Sector, in its scope of work includes the following activities and works:

- collects requests for issuance of decisions for completion of activity;
- in cooperation with the Department for Inspection Supervision in sports, examines the merits of a separate request for issuance of a decision for sports activity;
- prepares and proposes to the Director of the Agency for Youth and Sports for issuing decisions for performing sports activities;
- keeps a Register of entities that perform sports activity in the Republic of North Macedonia;
- prepares analyses, elaborations, reviews, information, reports and other materials.

*80.* Also, the Agency issues and abolishes decisions for performing sports activities by sport clubs, the Macedonian Olympic Committee and the National Sport Federations (LS, Articles 11, 12); issues opinions for inscription of these subjects into the Central Register of Macedonia; and issues licenses for sport management valid for eight years (LS, Article 14).

*C. Financing of Projects in the Field of Sports*

*81.* A particularly important issue that falls within the competence of the Agency is the area of financing projects in the field of sports. Project financing is a complex process and is achieved through the process of financing annual projects. These projects are very important because sport is an activity of great importance for the Republic of Macedonia. The system of vouchers (LS, Article 14-g) is also an element of the financing. The Agency prepares and determines a draft list which is evaluated, verified and ranked by the National Sports Federations that meet the criteria for using the funds from the tax exemption in accordance with paragraphs in the articles of Profit in tax law.

*82.* The Agency proposes an annual program for realization of public interest in sport. The program adoption is under the competence of the Government of the Republic of Macedonia.

*83.* Funds in the budget of the Republic of Macedonia are provided for the realization of the general interest in the field of sports. The funds realized on all grounds from the organization of the special games of chance are used for financing the sports for the sports federations and clubs through the Agency for Youth and Sports. The distribution of funds is done by the Government of the Republic of Macedonia with a decision based on a program submitted by the Agency for Youth and Sports. The Agency for Youth and Sports prepares the program on the basis of projects submitted by sports federations and clubs, as well as on the basis of its own projects for the promotion of sports, which specify the amount of funds and the purpose for their use (LGC, Article 16).

*84.* The organizer of games of chance in a betting shop, on a monthly basis, for sports financing pays a special fee in the amount of 3%, which is calculated on the difference between the amount paid from all computers in all payment points of that organizer and the amount paid from all computers in all payment points, at the expense of the Agency for Youth and Sports (LGC, Article 79(2)).

*85.* The organizer of games of chance in a slot machine club, on a monthly basis, for financing the sport shall pay a special fee in the amount of 1.5%, which is calculated on the difference between the paid amount in all slot machines of that slot machine and the paid amount from all slot machines, in all business premises of the organizer on account of the Agency for Youth and Sports. The special fee is paid by the 15th of the month for the previous month (LGC, Article 94).

*86.* The procedure for distribution of these funds is Regulated by a Rulebook enacted by the Agency of Youth and Sports.[83]

---

83. Rulebook for the procedure of acquiring fees for sport, determined with Arts 79(2) and 94(2) of the Law on Games of Chance and Entertainment Law and the way of their distribution.

## II. The Sports Council

*87.* The Agency of Youth and Sport establishes an expert—advisory body—Sports Council, from the ranks of prominent professional, scientific, as well as other prominent workers in the field of sports. The council is composed of seven members appointed by the official who manages the body of the state administration responsible for the affairs in the field of sports for a term of four years. The council elects a president from among its members for a term of four years.

*88.* The Sports Council performs the following duties:

- participates in the preparation of the Program from Article 23 of LS;
- gives an opinion on the criteria for distribution of funds, measures and other acts adopted by the official who manages the body of the state administration responsible for the affairs in the field of sports;
- gives an opinion regarding the distribution of funds referred to in Article 23 paragraph 4 of LS;
- gives an opinion to the official who manages the body of the state administration responsible for the affairs in the field of sports for awarding the title of Ambassador of Sports of the Republic of Macedonia after a previously obtained opinion from the National Sports Federation; and
- performs other activities determined by this law entrusted to them by the official who manages the body of the state administration responsible for the affairs in the field of sports. The Sports Council submits a report on its work to the official who manages the body of the state administration responsible for the affairs in the field of sports at least once a year.

## §2. National Olympic Committee and Sports Associations

## I. Macedonian Olympic Committee

*89.* The Macedonian Olympic Committee (hereinafter "MOC") is the highest nongovernmental sports association whose constitutive members are the national sports federations from the Olympic sports. MOC is a member of and represents the national sports federations of the IOC. The MOC president is a person elected by a majority of votes from the total number of members of the MOC Assembly.

*90.* The person representing the MOC may be selected for a maximum of two four-year terms consecutively, and the same may be re-elected after a period of time of at least one full term.

*91.* The governing body of the IOC appoints a Secretary-General. The Secretary-General may be appointed a maximum of two consecutive times with a mandate of four years.

*92.* MOC is organized in accordance with the interests of national sports federations, with the principles of the Olympic movement, the Olympic Charter of the International Olympic Committee and in accordance with the LS. The MOC regulates the internal organization and way of working by statute. Concerning the competencies of MOC in its activities, MOC, in particular, realizes the following activities:

- participates in encouraging, helping and creating conditions for development of sports in the Republic;
- participates in the preparation of the Sports Development Program in the area of determining the goals and priorities of the development of sports;
- coordinates the activities of the national sports federations in the realization of the Olympic programs;
- determines it in accordance with the criteria and rules established by the International Olympic Committee composition of the Macedonian Olympics team; and
- performs other works and tasks determined by LS and by the statute.[84]

*93.* As far as the results at the Olympic Games are concerned, the summary includes two gold, five silver and six bronze medals. Specifically, the winners of the Olympic medals list include:[85]

- Blagoja Vidinic—Melbourne Olympics—1956—silver medal.
- Blagoja Vidinic—Olympic Games Rome—1960—gold medal.
- Blagoja Georgievski—Olympic Games Montreal—1976—silver medal.
- Ace Rusevski—Olympic Games Montreal—1976—bronze medal.
- Shaban Sejdiu—Moscow Olympics—1980—bronze medal.
- Shaban Sejdiu—Los Angeles Olympics—1984—bronze medal.
- Azis Salihu—Los Angeles Olympics—1984—bronze medal.
- Milko Gjurovski—Los Angeles Olympics 1984—bronze medal.
- Redzep Redzepovski—Olympic Games Los Angeles—1984—silver medal.
- Shaban Trstena—Los Angeles Olympics—1984—gold Medal.
- Shaban Trstena —Seoul Olympics—1988—silver medal.
- Stojna Vangelovska—Olympic Games Seoul—1988—silver medal.
- Mogamed Ibragimov—Sydney Olympics—2000—bronze medal.

## II. The National Federation for Sports and Recreation of the Disabled of Macedonia-Macedonian Paralympic Committee (NFSRDM-MPC)

*94.* According to the data of the MPC, the following key moments and personalities characterize the process of its foundation:[86] (1) On June 13, 1965, an

---

84. Articles 17–20, LS.
85. Data from the official webpage of the Macedonian Olympic Committee. See: https://mok.org.mk/site/mok Accessed Aug. 23, 2022.
86. The details of the process are described at the webpage of the MPC. *See*: http://fsrim.org.mk/za-nas/

establishment conference of the Association for Sport and Recreation of the Disabled of Macedonia was organized in the Sutjeska resort for the disabled in Ohrid. The first officials of the Association included: Boyko Zatenko as the first president, and in the further course of work, Reiz Shaqiri, Kiro Menkov, Angel Mojsovski, Prof. Dr. Nikola Hristov, Branimir Jovanovski and Kotse Dimov. (2) A special merit for the development of disabled sports in the Republic of Macedonia goes to the experts who for many years worked on the implementation of sports programs in the role of sports workers, especially Panche Pandilov, secretaries Slavko Jovevski, Ivica Glasnović, Savo Gerasimovski, Temelko Dojchinoski, as well as the current secretary Dragan Dojchinoski.[87]

*95.* Currently, the Paralympic Committee acts in accordance with the legal regulations related to the Law on Citizens' Associations and Foundations, the Law on Disabled Organizations and the Law on Sports. The National Federation for Sports and Recreation of the Disabled of Macedonia-MPC (NFSRDM-MPC) is a sports, voluntary, social and humanitarian organization whose key objective is to develop, create, unite and represent the sports and recreational activities of all disabled persons on the territory of the Republic of Macedonia, regardless of the type, degree and character of the disability, as well as the reasons for the placement of the disability. In addition to being registered in the Register of Citizens' Associations and Foundations, and the Register of National Disabled Organizations, by the Agency for Youth and Sports, NFSRDM-MPC has received a Decision to engage in sports activities in accordance with the Law on Sports. It conducts its activities in accordance with its norms, proposals and criteria as well as the norms, proposals and criteria of the International Paralympic Committee (IPC), of which it has been a member since 1994 when it was accepted as a regular member by acclamation at the General Assembly in Tokyo. NFSRDM-MPC, in organizing and implementing its activities, closely cooperates with the Agency for Youth and Sports of the Republic of Macedonia, the National Council of Disabled Organizations of Macedonia, and the Union of Sports Federations of Macedonia. NFSRDM-MPC also cooperates with other interested bodies, organizations and institutions in the country and outside it interested in the development of sports for persons with disabilities.

*96.* NFSRDM-MPC works on mass and systematic psychophysical rehabilitation of persons with disabilities through sports and sports recreation with the aim of preserving, strengthening, and improving the state of health of the remaining motor abilities of disabled persons, as well as their active and equal inclusion in social and the economic life of the Republic of Macedonia. For the successful implementation of the program activities, NFSRDM-MPC has formed municipal unions for sports and recreation of the disabled in twenty municipalities. The same, according to the geographical location, are regionalized into three regions. In view of the fact that it is a sports organization, a large part of the members are young people (14–30 years

---

87. *Ibid.*

old), but unfortunately, they are not covered by a training process in their municipalities to a satisfactory extent, primarily due to the financial difficulties of NFSRDM-MPC but also a lack of professional staff and sports facilities to implement the activities.[88]

*97.* The highest body is the Assembly, which has thirty-five representatives who, at the constitutive session, elect the president, an eleven-member Executive Board and a three-member Supervisory Board. Election sessions of the Assembly are held every four years, in the year immediately after the end of the summer Paralympic Games. The sports program, the calendar of sports competitions, the planning, organization and holding of the championships, the consideration of the rules and proposals for individual sports and categories of disability are the responsibility of the Professional Committee, which has five members. Within the Federation, there are twenty municipal sports and recreation associations for the disabled, and according to their geographical location, they are regionalized into three regions with regional headquarters in Skopje, Bitola and Kumanovo:

- In the first region: "Kisela Voda," "Chair," "Gazi Baba," "Centar," "Karposh" (all from Skopje), Tetovo and Gostivar.
- In the second region: Kumanovo, Veles, Shtip, Kochani, Gevgelija and Strumica.
- In the third region: Bitola, Prilep, Kavadartsi, Struga, Ohrid, Resen and Kichevo.[89]

NFSRDM-MPC is currently presided over by Branimir Jovanovski.

## III. Macedonian Sports Federations

### A. *General Framework*

*98.* The sports clubs from the same sport, as well as from the school, students and sports of the disabled, can join together in an appropriate National Sports Federation of the Republic of Macedonia because of:

- encouragement and promotion of the respective sport;
- implementation of the established program for the development of sports;
- harmonizing and coordinating the program activities of the affiliates members;
- organization and implementation of the competition system;
- advancement of professional work.

*99.* The National Sports Federation of the Republic of Macedonia (hereinafter "National Sports Federation"), in addition to the above, takes care of the state representations. Only one national sports federation can be founded in one sport. Decision on registration in the Register of Associations of the National sports federation

88. *Ibid.*
89. *Ibid.*

is taken by the Central Register in the case a of a positive opinion from the state administration body appropriate for the works from the field of sports is secured.

*100.* A national sports federation is a federation in which there are associated more than half of the sports clubs in the Republic of Macedonia that perform the same type of sport.

*101.* The Federation is represented by a person elected by a majority vote. A person representing the federation can be elected at most two four-year terms consecutively, and the same may be re-elected after a period of time of at least one full term.

*102.* The governing body of the national sports federation appoints a Secretary-General of the national sports federation. The assembly of national sports federations in team sports consists of the representatives from the first and second league clubs and the remaining club members in the federations, as well as representatives of sports coaches, veterans, judges and athletes from the respective sport proposed by their own organizational forms.

*103.* The assembly of national sports federations in individual sports is made up of the representatives of the clubs associated with the federations, as well as representatives of sports coaches, veterans, judges and athletes from the respective sports offered by their organizational forms.

*104.* In the national sports federations, the sports clubs compete at the highest level of competition in senior competition in sports in which a senior system of competitions is organized in more degrees, are united in an organizational form in accordance with the Law on associations and foundations (LAF) for the exercise of their rights and interests.

*105.* The clubs must also include youth clubs that compete in the system of competitions organized for the youth categories in the respective sport.

*106.* The organizational form of association submits to the Assembly of the Federation proposals for the determination of the system of matches, the choice of the sponsor of the league, the broadcasting rights of competitions and other issues related to maintaining the highest degree of competitions in senior competition. National sports federations provide premises and other conditions for operation of the organizational form of the associations.

*107.* The governing body of the national sports federation should include at least two lawyers and two economists as members. Kinship (up to the second degree) among each other, as well as capital or management relations, are obstacles to election of the members of the governing body of the national sports federation, the Secretary-General, and the president of the national sports federation. The members of the management body of the national sports federation should not be employees or members of management bodies in a company in which it has dominant ownership, the president of the national sports federation. The president of the governing body of the national sports federation may not have ownership shares or be part of the founders' associations in the sports clubs for which they are appointed.[90]

*108.* For the purpose of overview of the structure, activities and management concept of the sports federations system in Macedonia, on this occasion, three of the larger federations will be analyzed, i.e., the Football Federation of Macedonia (FFM), the Basketball Federation of Macedonia and the Handball Federation of Macedonia (RFM). In accordance with the primary and secondary sport legislation, the other federations have adopted a similar approach.

## B. *Football Federation of Macedonia (FFM)*

### 1. General Characteristics and Aims

*109.* The main legal source of the FFM is the Statute of the Football Federation of Macedonia (SFFM).[91] According to SFFM, FFM is an independent, voluntary, nonprofit, national organization in the field of football sport, established on the basis of the positive legal regulations of the Republic of Macedonia, registered in the relevant register kept in the Central Register of the Republic of Macedonia as an association, in accordance with the LAF and the Law on Sports of Republic of Macedonia (Article 1, SFFM). FFM, as a national sports federation, has the exclusive competence to organize and arrange football sports on the territory of the Republic of Macedonia.[92] FFM is a nonpolitical and nonprofit sports organization based on the principles of integrity and sportsmanship in accordance with the principles of fair play, founded on August 16, 1948. Independence, rights, and obligations of the FFM arise and are regulated by the acts of FFM, Fédération Internationale de Football Association (FIFA),Union of European Football Associations (UEFA) and the provisions of the Law on sport through which the autonomy or independence of FFM is ensured. The headquarters of the FFM is in Skopje, at the address bul. ASNOM number 21. Article 4 of SFFM describes the flag, the emblem, the seal, and the stamp.

*110.* The FFM was established and registered for achieving the following goals: (1) continuous improvement and affirmation, regulation and control of football sport on the territory of the Republic of Macedonia in the spirit of fair play and its unifying, educational, cultural and humanitarian values, especially with assistance with youth programs and development programs; promoting and caring for the ethical, fair conduct and integrity of football game; (2) encourages the development of club and national football; (3) encourages and develops amateur and professional football; (4) encourages and maintains the competitive spirit of the football game; (5)

---

90. Articles 14–14 C, LS.
91. Available in Macedonian at: https://ffm.mk/media/files/st%D0%90tut-n%D0%90-ffm-2018.pdf.
92. Article 2, SFFM.

encourages the development of the football game in the spirit of fair play and non-discrimination on any grounds; (6) encourages the development of professionalism of all members of FFM; (7) coordinates the activities and takes care of protection of the interests of all its members; (8) directs and educates all members of the football organization regarding the prevention of use and harm from the use of illicit stimulants; (9) takes care of protecting the integrity of the competition through takeovers activities to prevent negative phenomena in football; (10) represents the Republic of Macedonia in international sports relations related to football in all its forms; (11) develops cooperation with other sports organizations in the Republic of Macedonia; (12) develops international sports cooperation and maintains constant contacts and cooperation with FIFA, UEFA, and other football associations and their members; (13) monitors the achievement of goals and their amendment.[93]

*111.* To achieve its goals, FFM undertakes the following tasks: (1) organizes and supervises the competition in all categories of football in compliance with this Statute and the general acts of FFM; (2) normatively regulates, organizes and administers football activities on the territory of the Republic of Macedonia; (3) normatively regulates the rights and obligations of the members of FFM, their status, adopts legal acts and informs them about the rights, obligations that arise from the statutes of FIFA and UEFA; (4) to encourage professional work, organize and perform training on all participants in the football game, such as players, referees, coaches, medical experts, delegates, administrators and other football experts; (5) normatively regulates the issues related to the status of clubs, players, coaches, referees and other participants in the football game and related issues registration of football organizations, players, officials; (6) organizes international, qualifying and friendly matches for everyone national football teams; (7) creates conditions for financing the activities of the national teams, on other international football activities, the work of FFM bodies and General Secretariat; (8) exercises control and takes all means to prevent any kind of activities that could jeopardize the integrity of a match, competition or may lead to abuse of the football game; (9) is dedicated to the application of anti-doping measures in football; (10) implements the Statute, regulations, directives and decisions of FIFA, UEFA, as well as the Rules of the Football Game and ensures their application by members; (11) performs other activities that are of interest to football in the Republic of Macedonia.[94]

*112.* FFM prepares programs and can establish subsidiaries and companies to achieve its goals. To promote the football game, FFM can arrange the sale of sports equipment, props and other products branded with the FFM logo.[95]

*113.* FFM is a member of the Macedonian Olympic Committee and the Association of Sports federations of the Republic of Macedonia. FFM is a full member of FIFA and UEFA. With full membership in FIFA, FFM was acquired at the FIFA

93. Article 5, SFFM.
94. Article 6. SFFM.
95. *Ibid.*

Congress held in Chicago on June 16, 1994. With full membership in UEFA, FFM was acquired at the UEFA Congress held on April 28, 1994.[96]

*114.* FFM as a member of FIFA and UEFA is committed to comply with FIFA statutes, regulations, directives and decisions, and UEFA. Furthermore, it is committed to respecting the FIFA Code of Ethics, the rules of the football game, in a manner prescribed by International Football Association Board (IFAB). FFM also participates in the work of FIFA and UEFA and competitions organized by FIFA and UEFA on a representative and club level, for which it nominates its representatives for FIFA and UEFA bodies.[97] FFM recognizes the competence of CAS and will respect the decisions made as determined in the statutes of FIFA and UEFA in accordance with the positive legal regulations of the Republic of Macedonia and refers to the resolution of disputes in the last instance to an independent and impartial Arbitral Tribunal, in arbitration proceedings unless otherwise determined by the positive legal regulations of the Republic of Macedonia.[98] Other commitments of FFM include: (1) respect the principles of loyalty, integrity and sportsmanship in compliance with the principles of fair play; (2) respect the international football calendar; (3) representation and protection of the interests of its clubs in international relationships; (4) organization and play in international football matches accordingly FIFA and UEFA rules; (5) fulfillment of the financial obligations towards FIFA and UEFA; (6) taking care of other rights and obligations arising from the statutes, FIFA and UEFA regulations and decisions; (7) providing FFM members, clubs, players, referees, coaches and their associations as well as other officials to respect the obligations of this provision by implementing them in the statutes of their organizations.[99]

*115.* FFM is neutral on issues related to politics and religion. Discrimination of any kind, including hate speech targeted against a country, natural person or group of persons on account of ethnic origin, gender, language, religion, politics or any other reason, is strictly forbidden and punishable in accordance with the FFM Disciplinary Rulebook.[100] FFM, as a socially and socially responsible entity, promotes friendly relations between members, clubs, officials and players and their interaction with other socially and socially vulnerable categories.[101]

*116.* Any legal and natural person related in any way to organized football in the Republic of Macedonia has an obligation to respect the statutes, the rules and other acts of FFM, UEFA and FIFA, as well as the principles of fair play, loyalty, integrity and sporting behavior. All members of organs and bodies of FFM and officials in the execution of their activities must comply with the provisions of the Code of Ethics.[102] In order to resolve disputes that may arise between the members, clubs,

96. Article 7, SFFM.
97. Article 8, SFFM.
98. *Ibid.*
99. *Ibid.*
100. Article 9, SFFM.
101. Article 10, SFFM.
102. Article 11, SFFM.

officials and players, FFM establishes an institutional way, prescribes procedures, and determines the bodies that will have the authority to dismiss such disputes.[103]

*117.* The Management Board of FFM regulates the status of the players accordingly to the provisions of the FIFA Rules on the Status and Transfer of Players. FFM and each of its members who organize the competition compete in accordance with the Rules of the Game issued by IFAB. The adoption, amendment and supplementation of the Rules of the Game is exclusive competence of IFAB. Adoption and amendment of the Rules of the game of futsal and Beach soccer is the exclusive responsibility of FIFA. The official language of FFM is the Macedonian language. Albanian as an official language is used in accordance with the Constitution and the laws of the Republic of Macedonia; the other languages as official languages are applied in accordance with the Constitution and the laws of the Republic of Macedonia.[104]

## 2. Membership in FFM

*118.* The Assembly of FFM decides on issues related to the admission, suspension and expulsion of a member. The admission procedure begins with the submission of an application for admission to the FFM Management Board. With the application, the applicant is obliged to submit the following documentation: decision for entry in the Central Register and current status dated submission of the request; decision for performing sports activity; copy of the statute and other adopted acts; copy of the minutes from the last or constitutive assembly; list of associate members; decision of the assembly on the motives and goals for membership; statement for acceptance and respect of the decisions, directives and acts of FFM, UEFA and FIFA given by the applicant and statements made by its members; statement of compliance with the Rules of the game of football and the implementation of IFAB decisions; statement of acceptance of the jurisdiction of the selected sports arbitrator tribunal recognized by FFM; statement of acceptance of the competence of CAS; and a statement by which the applicant refrains from filing lawsuits for settlement of disputes before regular courts except in cases where the legal solutions exclusively refer to the settlement of disputes before regular courts. The Management Board of FFM has the right to request additional documentation depending on the basis for entry into membership. The Management Board, at the next session of the General Assembly, submits the application and opinions regarding the submitted application. The final decision for membership is made by the Assembly of FFM.[105]

*119.* The FFM Assembly may exclude or suspend the member. The suspension of a member can be imposed for a maximum of two years. The basis for excluding or imposing a suspension may be gross and/or constant violation of the provisions

103. Article 12, SFFM.
104. Articles 13–15, SFFM.
105. Article 16, SFFM.

of the Statute of FFM, noncompliance with financial and other obligations arising from decisions, directives and acts of FFM, UEFA and FIFA; filing lawsuits by the member and/or its members for resolving sports-related disputes before regular courts unless such a solution is provided by a legal solution in accordance with the positive legal ones regulations of the Republic of Macedonia without exception; endangering the unity of FFM; and loss of the characteristics that were necessary for entry into membership. Between two sessions of the assembly, the Executive decides on the suspension of a member FFM Board. The Management Board of FFM determines the legal and sports consequences which should be borne by the members of the suspended member. The Management Board may withdraw the suspension even before the maintenance of the session of the Assembly if the reasons for pronouncing the suspension cease. During the suspension of the member, the membership rights are dormant.[106] The member can apply to leave the membership. The request should be submitted no later than six months before the expiration of the calendar year. Withdrawal from membership at your own request or due to expulsion does not release the member from the financial obligations towards FFM and the other members of FFM, UEFA and FIFA and their members.[107]

*120.* In addition to leaving and expelling from membership, the member loses the status of member by force of law upon its termination. After losing the status of a member, the member loses all the rights he/she derives from membership in FFM. The membership in FFM is acquired: on the basis of territorial affiliation which may be municipal, urban and/or regional; and based on the affiliation of a certain group of football stakeholders.

*121.* The following entities can be members of FFM: Territorial football organizations and Organizations of football stakeholders.[108]

*122.* Territorial football organizations that have gained member status based on territorial affiliation are fully responsible for the management, administering and organizing of football matches on their own territory. Territorial organizations can be organized on:

- municipal level, as Municipal Football Associations with the abbreviated name municipal football associations (OFS);
- level of the city of Skopje, as the Football Association of the city of Skopje, result of association of municipal football unions on the territory of the city of Skopje;
- level of the region, as regional football associations, the result of the association of municipal football associations on the territory of a certain region with the abbreviated name Regional Football Associations (RFS).

---

106. Article 17, SFFM.
107. Article 18, SFFM.
108. Articles 19–21, SFFM.

*123.* A member who has not been accepted as a member of FFM cannot join RFS. The General Assembly of FFM decides on the manner and type of involvement of territorial football organizations in the structure of FFM.[109]

*124.* Territorial football organizations have the following competencies:

(1) regulate the internal organization and work in accordance with this statute and other acts of FFM;
(2) carry out programs for development of football sport on the territory that they occupy;
(3) organize and manage competitions in their own league's territory in accordance with this statute and the acts of FFM;
(4) give opinions and suggestions on issues related to the work of FFM;
(5) provide proposals for amendments to the Statute and acts of FFM;
(6) elect representatives for bodies of their territorial organization;
(7) participate in the election of representatives for FFM bodies;
(8) they have other competencies determined by the acts of the territorial organization in accordance with this Statute and the acts of FFM.

*125.* The statutes of territorial football organizations must be in accordance with this Statute and the acts of FFM. Organizations that have gained member status on the basis of association of football stakeholders are fully responsible for exercising their rights and the obligations of the associated stakeholders.[110]

*126.* The following organizations of football stakeholders can be members of FFM: (1) Association of clubs from the first league; (2) Association of clubs from the second league; (3) Association of women's football clubs; (4) Association of futsal clubs; (5) Association of Judges; (6) Association of coaches; (7) Football Association; (8) Association of beach soccer clubs.

*127.* Football stakeholder organizations acquire membership rights after the reception by the General Assembly of FFM. The statutes of football stakeholder organizations must comply with the Statute of FFM. They are members of the OFS as basic territorial football organizations, clubs, and organizations related to a particular football or profession required for advancing the football process. In the RFS and the city of Skopje, territorial football organizations are members of OFS with its clubs and organizations related to a certain football profession or profession needed to advance the football process.

*128.* OFS derives rights and has obligations from membership if: it has organized a municipal football league with at least six clubs in male or female competition; the structure has an organization of football referees with at least ten referees; in the structure, there is an organization of football coaches with at least six coaches

109. Article 22, SFFM.
110. Articles 23–24, SFFM.

who have obtained a license in accordance with the acts of FFM; meets all spatial, technical and personnel conditions determined by the acts on FFM.[111]

## 3. Football Clubs

*129.* A football club is a basic football organization that can be amateur and/or professional and engaged in football due to achieving competitive results and other sports interests. A football club is a legal entity that can be established by legal or natural persons, is established as a sports organization in accordance with the positive legal regulations and, in its form, can be an association or a type of company. A football club is established by an act of establishment in accordance with the law by enrolling in the register kept by a competent state body.

*130.* Football clubs are indirect members of FFM; membership of FFM enters with the act of registration in the Municipal Football Association, where territorial registration and publication of the registration in the official list of FFM "Makfootball" are in accordance with the acts of FFM. To claim membership rights, football clubs have an obligation to take active participation in organized competitions in the football organization of FFM (Article 29, SFFM).

*131.* Active participation in organized football competitions FFM organization allows the club to take part in organized international competitions through won sports results and additional criteria provided by the acts of FFM. A football club, in terms of Article 50 of the Statute, is a club whose senior team competes in a regular FFM competition or a club that actively competes with at least two teams from young categories in constant competition of FFM at least three competitive seasons in continuity. Under the youth categories in the sense of the previous paragraph are considered: youth, cadets, pioneers, junior pioneers, and roosters. The organization and functioning of the football club are determined by the statute and the rules of the club that must be in accordance with this Statute and the acts of FFM, UEFA, FIFA and the positive legal regulations of the Republic of Macedonia. The players and the officials of the club are registered in accordance with the acts of FFM in the Municipal Football Associations, and there is an obligation for them to submit a written statement that they accept the acts of FFM, UEFA and FIFA.[112]

## 4. Professional Expert Football Organizations

*132.* Football experts and football experts for the purpose of arranging professional issues and realization of issues of common interest within territorial football organizations can be grouped into professional organizations related to the profession. These professional organizations specially deal with professional issues related to football and the football game that may relate to referees and trials, coaches and

111. Articles 24–27, SFFM.
112. Articles 28–32, SFFM.

coaching work, sports medicine issues, anti-doping, security and other football-related issues. Professional trade organizations do not have the status of legal entities, and unlike organizations of football, stakeholders perform their function on a local/regional level and are an integral part of the territorial football organization. The professional-professional football organization takes care of the selection and training of experts in their field in accordance with the goals of territorial football organization and FFM. The training of professionals for performing activities in the profession on the territory of RM is performed under the supervision of FFM. Individual and common goals are achieved through the participation of expert persons in the activities of the territorial organization and FFM. Professional organizations have their own acts that should be in accordance with the positive legal regulations, the acts of the territorial organization, FFM, UEFA and FIFA and approved by the Boards of territorial organizations. Professional trade organizations submit an application for membership in territorial organization; the application is submitted on a form prescribed by FFM for each profession separately and should be supported by at least:

- Ten judges for professional organizations related to judges and trials;
- Six trainers for professional organizations related to professional coaching;
- Three medical professionals for professional organizations in the field of medicine and anti-doping.

*133.* The membership of the sports football workers is regulated by the territorial one football organization in accordance with the Rulebook adopted by the Board of FFM and other acts of FFM. Members of professional organizations for judges and trial and professional coaching work registered in territorial organizations can be united nationally in Football Stakeholder Organizations.[113]

## 5. Association of Clubs and Basic Football

*134.* Club associations are subordinated to FFM. Club associations are obliged to follow the directions, recommendations and directives given by FFM. FFM with a special act will regulate the rights, obligations and competencies of club associations, including the manner of adoption of the amendments and amendments to the statutes, adoption of other acts, rulebooks, and propositions.

*135.* Basic football is football that is not top and professional regardless of the type of football game, playground dimensions, ability, gender and age of players, race, religion and nationality. Basic football includes activities in the field of children's football, school football, women's soccer, veteran soccer, soccer for people with special needs, etc. Basic football promotes the educational function of the sport, fair play, understanding, tolerance and responsibility through sports. FFM pays special attention to Basic Football through programs involving the target groups and organizing a competition in children's and school football. For activities

113. Article 33, SFFM.

related to basic football, each territorial football organization, in cooperation with the Board of FFM, appoints coordinators who implement the program, plans and calendar of activities adopted by the Board of FFM.[114]

6. Membership Rights and Duties

*136.* FFM members have the right to:

– be called in accordance with the established procedure, to participate in the work of the Assembly and through its elected representatives-delegates of the Assembly FFM to exercise their right to vote;
– give proposals for the agenda for a session of the Assembly;
– propose candidates for the bodies of FFM;
– be informed about the activities and work of FFM through the bodies of FFM and the official list of FFM "Makfootball";
– participate in competitions and/or other activities organized by them FFM;
– exercise all other rights arising from this Statute, rulebooks, decisions and other acts of FFM.

*137.* The manner of exercising these rights is subject to further regulation by the provisions of this Statute.

*138.* The members of FFM have the following obligations:

– to fully adhere to and respect the Statute, the rulebooks, decisions of FFM, UEFA and FIFA and to ensure that their members, clubs, players, referees, coaches and their organizations, as well as other officials persons, will comply with the obligations of this provision by implementing them in their statutes;
– to obey the rules of the football game in a manner prescribed by IFAB;
– to adopt a statutory provision recognizing the competence of the CAS in case of dispute and will abide by the decisions taken in a manner specified in the statutes of FIFA and UEFA and the positive legal regulations of the Republic of Macedonia;
– to adopt a statutory provision recognizing the competence of an independent and impartial Arbitral Tribunal recognized by FFM and with which it will be obliged and will oblige their members not to dispute disputes of a sports nature and submit to a decision before the regular courts in accordance with the positive legal regulations of the Republic of Macedonia;
– to resolve any possible misunderstandings within the football organization through dialog and solutions that are in the interest of football on the territory of the Republic of Macedonia;
– to keep a register of members, to regularly update the register upon request to submit it to the General Secretariat of FFM;

114. Articles 34–35, SFFM.

- to take care and protect the interests of FFM and refrain from any activities contrary to the interests of FFM;
- to respect the principles of loyalty, integrity and sportsmanship in compliance with the principles of fair play;
- to maintain sports activity and participate in competitions and/or events organized by FFM or its members;
- to report on changes in their acts;
- to fully fulfill the financial obligations towards FFM;
- to guarantee full independence during the elections for an administrative body and the election and appointment of members of other bodies;
- to inform FFM in writing about the date and place of holding a session of the Assembly and request the presence of an authorized representative from FFM at least ten days before the day of the assembly;
- not to maintain any relations and activities of a sports nature with entities that are not recognized, excluded or suspended;
- to participate in the work of the Assembly of FFM, elect or propose delegates for the Assembly of FFM;
- to participate in the decision-making process of the Assembly of FFM and other organs and bodies of FFM;
- not to allow discrimination of any kind against a country, private persons or group of persons on the basis of ethnic origin, race, sex, language, religion, policy or other reason;
- to inform FFM before entering into direct communication with UEFA and FIFA;
- to harmonize their statutes and other acts with the Statute and the acts of FFM;
- to record the adopted decisions with number and date in a special book of decisions independent of the ledger to be submitted to FFM fifteen days after the end of the calendar year for the previous year;
- to enter a statutory provision by which the Management Board of FFM recognizes powers to initiate proceedings for the taking of measures for fulfillment of provisions of the Statute;
- to take care of other rights and obligations arising from the statute, acts and decisions of FFM, UEFA and FIFA.

*139.* Failure to comply with the above obligations may lead to the imposition of disciplinary measures in accordance with this Statute and the Disciplinary Rulebook of FFM. Decisions made by bodies that are not elected in a prescribed manner do not have legal action and are not recognized within the football organization.

*140.* FFM members and their members have an obligation to pay attention to the integrity of the competition. No legal and/or natural persons (including subsidiaries and groupings or affiliated companies) must not have control over more than a club in order to prevent endangering the integrity of individual competition and/or competition.

*141.* Clubs, at the same time, cannot be direct members of more than one FFM territorial football organization. FFM members cannot be direct members of another at the same time football association—members of UEFA and FIFA.[115]

## 7. Organization of FFM

*142.* The FFM organization includes the following bodies: (1) General Assembly—the highest statutory collegial body; (2) Supervisory Board; (3) Election and Verification Commission; (4) President; (5) Management Board —Executive statutory collegial body; (6) Emergency Board; and (7) Other Committees and Boards—Consultative Bodies of the Management Board. FFM also has an Ethics Board, Appeals Commission, and General Secretariat as an Administrative body.[116]

*143.* The bodies of FFM are elected or appointed in a prescribed procedure without influence of external third parties. Candidates for a body or body of FFM are proposed by the members of FFM and/or The President of FFM and/or the Board of FFM. All members of the bodies of FFM have an obligation to perform a function to adhere to the ethical principles of FFM and FIFA. The members of the bodies of FFM have an obligation to be excluded from voting whenever a decision is made on an issue on which there is or may be a conflict of interests. All members of organs and bodies of FFM are elected for a term of four years, including the management structure of the General Secretariat. The members of the bodies of FFM have the right to one vote with exception as in the provisions of this Statute. In the decision-making process of the bodies of FFM is not allowed voting through an authorized person. In the decision-making process of certain bodies arranged with further provisions of this Statute, voting by conference call is allowed. A member of a statutory body cannot be for the duration of the mandate member of the Licensing Bodies. A member of a statutory body cannot be for the duration of the mandate member and of another statutory body with the exception in the provisions of this Statute. General provisions for the election of members.[117]

### a. General Assembly

*144.* The General Assembly is the highest statutory body of FFM. The General Assembly works in sessions. The sessions of the General Assembly can be regular and extraordinary. Regular sessions are convened once a year. Extraordinary sessions are convened under conditions determined by this Statute. The sessions of the General Assembly are convened by the Board of FFM. The sessions of the General Assembly are chaired by the President of FFM. In the absence of the President, the

---

115. Articles 36–40, SFFM.
116. Articles 40–41, SFFM.
117. Article 42, SFFM.

sessions are chaired by the oldest delegate from the ranks of delegates to the General Assembly. An Extraordinary Session of the General Assembly may be convened by the Management Board of FFM or the members of FFM under conditions determined by this Statute.

*145*. The Assembly consists of delegates-representatives of the members of FFM. The structure of the delegates is determined by the provisions of this Statute. The work of the General Assembly is regulated by the Rules of Procedure. The Rules of Procedure of the General Assembly are adopted by a majority of those present delegates.[118]

*146*. The General Assembly of FFM has the following competencies:[119]

(1) decides on amendments to the Statute and the decisions of the Assembly;
(2) decides on amending and supplementing the goals of FFM;
(3) decides on internal organization and organizational forms;
(4) decides on status changes;
(5) adopts the Rules of Procedure of the Assembly and amendments and additions to it;
(6) decides on the adoption of the Rulebook on elections and verification and amendments to it;
(7) decides on the adoption and amendments to the rules of operation of the Supervisory Authority;
(8) decides to change the competition system;
(9) makes a decision for adoption of the financial plan (budget) of FFM;
(10) adopts the final account of FFM and decides on the deployment of surplus revenue and loss coverage;
(11) adopts the work report of the President and the Management Board;
(12) adopts the reports on the work of the other statutory bodies;
(13) adopts the report of the independent auditor;
(14) adopts the minutes of the assembly from the previous session if it is not adopted in any other way provided by this Statute;
(15) adopts, changes and/or supplements the agenda for the subject session;
(16) appoints three delegates from three members to verify the minutes of the assembly;
(17) appoints a minute taker and persons for counting votes from the ranks of the General Secretariat;
(18) decides on the election and confidence of the President and the Management Board of FFM;
(19) decides on dismissal of members of the Board of FFM;
(20) decides on the election and dismissal of members of the Supervisory Body of FFM;
(21) decides on the election and dismissal of members of the Legal Bodies of FFM;

118. Articles 45–47, SFFM.
119. Article 58, SFFM.

(22) decides on the election and dismissal of members of the Election Commission and FFM verification;
(23) elects an authorized Audit House;
(24) decides on admission, suspension and expulsion of a member;
(25) decides on association and status of associate members;
(26) decides on the manner of inclusion of the associated territorial football organizations in the structure of FFM;
(27) decides on the appointment of persons with special merits and the appointment of honorary member and honorary president upon the proposal of the Board;
(28) establishes a program for the development and promotion of football in the Republic of Macedonia;
(29) analyzes the conditions for dissolution of FFM and brings appropriate decisions on the same;
(30) decides on other issues within its competence in accordance with the provisions of this Statute and the positive legal regulations;
(31) decides on the requests of the members in accordance with the acts of FFM; and
(32) may authorize the Management Board of FFM to decide on issues within its competence.

*147.* The basic rule is that the Assembly makes decisions by a majority of delegates present. An exception to the basic rule for decision-making is voting by the following items on the agenda, the adoption of which is a necessary qualified majority of two-thirds of the delegates present, as follows:

– amendments to the Statute;
– election of a President in the first round;
– expulsion of a member.

*148.* For the adoption of the items on the agenda: trust of the President and the Managing Director board and analysis of the conditions for dissolution and dissolution of FFM, it is necessary to have a qualified majority of two-thirds of the total number of delegates representing the members.[120]

b. Supervisory Board

*149.* The Supervisory Board is a collegial body composed of five members, one of which is the chairman and one deputy chairman. The election of the members of the board is done by the General Assembly on the proposal of the FFM Management Board. The valid decision of the Board requires the presence of more than half of the total number of members. The Board makes decisions by a majority vote of the members present. The Chairman and Deputy Chairman of the Supervisory Board should possess expert knowledge in the field of law or finance (Article 84, SFFM).

---

120. Article 62, SFFM.

*150.* The Supervisory Board convenes the Chairman of the Board. If necessary, the Supervisory Board may convene the President of FFM. The Supervisory Board controls the operation, the execution of the financial plan, purposeful and rational use of funds as well as compliance with working with positive legal regulations. The Supervisory Board submits a report on the findings of the operation. The manner of work and tasks of the Supervisory Board are determined by Rulebook for the organization of FFM.[121]

c. Election and Verification Commission

*151.* The Election and Verification Commission is a collegial body. The election of the members of the Commission is done by the General Assembly on a proposal of the Board of FFM. The commission sits in full force and makes decisions with a majority of votes of the members present. The members of the Commission should have expert knowledge in the field of law and sports operations.

*152.* The Commission has the competence:

- to organize, coordinate and supervise the election process regulated by the provisions of this Statute and the Rulebook on elections;
- to determine the mandates of the delegates and propose them to the assembly verification of the same;
- to determine the quorum for the work of the General Assembly.

*153.* The Election Rulebook additionally determines the competence, composition and manner of action of this Commission.[122]

d. President

*154.* The president of FFM represents the FFM in legal transactions in the country and abroad. The president of FFM is an authorized signatory, by function, on the accounts, financial and legal documentation arising from the operation of FFM. The president may authorize the Secretary-General and/or a member of the Management Board to sign financial and/or legal documentation from its competence.

*155.* At the proposal of the competent body of the members of FFM, the president of FFM elects the General Assembly from among the delegates of the General Assembly in a prescribed procedure in accordance with the criteria set out in this Statute. In case the members of FFM do not have competent authority in their statutes body, the competent body is considered to be the assembly of the member. The President of FFM is ex officio president of the General Assembly and president of the Board of FFM. The mandate of the president in accordance with the provisions of this Statute is four years with the right of re-election.

121. Articles 83–85, SFFM.
122. Articles 86–89, SFFM.

*156.* The president of FFM has the following competencies:

- presides over the sessions of the General Assembly and signs the acts and decisions of the General Assembly;
- convenes them, proposes an agenda and chairs the sessions of the Management Board and the Emergency Board and signs all acts and decisions arising from the operation of these bodies;
- assigns to the members of the Management Board coordination tasks and function of Chairman of the standing and ad hoc committees of the Management Board;
- monitors the implementation of the decisions adopted by the General Assembly, FFM Management Board and Emergency Board;
- monitors the work of the statutory bodies in order to achieve the goals set out in this Statute;
- proposes vice presidents of the Management Board of FFM;
- monitors and manages the work of the administrative body of FFM;
- proposes the election and dismissal of the Secretary-General and the management structure of FFM.

*157.* The other competencies of the president are regulated in the Rulebook on organization of FFM.

*158.* In case of temporary or permanent impediment of the president to perform the function of Chairman of the Management Board and the Emergency Board, the function of a proposal of the president or the Management Board shall be performed by one of the vice presidents until the termination of the circumstances that led to the impediment to the performance of the function. If the impediment to the performance of the function lasts more than six months, a session of the General Assembly is scheduled, regular or extraordinary, in order to elect the president of FFM for the remaining term of office.[123]

e. Management Board

*159.* The Management Board is the executive body of FFM. The members of the Board are elected by the General Assembly on the proposal of the members of FFM. Each member may nominate one candidate for the Management Board of FFM. Proposals for a candidate for a member of the Board, together with the documentation from which it can determine whether the candidate meets the requirements for candidacy referred to in Article 43 of the Statute, are submitted no later than twenty days before the day of the session of the Assembly of FFM to the Election Commission and FFM verification. The Commission for Elections and Verification of FFM, after receiving the proposals from the members, prepares a final list/s of candidates, which, together with the daily draft order and other materials for the assembly, are submitted to the members of FFM.

123. Articles 90–93, SFFM.

*160.* The Management Board has fifteen members and consists of the president, the vice presidents and twelve members.

*161.* As an exception in accordance with Article 70 of this Statute, the Management Board may count a maximum of nineteen members. The President of the Management Board is the President of FFM. The members of the Management Board at the constitutive session on the proposal of the President from their own ranks elect vice presidents.

*162.* The mandate of the members of the Management Board in accordance with the provisions of this Statute is four years. The mandate of the members of the Management Board starts after the end of the session of the General Assembly and lasts until the end of the session of the General Assembly, on which a new composition of the Management Board is elected in the fourth year of their mandate. The members of the Management Board can be re-elected (Article 97, SFFM).

*163.* For the duration of the mandate, with the exception of the provisions of this Statute, the members of the Management Board may not be members of the General Assembly and its bodies, Legal Bodies, Licensing Bodies, Arbitration Tribunal and the administrative body of FFM (Article 98, SFFM).

*164.* The mandate of the members of the Board, as well as of the delegates of the assembly, will be considered for termination in case of:

- determination of permanent incapacity for performing the function or death;
- final court verdict by which the member has been sentenced to imprisonment for a period of six months or more;
- pronounced disciplinary measure prohibition to perform a function for a period of six months and more by a body of FFM or confirmed by a body of FFM;
- unjustified absence from more than three consecutive sessions;
- resignation.[124]

*165.* The meetings of the Management Board are scheduled and chaired by the president of FFM. The meetings of the Management Board are not public. In addition to the members of the Management Board, the sessions are attended by: the Secretary-General and persons from the General Secretariat in accordance with the competence they have in the advisory role. At the request of the president, the session without the right to vote may invite other persons to attend (Article 102, SFFM).

*166.* The Management Board holds at least six sessions during one calendar year. At the request of at least half of the members of the Management Board, the President shall schedule a meeting within twenty-one days from the date of submission of the request. Failure to comply with the request from the previous paragraph

124. Articles 94–99, SFFM.

allows the members to schedule the session independently and to inform the Secretary-General of FFM (Article 103, SFFM).

*167.* The Management Board has the following competencies:

- organizes the sessions of the General Assembly;
- determines the proposals for amendment of the Statute and other acts within the competence of the Assembly;
- adopts rulebooks, propositions and other acts that are not within its competence at the General Assembly;
- determines the financial statements—the final account and proposes financial plan-budget;
- proposes to the Assembly the election of an independent Audit House;
- reviews and determines the audit report;
- decides on the suspension of a member between two sessions of the Assembly of FFM;
- prepares a report on the work;
- proposes to the Assembly honorary members and honorary president;
- monitors the execution of the decisions of the General Assembly;
- performs other tasks entrusted to him by the General Assembly;
- organizes competitions in the first, second and third degree in senior and in youth categories in football, women's football, futsal, beach football;
- organizes competitions in children's football and other categories from basic football;
- proposes a change in the system for competition in all categories of football and adopts changes in the system of competition in futsal and women's football;
- adopts the calendars for competition in all categories;
- adopts lists of judges, controllers, delegates and other officials for competitions organized by FFM;
- decides on the initiated requests for protection of rulebooks in accordance with the acts on FFM.
- annuls and revokes decisions of its bodies on extraordinary legal remedies;
- decides on the appointment of additional members of the Management Board in accordance with Articles 70 and 100 of this Statute;
- on the proposal of the president, elects vice presidents of the Management Board;
- in case of an impediment to the performance of the function by the President, elects the vice president who will temporarily perform the function;
- appoints and dismisses the chairpersons, deputies and other members of permanent and ad hoc bodies;
- at the proposal of the members, selects and determines a list of arbitrators for Arbitral Tribunal;
- under special circumstances determined by the Rulebook for the organization of FFM, by consensus, may suspend from performing the function of a member of a statutory body to the next session of the General Assembly;
- reviews and adopts the reports of the permanent and ad hoc bodies;
- supervises all activities of the bodies under its competence;

- reviews, determines and submits to the Assembly the annual reports of other statutory bodies;
- decides on issues related to the work of the members of FFM;
- assesses the compliance of the statutes and other acts of the members with FFM acts;
- adopts the organization of the General Secretariat;
- upon the proposal of the President, appoints and dismisses the General Secretary of FFM;
- upon the proposal of the President, appoints and dismisses the managerial structure of FFM;
- decides on all types of cooperation and international issues;
- decides on issues related to international football and the organization of international competitions;
- organizes and supports events of social character;
- takes care of the implementation of the decisions and acts arising from UEFA and FIFA Statutes;
- adopts development programs for all football categories and football stakeholder organizations;
- appoints and dismisses the selectors and the professional staff of all national teams;
- determines the commercial policy and strategy of FFM;
- decides on awards, recognitions and donations that are not within the competence of the assembly;
- decides on the amount of membership fees;
- provides funds for expenses not provided for in the budget in amount of 20% of the budget for the previous calendar year;
- decides on the amount of fees for submissions on various grounds;
- decides on other issues that are not within the competence of other statutory bodies.

*168.* The Management Board, with a special act/decision, determines the criteria and manner of awarding prizes and recognitions for special contributions and development of football sport.

*169.* The Management Board may delegate some of the competencies to its members' permanent and ad hoc bodies. The Management Board may be part of the competencies related to the organization of competitions and competitions to delegate to members. The competencies from the previous paragraph are regulated by the Rulebook on organization on FFM.[125]

f. Emergency Board

*170.* The Emergency Board is a body of the Management Board composed of three members: the president, one of the vice presidents and one member of the

125. Articles 100–109, SFFM.

Management Board appointed by the president. In case of absence of the vice president from paragraph 1 of this article, the president calls the other vice president, and in case of impediment, another member of the Management Board. The Emergency Board decides between two sessions of the Emergency Management Board issues within the competence of the Management Board. The Emergency Committee is convened and chaired by the president.

*171.* For a valid decision, it is necessary for the Emergency Board to sit in full composition. Decisions are made by a majority of the total number of votes. All decisions of the emergency board take effect immediately and will be given confirmation at the next meeting of the Management Board. The board can decide otherwise, in which case the decisions are they are abolished, considered and re-decided. The legal consequences of the revoked decisions remain!

*172.* In the event of a conflict of interest, any member of the Emergency Board should be exempt from decision-making independently or ex officio. In case of conflict of interests between the president and the vice president from a member 110 paragraph 1 of this Statute, the Emergency Committee is chaired by the other vice president. In case of impediment of the other vice president, the Emergency Board is chaired by the member of the Board with the longest experience as a member of the Board.

*173.* The Emergency Board makes decisions at meetings for which minutes are drawn up by the Secretary-General. Decisions can be made without attending electronically via submitting the agenda and declaring by e-mail or via conference connection. If decisions are made electronically or by conference call, minutes shall be drawn up for the same, signed by the president and the Secretary-General (if applicable); in case of inapplicability, the minutes confirm the management structure of FFM on the day of decision-making. The minutes from the previous paragraph should be signed by all members of the Emergency Board before making confirmation decisions by Management Board.[126]

g. Other Commissions

*174.* The Management Board of FFM, for achieving the goals, part of the competencies regarding the implementation of activities, organizing and decision-making, can delegate to the following standing bodies (committees and boards): (1) Competition Commission; (2) Youth Commission; (3) Commission for Women's Football; (4) Futsal Commission; (5) Commission for Basic Football; (6) Commission for Status of Football Players; (7) Commission for Verification of Contracts and Registration; (8) Legal Commission; (9) Finance Commission; (10) Commission for International Activities; (11) Security Commission; (12) Infrastructure Commission; (13) Commission for Fair Play; (14) Commission for Medicine and Anti-doping; (15) Commission for Social Responsibility; (16) Commission for Media and Marketing.

126. Articles 110–113, SFFM.

*175.* The president appoints the chairmen of the standing committees from among the members of the Management Board of FFM, with the exception of the chairmen of the commissions for which it will be determined that expertise in an appropriate field is required. A member of the Management Board may not chair more than one permanent member commission. The president, when appointing the chairpersons of the bodies of the Management Board, pays attention to the professional qualifications required to perform work within the scope of the competencies of the designated body. The Deputy Chairs and the members of the standing bodies are elected by the Management Board at the proposal of the members of FFM.[127]

h. Boards, Committees and Licensing Bodies

*176.* The Management Board establishes the following permanent boards: (1) Board of Judges; (2) Board of Coaches. The composition and competencies of the Judicial and Coaching Board are determined by Rulebook for organization of FFM.[128]

*177.* The board, in the interest of the clubs in order to overcome the disputes and other issues arising from the competition, may form boards composed of representatives of the clubs competing in the first and second degree. The manner of work of these boards will be determined by the Rules of Procedure adopted by the Board of FFM. The board, in order to protect the interests of the players, can form a Board of Footballers. As an advisory body, the Management Board may also establish a Board of experienced and proven former footballers. The Management Board may establish ad hoc bodies for a specific purpose and for a specific purpose time. The Management Board, with a decision for formation, determines the composition, goals, rights, obligations and deadlines for submitting reports to the bodies. The Management Board, with a special act—Rulebook for organization of FFM—determines the composition, goals, competencies, rights, obligations, procedures and manner of decision-making of standing and ad hoc bodies.[129]

*178.* In order to develop and improve club management, club administration and respect for financial fair play, FFM, in cooperation with UEFA, adopts licensing rules and sets standardization criteria in the operation of football clubs.[130]

*179.* The participation of the clubs in the competition system of FFM and UEFA is conditioned by the sports result and the fulfillment of the licensing criteria. The procedure for determining the fulfillment of the criteria is implemented by FFM licensing bodies. FFM licenses are:

– Licensing Commission.

127. Article 114, SFFM.
128. Article 115, SFFM.
129. Articles 116–118, SFFM.
130. Article 119, SFFM.

– Licensing Appeals Commission.[131]

*180.* The Licensing Commission is the body that decides in the first instance on the fulfillment of the licensing criteria by the applicant clubs, as prescribed in the Rulebook on licensing of clubs participating in competitions organized by UEFA and the Club Licensing Regulations, which compete in national competitions.[132]

*181.* The Licensing Commission is elected by the Management Board of FFM with a mandate of four years; it is composed of five members, of which, among other conditions provided by the Statute, one member should be an experienced lawyer and one member should have experience and financial education in the field of auditing and accounting.[133]

*182.* The Commission has the competence to take into account the fulfillment of the foreseen criteria to issue or not to issue a license for the relevant competition. The Licensing Commission may decide on other issues determined by acts of FFM. For the valid work of the commission, the presence of more than half of the total number of members is required. The decisions of the commission are made by a majority of the members present; in the event of an equal number of votes, the chairman's vote shall be decisive. As an exception, decisions can be made without attendance, electronically by submitting an agenda and declaring by e-mail or by conference connection. If decisions are made electronically or by conference call, a report shall be drawn up and signed by the present members, and the Secretary-General shall, if not applicable, sign the minutes. The minutes from the previous paragraph, additionally within the deadline determined by the Rules of Procedure for work, are signed by the members of the Commission who participated in the decision-making. The other issues related to the composition, competencies and procedure are subject to the regulation of the subject Rulebook for licensing of clubs.[134]

*183.* The Licensing Appeals Commission has five members; in addition to which other conditions provided by the Statute, one member should be an experienced lawyer and one member to have experience and financial education in the field of auditing and accounting. The Commission has the authority to decide on appeals against first-instance decisions of applicant clubs. For the valid work of the commission, the presence of more than half of the total number of members. Decisions of the commission are made by a majority of the members present; in case of an equal number of votes, the chairman's vote is decisive. The other issues related to the composition, competencies and procedure are subject to the regulation of the subject Rulebook for licensing of clubs.[135]

---

131. Article 120, SFFM.
132. Article 121, SFFM.
133. Article 122, SFFM.
134. Article 123, SFFM.
135. Article 124, SFFM.

i. Legal Bodies

*184.* The legal bodies of FFM have the authority to act upon the grounds of suspicion of noncompliance with the acts of FFM and/or determination of violation of the rules of the football game set out in the Rules of the football game, The Rulebook and the Proposals of the respective competition and other acts of FFM, to conduct investigative actions, initiate and conduct proceedings, hear parties and witnesses in proceedings, make decisions, impose disciplinary measures.[136]

*185.* Legal authorities can be inhospitable and collegial. The legal bodies are elected by the General Assembly on the proposal of the Management Board. The members of the legal bodies, in accordance with the provisions of the Statute, have a mandate of four years, and they can be re-elected. Candidates for chairpersons and deputy chairpersons of legal bodies, in addition to the general conditions provided by the provisions of the Statute, it is necessary to have knowledge, skills and expertise in a particular field necessary for decision-making within the body.[137]

*186.* The collegial legal bodies sit and decide at sessions. The stainless steel authority shall issue a report on the activities it undertakes. The legal bodies derive their competence from the Statute, the Rulebook for organization, the Disciplinary Rulebook, the Code of Ethics and other acts that regulate the subject.[138]

*187.* If for the duration of the term of the members of the collegial legal bodies, due to inability to perform the function of some of the members, disable the work of the body, the Board appoints a replacement until termination on the reasons for the impediment or until the next session of the General Assembly when a selection will be made for the vacant position in accordance with the provisions of the Statute.[139]

8. Disciplinary Measures

*188.* Disciplinary measures are imposed on legal entities and individuals.[140] Legal authorities that have the authority to impose disciplinary measures may

136. Article 125, SFFM.
137. Article 126, SFFM.
138. Article 127, SFFM.
139. Article 128, SFFM.
140. Article 129, SFFM.

impose a suspension as a temporary measure until a disciplinary sanction is imposed, and disciplinary punishment is as follows:

- warning;
- fine;
- time measure;
- official result;
- deduction of points;
- expulsion from the club;
- exclusion from a football organization;
- exclusion from the league and return to a lower level of competition, i.e., elimination from further competition;
- return of the award.

*189.* Reprimand is issued to legal entities and individuals for violations committed under mitigating circumstances, which makes them particularly light. A fine is imposed on legal entities and individuals in denars or euros denar counter value, more closely regulated by the FFM Disciplinary Rulebook.

*190.* Time measure for individuals can be:

- ban on performance;
- lifetime ban on performance;
- ban on access to changing rooms and/or spare bench;
- ban on access to the stadium;
- prohibition to perform a certain function for a certain time;
- prohibition to perform all functions for a certain time;
- ban on participation in any football-related activity;
- Determining compulsory participation in an educational/social program character.

*191.* A temporary penalty for legal entities can be:

- prohibition of playing a match on a certain field;
- playing a certain number of matches without the presence of spectators.

*192.* The penalty of deprivation of points is imposed on legal entities, and the competent legal entity authority may impose it with:

- deduction of points from the current point balance, i.e., from the won or points that the club will win in the current championship;
- ban on transferring a football player;
- deduction of points from the next championship (negative points).

*193.* The penalty of returning the award is imposed on legal entities and individuals for violations regulated by the Disciplinary Rulebook and the Code of Ethics of FFM. Suspension as a temporary measure can be imposed both physically and legally persons (Article 130, SFFM).

*194.* At the same time and for the same misdemeanor, the competent legal authority may pronounce cumulatively several types of measures as main and secondary penalties. At the same time and for different offenses, the competent legal authority may impose a joint measure. Disciplinary measures can be imposed on all entities in football organization regardless of the degree and rank in which the function is performed. The procedure and disciplinary measures imposed by the competent legal authorities FFM bodies are regulated by the FFM Disciplinary Rulebook, in accordance with the FIFA Code of Discipline, Code of Ethics and other acts governing the subject matter.[141]

*195.* According to Article 132 of SFFM, the legal bodies of FFM are:

- Disciplinary inspector;
- Disciplinary Commission;
- Ethics Board;
- Complaints Commission.

*196.* The disciplinary inspector of FFM is a stainless legal body that elects him to the General Assembly at the proposal of the Management Board of FFM.[142] The disciplinary inspector, according to Article 134 of SFFM, has the competence:

- to conduct investigative actions and undertake activities related to investigative actions;
- to file a report for initiating a disciplinary procedure or a report before the Ethics Board of FFM for noncompliance with the Statute and acts of FFM by all subjects of disciplinary responsibility;
- to file an appeal and an extraordinary legal remedy.

*197.* The disciplinary inspector should possess expert knowledge in the field of the right. The work and manner of action of the Disciplinary Inspector will be regulated by the Rulebook for organization of FFM.[143]

## 9. Disciplinary Commission

*198.* The FFM Disciplinary Commission is a collegial body composed of five members, one chairman and one vice-chairman. The chairperson and the deputy chairperson should possess expert knowledge from the field of law. The election of

141. Article 131, SFFM.
142. Article 133, SFFM.
143. Article 134, SFFM.

the members of the commission is done by the General Assembly on a proposal of the Board of FFM. For a valid session of the Commission, the presence of more than half of the total number of members. Decisions are made by the Commission by a majority vote of the members present.[144]

*199.* The Chairman of the Disciplinary Commission may, from the ranks of the Commission, appoint members who will have the authority to perform the function in the capacity of disciplinary commissioner when it comes to competition-related offenses in youth categories, women's soccer and futsal.[145]

*200.* The commission acts upon a report for a disciplinary misdemeanor or after an official duty in accordance with the provisions of the Disciplinary Rulebook of FFM and other acts where disciplinary offenses and measures are provided. The Commission decides in the first instance on:

- disciplinary offenses arising from the rules of the game, sports behavior and organization of the competitions organized by FFM;
- disciplinary offenses arising from noncompliance with the provisions of the Statute, acts, directives, conclusions, decisions and other writings of FFM, UEFA and FIFA by the bodies of FFM; arising from their members, organs and bodies; as well as all other unmentioned categories legal and natural persons involved in the football organization regardless of the degree and the function they perform.[146]

*201.* The Ethics Board of FFM is a collegial body composed of five members: one chairman, one deputy chairman and three members. The Ethics Board has an expert investigative body composed of one member of the board elected on the proposal of the chairman, Disciplinary Inspector of FFM and FFM Integrity Officer. The expert body for investigations performs investigative actions at the request of the Board. The election of the members of the Ethics Board is done by the General Assembly of proposal of the Board of FFM. For a valid meeting of the Ethics Board, the presence of more is required from half of the total number of members. The Board makes decisions by a majority vote of the members present.[147]

*202.* The Chairman and Vice-Chairman of the Ethics Board should own professional knowledge in the field of law. The member of the Ethics Board who is part of the Investigative Body should possess the necessary skills and professional knowledge.[148]

---

144. Article 135, SFFM.
145. Article 136, SFFM.
146. Article 137, SFFM.
147. Article 138, SFFM
148. Article 139, SFFM.

## 10. Ethics Board

*203.* The Ethics Board is responsible for monitoring the work of the football team organization aimed at recognizing irregularities, including corruption, betting, unauthorized influence on the course and outcome of football matches, immoral and unethical activities and methods of work in the football organization. The Ethics Board imposes measures on all those directly or indirectly involved entities in the football organization based on the Statute, the Code of Ethics of FFM, the FFM Disciplinary Rulebook and other related acts and regulations of the subject matter. The Ethics Board may have other responsibilities; the manner of acting, decision-making and competencies of the Ethics Board are regulated in the Rulebook on organization of FFM.[149]

*204.* The FFM Appeals Commission is a collegial body composed of five members, of which one is a chairperson and one deputy chairperson. The election of the members of the commission is done by the General Assembly on a proposal of the Board of FFM. For a valid session of the Commission, the presence of more than half of the total number of members. Decisions are made by the Commission by a majority vote of the members present (Article 141, SFFM).

*205.* The Chairman and Deputy Chairman of the Appeals Commission should possess expert knowledge in the field of law.[150]

*206.* The Appeals Commission shall act in accordance with the provisions of the Statute, FFM Disciplinary Rulebook, FFM Code of Ethics, Rulebook on FFM elections and other acts where two-stage decision-making is envisaged. The exception from paragraph 1 of the article is the process of licensing clubs for national or UEFA competition.[151]

## 11. Appeals Commission

*207.* The subject of appeal are the decisions of the first-instance legal bodies that, at the time of filing an appeal, have not become final. Decisions of other first-instance bodies that, at the time of filing the appeal, did not become final, including permanent bodies of the governing bodies that conduct the competition, decide on issues related to the status of players, referees, coaching issues and more.[152] No appeal is allowed against the decisions of the Appeals Commission; they are final.[153] Upon completion of the second-instance procedure, the interested parties,

149. Article 140, SFFM.
150. Article 142, SFFM.
151. Article 143, SFFM.
152. Article 144, SFFM.
153. Article 145, SFFM.

in accordance with the prescribed rules, may submit extraordinary remedies regulated by the FFM Disciplinary Rulebook.[154]

## 12. General Secretariat

*208.* The General Secretariat is the administrative body of the FFM. The organization of the General Secretariat is regulated by the Rulebook on organization of FFM. The General Secretariat is managed by the President of FFM as a person who represents FFM in legal transactions.[155]

*209.* At the proposal of the President, the Management Board appoints a management structure of the General Secretariat. The Secretary-General and the department managers should have high education, professional knowledge in the field of the relevant sector, experience in football administrative work of at least five years, and knowledge of acts of FFM, UEFA and FIFA. The Secretary-General and the Department Managers have a mandate of four years with the right of re-election. For coordination and management of the work of the national teams, FFM hires a technical director or development director and a coordinator who actively participates in the work of national teams.[156]

*210.* The President may delegate some of the powers relating to management and financial operations of the General Secretariat, including the signing of financial documents of the Secretary-General. The Secretary-General is responsible for executing FFM's financial plan. The Secretary-General, in cooperation with the department managers, coordinates the work of the organs and bodies of FFM and is responsible for the work of the General Secretariat. The Secretary-General attends the meetings of the Management Board without voting rights. The competencies of the Secretary-General are regulated by a Rulebook on organization of FFM.[157]

*211.* The General Secretariat has the following tasks:

- performs preparations and administrative-technical works for organizing and holding the General Assembly of FFM;
- organizes the sessions, administratively supports them, executes them, implements the decisions of the statutory bodies, permanent and ad hoc bodies;
- performs activities related to the organization of domestic and international competitions;
- organizes events for promotion and development of football in the Republic of Macedonia;
- implements the decisions of the bodies of FFM;
- prepares draft decisions and acts of FFM;

154. Article 146, SFFM.
155. Article 147, SFFM.
156. Article 148, SFFM.
157. Article 149, SFFM.

- keeps books for financial and material operations;
- keeps ledgers and archives;
- keeps records of registered clubs, players, professional contracts with players, coaches, etc.;
- keeps records of active football referees, controllers and mentors; organizes conducting exams for judges, etc.;
- organizes seminars and workshops, implements an education system of coaches, referees, etc.;
- proposes amendments to acts for systematization and regulation of the internal organization of the General Secretariat to the Board of FFM;
- performs other tasks necessary to achieve the goals defined in the Statute.

*212.* Employees of the General Secretariat may not be members of the statutory bodies and bodies of FFM, the standing committees and boards, as well as members of bodies and organs of the members of FFM, with the exception provided by the provisions of the Statute. Employees of the administrative body, for the duration of the contract for employment, may participate in the work of the bodies of UEFA and FIFA, as well as perform functions in UEFA and FIFA.[158]

## 13. Competitions

*213.* FFM is responsible for organizing all types of football competitions held in the territory of the Republic of Macedonia. FFM organizes championships and a bunch of senior and youth competitions categories 11v11, in male and female competition. FFM can also organize friendly domestic or international competitions and/or tournaments. The manner of organization, the conditions under which they are organized, the criteria and the rest are described in the FFM Competition Rules. For each competition before the start of the season, the Management Board adopts Propositions that set out the rules of the competition in more detail.[159]

*214.* FFM may be part of the authority to organize competitions and convey competitions to its members.[160]

*215.* Before each competition season/year, the competition organizer prepares a competition calendar that should be aligned with the calendar of a higher level of competition at home. The FFM competition calendar needs to be coordinated and harmonized with the FIFA International Calendar.[161]

158. Article 151, SFFM.
159. Article 152, SFFM.
160. Article 153, SFFM.
161. Article 154, SFFM.

*216.* Clubs provide participation in a higher level of competition with cumulative fulfillment of the following criteria:

(1) achieved sports result;
(2) meeting the licensing criteria for the competition levels where it is prescribed;
(3) fulfillment of other criteria determined by the body that adopts Competition Propositions.[162]

*217.* Clubs provide participation in international competitions with cumulative meeting the following criteria:

(1) achieved sports result;
(2) fulfillment of licensing criteria;
(3) fulfillment of other criteria determined by the body that organizes the competition (Article 156, SFFM).

*218.* FIFA, UEFA or other confederations depending on the venue, have exclusive authority to organize international competitions and competitions. FFM, FFM members, and clubs as indirect members can organize international competitions and contests only if, for the same, they have the approval of the competent authority of FIFA, UEFA and FFM, respectively.[163]

*219.* FFM, members of FFM, clubs, football players, and officials under no circumstances may occur or enter into organization agreements or participation in international competitions and/or competitions if they organize or participate in an association/union that is not a member of FIFA or is a member of temporary status of one of the confederations, without the approval of FIFA.[164]

*220.* The FFM and its members, as organizers of the respective competitions, own all the rights arising from competitions and the subject competition as well as from other events whose organization they have in charge. The rights from paragraph one of this provision include financial rights, image and/or sound distribution, including but not limited to: transmission in live, recording or excerpt via audiovisual and/or audio media, reproduction and broadcasting rights, multimedia rights, data transfer rights from competitions, marketing rights, promotion rights and intangible rights like what are the marks, emblem, logo and other rights arising from the Copyright Act and other related rights and industrial property.[165]

162. Article 155, SFFM.
163. Article 157, SFFM.
164. Article 158, SFFM.
165. Article 159, SFFM.

*221.* Terms, method of use, responsibility for distribution, exclusivity, rights and obligations arising from the management of rights subject to this provision, including the rights of clubs which, as participants in the competition, appear as organizers of the competitions, are regulated by a special Rulebook on the use of media and other rights adopted from the Board of FFM.[166]

## 14. Normative and Financial Activities

*222.* The general acts of FFM constitute but are not limited to the Statute, rules, competition regulations, rules of procedure and more. The individual acts of FFM constitute but are not limited to decisions which are brought by the competent bodies of FFM, conclusions, criteria and more.[167]

*223.* The statute is a basic constitutive legal act of FFM. All other general and individual acts of FFM and the members of FFM must be in accordance with the Statute.[168]

*224.* Rules are general acts that regulate sports legislation in connection with a specific activity arising from the goals of FFM. Decisions are individual legal acts based on the sports legislation of FFM, which give direction to legal entities and individuals in accordance with the Statute, regulate, determine, name, and pronounce a certain act or non-act.[169]

*225.* The work of referees and coaches as separate football categories is regulated by the Rulebook on Judges and Trials and the Rulebook on the Status and Work of Coaches. The Management Board of FFM obligatorily determines disciplinary rules; competition rules; rules for registration, status and transfer of players and licensing rules. Depending on whether it is a domestic or international competition licensing rules are systematized in:

- Rulebook on licensing of clubs for domestic competition;
- Rulebook on licensing of clubs for competitions organized by UEFA;
- Rulebook on licensing of clubs for competitions organized by UEFA must comply with the UEFA Club Licensing Regulations and financially fair play. According to the licensing rules, the club licensing process is managed by the Licensing Bodies in cooperation with the Licensing Department of FFM.[170]

*226.* "Makfootball" is an official list of FFM. The decisions of the organs and bodies of FFM announced for informative character, competition calendars, tables, acts, and registrations of players and clubs are published in the official list of FFM

166. Article 160, SFFM.
167. Article 161, SFFM.
168. Article 162, SFFM.
169. Article 163, SFFM.
170. Article 164, SFFM.

"Makfootball" in accordance with the adopted decisions and acts of FFM. The composition of the editorial board of the official list "Makfootball" and the competence is determined by the Rulebook for organization of FFM. FFM acts, decisions, schedules, calendars, press releases, and more can also be published on the FFM website.[171]

*227.* For all disputes between members, players, mediators, coaches, referees, clubs and other individuals and legal entities that undertake and/or perform sports activities related to the football game are directed to perform them by negotiating the jurisdiction of an independent Arbitral Tribunal recognized by FFM without the involvement of the regular courts of the Republic of Macedonia. The submission of disputes, as in paragraph 1 of this provision, is mandatory in all cases for which there is no provision prohibiting arbitration dispute resolution in accordance with the positive legal regulations of the Republic of Macedonia.[172]

*228.* The composition, competencies and procedure for arbitration of disputes are regulated with a special rulebook.[173]

*229.* The financial period of FFM starts on January 1 and ends on December 31 in the current year; it is one year and coincides with the calendar year.[174]

*230.* FFM has a denar and foreign currency account in one or more banks.[175]

*231.* The financial operations of FFM are conducted in accordance with the positive legal requirements regulations in the Republic of Macedonia in the field of finance and accounting in accordance with established accounting principles. The financial operations of FFM are subject to a regular annual audit conducted by an independent audit firm. The Independent Auditor is elected by the General Assembly at the suggestion of the Management Board for a period of four years. The independent auditor is responsible for auditing the financial statements previously subject to review by the Financial Commission of FFM and submitting and presenting the audit report to the General Assembly of FFM.[176]

*232.* According to Article 171 of SFFM, FFM generates revenues from:

– membership fee;
– TV and other media rights;
– wills, legacies;
– donations and sponsorship related to marketing activities;

171. Article 165, SFFM.
172. Article 166, SFFM.
173. Article 167, SFFM.
174. Article 168, SFFM.
175. Article 169, SFFM.
176. Article 170, SFFM.

- revenues from UEFA and FIFA to achieve the goals of FFM, which includes, but does not restrict, encourage and develop football activities, infrastructural projects, administration, etc.;
- fees and prizes for participation in international competitions and other revenues for which decisions have been made by the competent bodies of UEFA, FIFA and other domestic and international organizations;
- the budget of the Republic of Macedonia for development and support of football in the Republic of Macedonia;
- fees from members, clubs and other football entities for participation, payment fees and fines in accordance with decisions made by the competent authorities of FFM;
- publishing brochures, publications, professional information bulletins, etc.;
- rents;
- commercial rights that include but are not limited to the sale of fan props, balls, jerseys, hats, badges and more with the logo of FFM in order to promote FFM activities;
- income from tickets from domestic and international competitions;
- other unmentioned income in accordance with the law and the goals determined in the Statute.

*233.* FFM for the realization of the activities arising from the goals set in the Statute covers:

- the costs determined by the financial plan—the budget of FFM;
- expenses approved by the General Assembly;
- the costs that the Management Board will approve within its own powers;
- all other costs necessary for the realization of activities that arise from goals.[177]

*234.* Each member of FFM has a special account on which FFM records and resides liabilities and receivables of FFM and the member in accordance with the positive legal regulations.[178]

*235.* The General Assembly may, on the proposal of the Management Board, decide membership fees for its members. The membership fee is the same for all members.[179]

*236.* The Management Board of FFM can appoint the members and/or clubs from First and/or Second MFL, which organizes international competitions, to submit reports on realized income from the subject match/tournament. The income report is submitted on a form prescribed by FFM, according to which a fee is paid which cannot be more than 3% of the realized net income for the benefit of the territorial football organization and/or the FFM.[180]

177. Article 172, SFFM.
178. Article 173, SFFM.
179. Article 174, SFFM.
180. Article 175, SFFM.

15. Potential Termination of the Work of FFM

*237.* FFM may cease to operate under conditions determined by the Statute in compliance with positive legal regulations. In case of termination of work, the property of FFM is managed by a body selected on the session of the General Assembly at which the decision to terminate the work is a "bonus pater familias" to create conditions for re-formation with consent of UEFA and FIFA.[181]

## *C. Handball Federation of Macedonia*

1. Position of the Federation

*238.* With the Statute of the RFM, in accordance with the Law on Sports and other laws and regulations, as well as the Statute and other acts of European Handball Federation (EHF) and the International Handball Federation (IHF), are regulated: name and the seat of the Handball Federation of Macedonia (hereinafter "RFM"); goals and the tasks of the RFM, forms and manner of action; conditions and procedure of establishment; the association in RFM and the conditions for that; RFM membership in other unions, federations and international associations; seal, stamp and other features; representation and representation in legal transactions and against third parties; bodies, the manner of their selection, the duration of the mandate of the bodies and the manner of decision-making of the members, the competence and the manner of work; acquisition and disposal of property and financing, i.e., spending of the means for performing the activity; supervision; the representation of Macedonian handball; the functions and responsibilities for their performance; work programs and plans; security; making the public work; recognitions and awards; administration; status changes in the status of public interest organizations; termination of the work of RFM; handling of property and assets in case of termination of the RFM; as well as other issues determined by law regarding the work of RFM.[182]

*239.* RFM is an association created by the Association of handball clubs, the Association of handball referees, the Association of Handball Controllers and the Association of handball coaches in the Republic of Macedonia for the purpose of achieving and harmonizing the individual with general and common interests in the popularization and development of handball, as well as for the purpose of establishing and building an international program of handball sports cooperation and other programs of common interest. A handball club registered as an association may cease to operate as an association and be registered as a trading company for performing sports activity. The Handball Federation recognizes the continuity of the achieved result of the trading company that was created by registering from a sports association whose legal heir is the trading company.[183]

181. Article 177, SFFM.
182. Article 1, Statute of the Handball Federation of Macedonia (SHFM).
183. Article 2, SHFM.

*240.* RFM is the only sports federation in the Republic of Macedonia in handball. The members of RFM, leagues or any groups of clubs or associations are subordinated to RFM and cannot operate outside RFM. RFM is recognized by EHF and IHF. RFM has the status of a legal entity of public interest, with rights and obligations and responsibilities determined by the Constitution, Law and other regulations, the Statute, as well as by the Statute and other acts of EHF. RFM cannot be transformed into another type of legal entity.[184]

*241.* RFM is responsible for its obligations with its property and assets.[185]

*242.* RFM cannot perform economic activity. RFM may establish limited liability companies (LLCs) and joint-stock companies for realization of funds for financing the functions of the federation and for the purpose of realization of its goals.[186]

*243.* Political, religious and religious organizations and actions are prohibited in the RFM. The actions referred to in paragraph 1 are also undertaken by the competent authorities in the RFM. The bodies of RFM are obliged to inform the basic public prosecutor if the existence of political, religious and religious organizations is determined and acting in the RFM and its members, contrary to the Law.[187]

*244.* Disputed issues related to the organization of handball and the maintenance of sports competitions and other issues regulated by the acts of the RFM within the established jurisdiction are decided by the bodies of the RFM. Following the final decisions of the bodies of the RFM, no litigation can be conducted. As an exception, court and other proceedings may be instituted on labor matters and obligation relations and material-financial affairs.[188]

*245.* The Assembly, at the proposal of the Board of Directors, may grant him the status of honorary president or honorary membership of a person for special merits for Macedonian handball. Honorary presidents may attend the Assembly and the sessions of the Board of Directors in an advisory role but do not have the right to vote.[189]

## 2. Name, Seat, Aims, Tasks and Other Characteristics of the Federation

*246.* The name of the national sports federation is the Handball Federation of Macedonia.[190]

---

184. Article 3, SHFM.
185. Article 4, SHFM.
186. Article 5, SHFM.
187. Article 6, SHFM.
188. Article 7, SHFM.
189. Article 8, SHFM.
190. Article 9, SHFM.

*247.* The headquarters of RFM is in Skopje, on Blvd. Kuzman Josifovski-Pitu No. 15.[191]

*248.* RFM, in statutory, programmatic and other documents rounded and directed system:

(1) considers all issues related to Macedonian handball;
(2) determines the keeping of records for the purpose of organized monitoring and improvement of the situation and the development of handball sport (according to Article 68 of the Law on Sports of the Republic of Macedonia—Official Gazette No. 81/08 from July 7, 2008);
(3) promotes handball in the Republic of Macedonia in the spirit of peace, understanding and fair play, without any discriminations regarding politics, gender, religion, race and ethnicity;
(4) encourages sports activities in the realization of the RFM program as well as the activity of children and youth within the RFM (according to Article 22 of the Law on Sports of the Republic of Macedonia);
(5) respects and protects the interests of each member of the RFM and resolves disputes between them;
(6) encourages and promotes the handball sport;
(7) implements established programs related to the development of handball;
(8) is the holder of the coordination of the program activities of the handball clubs, ORS, GRS and ZRSM, ZRKM and ZRTM;
(9) organizes and implements the system in all levels of competition in handball on the territory of the Republic of Macedonia;
(10) is the bearer of the care for the development of the professional work and the training of the professional staff in handball sport;
(11) takes care of health protection and control, health examination of the handball players (according to Article 52 of the Law on Sports);
(12) takes care of the Convention on Anti-Doping Control in the Republic of Macedonia (according to Article 55 from the Law on Sports);
(13) ensures consistent application of the rules and regulations of the handball game by handball clubs, ORS, GRS, ZRSM, ZRKM, ZRTM and their bodies;
(14) determines the status of the handball players in accordance with the regulations of the IHF, EHF, the Statute and other acts and regulations of RFM;
(15) based on the application for enrollment, RFM keeps a register of members and records of members of the bodies (according to Article 27 of the LAF—Official Gazette of RM No. 52 from April 16, 2010);
(16) organizations have tax and customs relief in accordance with the Law;
(17) performs other activities and tasks arising from the Law on Sports, the LAF, other laws and regulations, the Statute and other acts of the RFM, as well as the acts of EHF and IHF.[192]

---

191. Article 10, SHFM.
192. Article 11, SHFM.

*249.* Article 12 of Statute of the Handball Federation of Macedonia (SHFM) describes the seal, the stamp and other designations.

*250.* RFM has an emblem and a flag. The emblem of RFM is the flag of the Republic of Macedonia, inscription "Handball Federation of Macedonia" in three official languages determined by EHF in yellow, silhouette of a handball player in movement in white, on a red background with a yellow stripe. The dimensions of the flag are 400 cm × 200 cm, 200 cm × 100 cm or 160 cm × 80 cm.[193]

3. Membership

*251.* In RFM as the only national handball federation for the territory of the Republic of Macedonia, all handball clubs are united, which, according to the Law, are united in municipal handball unions and boards, and for the area of the City of Skopje in City Handball Union – Skopje.[194]

*252.* Municipal and City Handball Association of Skopje can be organized if it:

- unites at least five handball clubs that compete in any system of competitions organized by RFM.
- has a properly organized form and action of handball referees, controllers and coaches; and
- has a youth zone or regional league.

*253.* Handball clubs from the territory of a municipality, in which, according to the law provided conditions, there are no opportunities to organize a municipal handball union, can join the already formed municipal union in a neighboring municipality or organize municipal handball association with handball clubs from other neighboring municipalities, in which, there are also no conditions for the formation of special municipal handball unions. All handball clubs in the area of the City of Skopje unite in a single City Handball Association—Skopje (hereinafter "GRS"). The clubs united in municipal and GRS statutory regulate the mutual relations and competencies on issues of common interest.

*254.* The statutes of the members of RFM (clubs, ORS, GRS, ZRSM, ZRKM and ZRTM) must be harmonized with the Statute of RFM. The statutes, before their adoption, are confirmed by the Commission for Statute and regulations of RFM or the Commission for normative acts of RFM. The statutes and other acts of the members of the RFM, after their adoption, are mandatory to submit to RFM for documentation and records.[195]

193. Article 13, SHFM.
194. Article 14, SHFM.
195. Article 15, SHFM.

*255.* Membership in RFM is open. Clubs, unions, boards and professional associations apply for membership in RFM. To the request, they are obliged to submit: Statute; Verdict; decision by the body of the state administration in charge of sports affairs affirming that the conditions for performing sports activity are met; a statement that they accept the Statute and other acts of the RFM and will observe the principles of loyalty and integrity of RFM; confirmation from the relevant municipal, i.e., GRS that the club is associated in that union and confirmation from RFM or request to RFM that it is included in the system of competition. The Assembly of RFM receives new members of RFM. As an exception, a decision to admit a new member between two sessions of the Assembly may be brought by the Board of Directors of RFM but is obliged at the next session of the Assembly to propose it on the agenda for confirmation.[196]

*256.* A Club member of RFM can be excluded from the membership of RFM if he/she:

- loses his/her status as a member of RFM due to termination of competition;
- seriously violates the Statute or other act of the RFM;
- does not keep a register of members and records of members and bodies; and
- does not settle the financial obligations to RFM or EHF.

*257.* The expulsion of the members is decided by the Board of Directors. After the exclusion decision, a complaint can be filed with the Assembly within fifteen days. Prior to exclusion, the organs and bodies of the RFM may impose a suspension.[197]

*258.* RFM is a constituent member of the Macedonian Olympic Committee. RFM is a member of the EHF. RFM is a member of the IHF. RFM can join other handball or sports associations in the region in accordance with the Law.[198]

*259.* In performing the activity, RFM and the members of RFM will adhere to the decisions contained in the acts of the IHF, EHF and the regional association. In case of noncompliance of the acts of RFM with the acts from the previous paragraph, directly the decisions contained in the acts of the IHF and EHF are applied.[199]

---

196. Article 16, SHFM.
197. Article 17, SHFM.
198. Article 18, SHFM.
199. Article 19, SHFM.

## 4. Organs and Bodies of the Federation, Their Election and Competence

*260.* The bodies of RFM are:[200]

(1) Assembly
(2) Board of Directors
(3) Supervisory Commission.

*261.* The Assembly of RFM is the highest body of RFM. The Assembly of RFM consists of one representative from each handball club from the Super Men and Women Handball League, First and Second Men and Women Handball League, three representatives from the Association of Handball Referees of Macedonia, three representatives from the Association of Handball Controllers of Macedonia, three representatives from the Association of Handball Coaches of Macedonia, in accordance with the Statute. A team that is not competing in the regular system of competitions or gives up for any reason from competition in the league—the system of RFM has no right to vote in the assembly as well newly registered clubs (acquire the right to vote after verification of receipt of the Assembly of the RFM). The bodies of the RFM and the members of the bodies of RFM exercise their rights and duties exercise and perform on the basis of the Law, the Statute and other acts of the RFM. A member (delegate) in the RFM can be a citizen of the Republic of Macedonia. A delegate in the Assembly can only be a member, as proposed by the Associations listed in paragraph 1 of the article. For participation in the work of the Assembly, it is obligatory to submit power of attorney from the association—the club. The mandate of the representatives in the Assembly by the Citizens' Associations lasts four years. The mandate of the delegate begins to run with the verification of the same by the Verification Commission. The mandate of the Delegate of the Assembly ends:

- if he resigns;
- if he is revoked, i.e., replaced by the bodies of his association with a new representative;
- in case of death;
- if a measure is imposed on the competent disciplinary body by a final decision ban on performing functions in sports.[201]

*262.* The Assembly of the RFM:

- adopts Statutes, programs and other acts;
- adopts annual reports, directions and work plans;
- adopts financial plans and programs;
- elects committees and other bodies for the work of the Assembly:
  (1) Working Presidency (five members)
  (2) Minutes (one member)

---

200. Article 20, SHFM.
201. Article 21, SHFM.

(3) Minutes of the Minutes (two members)
(4) Verification Commission (three members)
(5) Candidacy Commission (three members)
(6) Commission for counting the votes (three members)
(7) Commission for conducting elections (three members)

- elects other commissions and other bodies for issues within its competence;
- elects bodies of the association;
- elects the President of the Assembly, who is also the President of the Board of RFM, who receives the mandatory right to form a list of candidates for the Board of RFM from prominent businessmen and sports workers;
- in case of termination of the mandate of the president, until the election of a new president, the function of the president is performed by the vice president as the acting president (not more than six months);
- dismisses the president of the Assembly—MB;
- adopts the list of members for the Board of RFM upon the proposal of the mandator;
- adopts the list of deputy members for the Board of RFM on the proposal of the handball clubs and the sponsoring companies of RFM;
- makes decisions for association in RFM or separation from other sports associations federations and for membership in international associations;
- concludes admission of new members and termination of membership upon proposal of the Board of RFM;
- makes decisions for establishment of trade companies, LLCs and joint-stock companies in accordance with the law;
- elects the Supervisory Commission of the RFM;
- makes a decision for the honorary president and honorary member;
- decides on recognitions and awards;
- makes decisions, programs, rulebooks, instructions, conclusions and other acts;
- gives authentic interpretations of the decisions it makes for their practical application;
- adopts a Rulebook for handball competitions;
- adopts the system for handball competitions at all levels of competition in the Republic of Macedonia;
- adopts Rules of Procedure of the Assembly;
- decides on requests and appeals for extraordinary mitigation of fines;
- reviews the work reports of the bodies and bodies it elects;
- makes decisions on the total disposal of funds and their disposal according to the conditions determined by law;
- establishes foundations and decides on their abolition (in accordance with Article 27 of the LAF—Official Gazette of RM no. 52 from April 16, 2010);
- adopts development program for four years;
- reviews and adopts a report on the activity of the Management Board of RFM;
- makes a decision with a two-thirds majority for termination of the work of RFM;
- gives an authentic interpretation of the provisions of the acts it adopts;
- performs other activities in accordance with the Statute and the general acts of the RFM;

– performs other activities in accordance with the Law on Sports of the Republic of Macedonia and the Law of Health centers and foundations.[202]

*263.* The sessions of the Assembly are convened by the president of the Assembly. A session of the Assembly can be convened as needed and at least once a year with a Proposal—agenda that is submitted (and published on the RFM website) to the representatives in the Assembly of the RFM within eight to fourteen days before the Session of the Assembly. The president of the RFM has the right in case of need to convene the Assembly immediately and in a shorter term and to explain the urgency at the session of the Assembly of the RFM. The president must schedule a session of the Assembly at the request of:

– the Board of Directors of RFM; or
– written request of one-third of the total number of members of the Association.

*264.* The submitter of the request for scheduling a session of the Assembly proposes an agenda and submits the entire material to the president of the RFM. The president must schedule a session of the Assembly within fourteen days. The session must be held within thirty days at the latest. If the president does not convene a session within fourteen days, the session of the Assembly shall be convened by the initiators. The entire material for the session is submitted within eight to fourteen days to the delegates of the Assembly. If the issue for which a session of the Assembly is convened and held at the request of the initiators refers to the trust of the president of the RFM or to the election of the bodies of the RFM, such a question may not be asked for at least six months.[203]

*265.* The Assembly works in sessions. The Assembly can work if it is attended by a majority of the total number of delegates to the Assembly (more than half of the total number of delegates to the Assembly). Each delegate of the Assembly has the right to one vote. The Assembly, as a rule, makes decisions by a majority vote of those present delegates. The Assembly, with a qualified (two-thirds) majority of the votes from the total number of the representatives in the Assembly, makes a decision for termination of the RF.[204]

*266.* The Assembly decides by public vote. Voting can be secret, if so decided by the Assembly, at the proposal of the president or a delegate supported by at least fifteen delegates to the Assembly. The proposal for a secret ballot is considered accepted if more than half of the delegates present have voted for it. For the adoption of the list of candidates for members of the Management Board of RFM, the Assembly conducts it by public voting.[205]

202. Article 22, SHFM.
203. Article 23, SHFM.
204. Article 24, SHFM.
205. Article 25, SHFM.

*267.* The manner of work and decision-making of the Assembly is regulated in more detail by the Rules of Procedure of the Assembly. The Rules of Procedure of the Assembly especially regulate the procedure for adoption and amendments to the acts within the competence of the Assembly, the submission of initiatives and proposals, authorized proposers for adoption of acts, rights and the duties of the representatives in the Assembly, the course of the sessions, the maintenance of order, minutes and other issues. The Rules of Procedure of the Assembly regulate the composition and work of permanent and occasional committees and bodies established by the Assembly.[206]

*268.* The number of representatives that make up the Assembly of the RFM is determined by the Assembly of RFM, at the proposal of the Board of RFM, and at the beginning of the session of the Assembly (according to Article 21 of the Statute of RFM).[207]

*269.* The number and composition of the bodies of the Assembly are proposed by the Board of RFM and determined by the Assembly at the session itself. The election of the president must be announced no later than sixty days before the expiration of the term for which they were elected and whose term expires. In case of early termination of the mandate of the president of the RFM, after any basis, the election of a new president is made no later than six months.[208]

*270.* The Assembly elects the president of the RFM from among the delegates by a majority vote of the total number of delegates present in the Assembly. The president of the Assembly is elected for a term of four years. A proposal for the election of a president may be submitted by at least twenty delegates to the Assembly. The election of the president of the RFM is done by secret ballot; voting can also be public, if so decided by the Assembly, on the proposal of a delegate supported by at least fifteen delegates to the Assembly. The proposal for public voting is considered accepted if more than half voted for it from the delegates present.[209]

*271.* The president of the Assembly is also the President of the Management Board of the RFM. The president of the Assembly and the Board of the RFM have the following rights and duties:

- represents RFM in the country and abroad;
- proposes the composition of the Management Board of RFM;
- manages the RFM and controls the consistent application of the Statute and the acts of the Assembly and the Management Board propose and take appropriate measures in this regard in accordance with the acts of the RFM;
- convenes and manages the sessions of the Assembly and the Management Board, proposes agenda, determines the place and date of the sessions;

206. Article 26, SHFM.
207. Article 27, SHFM.
208. Article 28, SHFM.
209. Article 29, SHFM.

- signs the acts adopted by the Assembly and the Management Board of RFM;
- keeps from performing the acts of the bodies that it considers to have been adopted contrary to a Law or other regulation, for which it informs the Assembly and the Management Board of RFM and submits them for re-decision or final decision;
- is the commander for execution and realization of the financial plan of RFM;
- exercises control over the financial operations of RFM and, if necessary, undertakes appropriate measures;
- takes measures and, in cooperation with other bodies, provides conditions for regularity in handball competition on the domestic and international stages;
- is responsible for his work before the Assembly of the RFM;
- performs other activities determined by the Statute and other general acts of the RFM, as well as activities decided by the Assembly of the RFM.[210]

*272.* The Assembly elects from among the delegates upon the proposal of the president of the RFM and vice president of the RFM with a majority vote of the total number of delegates in the Assembly. The vice president of the Assembly is elected for a term of four years. The election of the vice president of RFM is done by public voting; voting can be secret, if so decided by the Assembly, at the proposal of a delegate supported by at least fifteen delegates to the Assembly. The proposal for public voting is considered accepted if more than half voted for it from the delegates present. Vice president of the Assembly, ex officio, is also vice president of the Board of RFM. In the absence of the president, the function is performed by the vice president; in case of termination of the mandate of the president, until the election of a new president, the function of the president is performed by the vice president as the acting president (not more than six months).[211]

*273.* The Management Board is an executive body of the Assembly and RFM and has thirteen to seventeen members. The members of the Board of RFM have one deputy each, who will be appointed by the handball clubs and sponsoring companies, which in the absence of the member of the Board of RFM replace and fully participate and decide in the work of the Board of RFM. At the suggestion of handball clubs and sponsoring companies, the election of deputy members of the Management Board of RFM is performed by the Management Board at its regular session. The Board of RFM elects three vice presidents from among its members. The mandate of the president, the vice presidents, the members of the Management Board and their deputies lasts four years. The rights and duties of the vice presidents are determined by the Rules of Procedure of MB of RFM. Members of the Management Board of RFM can also be persons who are not citizens of the Republic of Macedonia but not more than one-third of the total number of members of the Management Board of RFM.[212]

210. Article 30, SHFM.
211. Article 31, SHFM.
212. Article 32, SHFM.

*274.* In case of evident inactivity of a member of the Board of RFM, at the proposal of the president of RFM, the Board of Directors may appoint a new member of the Board of RFM. At the first Assembly, on the proposal of the president, the inactive member is dismissed, and the newly appointed member is verified.[213]

*275.* RFM Board of Directors:

- prepares the sessions of the Assembly;
- executes and implements the decisions, positions and conclusions of the Assembly;
- determines the proposal, amendments to the Statute of the RFM, and other general acts of RFM;
- adopts normative acts within its competencies;
- Adopts a calendar for the competition season;
- Establishes the system of the state cup of competitions;
- Establishes transitional terms for handball players;
- Adopts a list of referees and delegate controllers for the league matches;
- Forms working bodies and commissions that are not within the competence of the Assembly and appoints their own presidents and members;
- manages and is responsible for the management of the property of RFM;
- makes decisions on procurement and alienation of fixed assets;
- makes decisions on travel and other expenses for business trips;
- appoints and dismisses the Secretary-General;
- appoints and dismisses directors of handball national teams;
- appoints and dismisses secretaries of the handball national teams;
- appoints and dismisses selectors and coaches of the handball national teams;
- adopts a rulebook for all national teams;
- adopts rulebooks, accepts agreements and concludes and terminates contracts;
- enables permanent professional development of the professional staff in the field of handball sport in the Republic of Macedonia;
- elects representatives in sports bodies and organizations;
- declares the best handball player, club, coach, referee, or delegate controller for the past season, as well as for a certain period;
- makes decisions and other acts for organization and work of the handball national teams of the Republic of Macedonia;
- forms and dissolves permanent and occasional commissions as auxiliary bodies of the Management Board;
- reviews the reports of the standing and occasional commissions;
- raises and presents current issues related to handball before the body of the state administration responsible for sports affairs (AMC), the IOC and other bodies and organizations in the Republic of Macedonia;
- issues an official bulletin through its commissions;
- appoints a security commissioner, i.e., an appropriate security commission;
- announces elections for representatives in the Assembly;

213. Article 33, SHFM.

- annuls, revokes or returns for reconsideration the decisions and decisions of its commissions and bodies if it finds that they are in conflict with the Statute and other acts of the RFM and makes a final decision on certain issues (protection of legality);
- implements and controls the handball championships at all levels of competition;
- initiates a procedure before its commissions for responsibility and dismissal of officials RFM staff;
- submits a report on its work to the Assembly of the RFM;
- decides on the transfer of certain authorizations from its competence to its own commissions, boards, unions, associations, etc., as well as for their confiscation;
- makes other decisions that will arise from the current operation;
- determines criteria for participation of athletes and sports teams from the Republic of Macedonia at international competitions;
- makes decisions for organization of handball matches of interest for the Republic of Macedonia;
- provides conditions, takes concrete measures for violation of interests and violation of the reputation of the handball sport and at the same time bears responsibilities for the matches, for their regularity at the level of the Republic of Macedonia;
- makes decisions and reports to referees, delegate supervisors, and sports teams in regional leagues, EHF and IHF;
- adopts Rules of Procedure of the Management Board of RFM;
- adopts an act for systematization of jobs;
- gives an authentic interpretation of the provisions of the acts it adopts; and
- performs other activities determined by the Statute and other acts of the RFM.[214]

*276.* The Board of Directors meets as needed and works in sessions. The board can work if it is attended by more than half of the total number of members of the Board of RFM. The Management Board is accountable for its work to the Assembly of the RFM. Each representative of the Board of RFM has the right to one vote. The sessions of the Management Board of RFM are convened by the president of the Management Board of RFM on his own initiative and manages their work. A meeting of the Management Board of RFM is convened as needed, with an invitation and a Proposed agenda submitted to the members of the Board of RFM within five days before its holding. If there is an urgency for making a Decision, in accordance with Article 3 item 11, “Decision-making without presence” from the LAF (Official Gazette of RM No. 52 from April 16, 2010) is a way through which the members of the Board of RFM can declare and adopt a valid decision, without holding a session, and by telephone conference or electronic mail consult with the Secretary-General or the Organizational Secretary, and the Decision must on the next regular session of the Board of RFM to verify it. The president of the RFM has the right in case of need to convene the Board of Directors immediately in a shorter period of time and to explain the urgency at the session of the Management Board of RFM.[215]

214. Article 34, SHFM.
215. Article 35, SHFM.

*277.* The Management Board of RFM decides by a majority vote of the present members. RFM Management Board, with a majority of votes from the total number of members in the RFM Management Board, elects three vice presidents of the Management Board of RFM. The voting of the Board of RFM, as a rule, is public, if at the proposal of the president or after at the request of one of the members who will be supported by at least one-third of the present members may be secret. Voting can also be by individual vote (by roll call) if so suggested by the president or a member who will be supported by at least one-third of the members of the Board of RFM. A member of the Board of RFM is excluded from voting on issues related to him, his spouse, a friend or a relative to a second degree, as well as questions relating to the club he is from delegated.[216]

*278.* The members of the Management Board exercise control over the operation, use and disposal of the funds of the federation, through the governing bodies, in a determined manner with the Statute.[217]

*279.* For the purpose of performing the statutory and program tasks and the Decisions of the Assembly and the Board of Directors, the Board of Directors forms.

*280.* Permanent bodies of the Management Board of RFM:

(1) Commission for normative acts.
(2) Registration Commission.
(3) Licensing Commission.
(4) Competition Commission (or Commissioner).
(5) Commission for conducting cup competitions.
(6) Second Instance Competition Commission.
(7) Commission for Sports Halls.
(8) Security Commission.
(9) Commission for organization of international competitions.
(10) Disciplinary Commission.
(11) Arbitration Commission.
(12) Health Commission.
(13) Commission for awards and recognitions.
(14) Commission for mass sports, sports for all and sports for women.
(15) Commission for professional issues at RFM.
(16) Commission for mini handball;
(17) Beach Handball Commission.
(18) Commission for pioneer, cadet and youth competitions.
(19) Commission for zone competitions.
(20) Marketing Commission.

216. Article 36, SHFM.
217. Article 37, SHFM.

*281.* If necessary, the Management Board of RFM can form other Organizing Boards and committees, commissions and bodies. The chairmen of the commissions and bodies are elected by the members of the commissions, a The presidents of the boards and committees are elected by the Board of RFM from among the prominent sports workers. A member of the commission is excluded from voting on issues related to him, his spouse, a friend or a relative to a second degree, as well as questions relating to the club he is delegated.[218]

*282.* The formation of boards, committees, commissions and bodies, their competence and powers, composition, duration of the mandate and the manner of their work and decision-making are more closely determined by the Rules of Procedure of the Management Board of the RFM or by decisions of the Management Board of the RFM.[219]

*283.* The Supervisory Commission is elected by the Assembly of the RFM and consists of three members. Members of the Supervisory Commission elect a president from among its members. The members of the Supervisory Commission cannot be members of others in the same time bodies of RFM. The mandate of the members lasts four years.[220]

*284.* The Supervisory Commission works in sessions. Supervisory Committee:

- supervises the proper implementation and application of the provisions of the Statute and other acts of the RFM that refer only to the material-financial operations, i.e., control over the intended use and disposal of RFM funds and revenues;
- supervises the execution of the decisions and other acts of the bodies of the RFM refer only to the material-financial operations, i.e., the control for the intended use and disposal of the funds and revenues of the RFM.
- proposes measures for prevention and elimination of the irregularities in the work of the bodies and RFM bodies from the aspect of material-financial operations;
- in certain cases, proposes to the Assembly the engagement of an independent audit body, and
- performs other activities and undertakes measures that are within the scope of their work.[221]

*285.* The Supervisory Commission submits a report on its entire work to the Assembly. If he/she assesses that he/she is subject to the commission within the competence of the RFM Management Board, he/she shall inform him/her about making certain decisions and conclusions. For the findings and ascertained phenomena, the Supervisory Commission indicates the bodies and bodies in whose

218. Article 38, SHFM.
219. Article 39, SHFM.
220. Article 40, SHFM.
221. Article 41, SHFM.

work they have been ascertained, and if the irregularities are not removed in time, informs the Assembly of the RFM about that.[222]

*286.* The bodies and the administration of RFM are obliged to the Supervisory Commission and the inspector from the Agency for Youth and Sports of the Republic of Macedonia in accordance with Article 70 paragraph 1 of the Law on sports (Official Gazette of the Republic of Macedonia No. 81/08 of July 7, 2008), to present all documents and data and create conditions for smooth acquaintance with relevant facts relevant to making a concrete decision.[223]

*287.* The association with the status of public interest whose annual budget is over EUR 20,000 in denars counter value according to the middle exchange rate of the National Bank of Macedonia (NBRM) is obliged to perform an independent annual audit of its financial operations. The audit report referred to in paragraph 1 of the Article shall be submitted together with the report from The Supervisory Commission at least once a year (according to the LAF (Official Gazette of RM No. 52 from April 16, 2010)).[224]

## 5. Representation of Macedonian Handball

*288.* The handball sport of the Republic of Macedonia in the country and abroad is represented by the handball national teams, handball clubs, representatives of RFM in bodies and forums of the international handball federations, if also the handball referees, delegate controllers and coaches entrusted with participation in international competitions.[225]

*289.* The rights, obligations and responsibilities of handball players, coaches, referees, delegate controllers and sports workers, and the handball clubs that the handball teams of The Republic of Macedonia arise from the obligation to represent the Republic of Macedonia and from the work program of the national teams for a certain period. Failure to meet the obligations that handball teams present is a difficult misdemeanor for which appropriate sanctions are imposed in accordance with the Disciplinary Rulebook of the RFM.[226]

*290.* The basic color of the equipment of the handball national teams of the Republic of Macedonia is in a color that corresponds to the combination of colors and symbols of the flag of the Republic of Macedonia.[227]

---

222. Article 42, SHFM.
223. Article 43, SHFM.
224. Article 44, SHFM.
225. Article 45, SHFM.
226. Article 46, SHFM.
227. Article 47 SHFM.

*291.* Handball players, professionals and sports workers, at the call of the authorized bodies and entities of the RFM, are obliged to participate in the national teams of the Republic of Macedonia to call and get involved in the activities of the national teams. Failure to report the call entails disciplinary action.[228]

*292.* The handball clubs from the Republic of Macedonia will provide their handball players, foreign nationals, to play for the national teams of their countries in accordance with the conditions and the criteria set out in the EHF and IHF Regulations regarding the status and transfer of handball players. In accordance with the conditions and criteria from the previous paragraph, RFM will strive to provide the right to play and prepare in the national teams of the Republic of Macedonia to handball players—citizens of the Republic of Macedonia who play in clubs of foreign countries.[229]

*293.* Acts of the RFM regulate all issues related to the handball national teams of the Republic of Macedonia, the provision of funds for the work of the national teams, the competence for leading the handball national teams, as well as the attitude of the handball players, professionals and handball clubs to handball national teams.[230]

*294.* The handball clubs from the Republic of Macedonia participate in international competitions in a manner and under conditions determined in accordance with the acts of the RFM. Handball clubs can participate in friendly and other international competitions only with the prior consent of the competent body of the RFM. Noncompliance with the decisions of the RFM bodies is punished in accordance with the acts of the RFM.[231]

## 6. Financial Means

*295.* For the realization of its goals and tasks, RFM realizes revenues that it uses under conditions and in a manner determined by law, the Statute and other acts of the RFM. The funds from paragraph 1 of this article RFM provides from the following sources:

- from the Budget of the Republic of Macedonia;
- from membership fees;
- from donations—sponsorships;
- from companies;
- from income from commercial rights;
- from sold tickets for matches of the national teams;
- from fines imposed by the competent authorities;

228. Article 48, SHFM.
229. Article 49, SHFM.
230. Article 50, SHFM.
231. Article 51, SHFM

– from gifts (in cash, good property rights); and
– from other sources of funds.[232]

*296.* RFM funds are allocated to cover material costs and for depreciation, for the functioning of the professional service of RFM, for common consumption, and for expansion of the material basis for other needs of the RFM in accordance with its acts. The allocation of funds is done with a financial plan of revenues and expenditures that are adopted at the end of the current year for the following year. The final distribution of funds is done with the final account of RFM. The disposal of the funds is decided by the Board of RFM within the authorizations of this Statute and other acts of RFM. Responsible for the legal use of funds within the financial plan of RFM is the Secretary-General of the RFM as Commander.[233]

## 7. Program and Plan of Work, Security Issues, Transparency and Acknowledgments

*297.* The goals and tasks of the RFM are realized with the programs and work plans that they have adopted by the Assembly of the RFM and other bodies of the RFM.[234]

*298.* Security in RFM, in the municipal and City handball union and in handball clubs is exercised in accordance with the law on prevention of violence and indecency behavior on sports fields in the Republic of Macedonia, the law on safety, the regulations of the IHF, EHF and acts adopted by the bodies of the RFM. For security issues, RFM appoints a commission, i.e., commissioners for security of RFM. Questions regarding the safety of the handball organization and the handball players' competitions are determined by acts of the RFM.[235]

*299.* The work of the RFM bodies is public.[236]

*300.* The bodies of the RFM are obliged to regularly and timely inform the public about their own work. The bodies of RFM are obliged to provide a way and conditions for informing the public about achieving the goals of the RFM, its activity and the use of funds. The public in the work of RFM is provided through the website of RFM, www.macedoniahandball.com, where the official bulletins and decisions of the bodies of RFM.[237]

*301.* The presidents of the bodies of RFM or a person appointed by the Board of RFM for public relations (spokesperson) to the representatives of the mass media

232. Article 52, SHFM.
233. Article 53, SHFM.
234. Article 54, SHFM.
235. Article 55, SHFM.
236. Article 56, SHFM.
237. Article 57, SHFM.

present data and information on the work of the bodies of the RFM. Representatives of the media can attend the sessions of the Assembly and other bodies of the RFM at the invitation of the president of the respective organ, i.e., the body. When at the sessions of the bodies of the RFM, issues are considered that constitute an official or other type of secret, the public is excluded.[238]

*302.* Clubs, teams, handball players, coaches, referees, delegate controllers and other Professional and sports workers can be rewarded for outstanding contributions to the execution of the set tasks and achieved results in the field of organization and promotion of handball in the Republic of Macedonia.[239]

*303.* Awards and recognitions are in the form of trophy features, recognitions and cash prizes.[240]

*304.* The manner of awarding recognitions and prizes is regulated by a special rulebook of the Board of RFM.[241]

## 8. Information Bulletin

*305.* In order to provide publicity in the work and timely information of the members for all important issues, in order to achieve the goals and tasks, RFM issues an official bulletin of its own bodies and commissions and publishes it on the RFM website www.macedoniahandball.com. The clubs, the handball players, are registered in the bulletin of the registration commission, as well as decisions and solutions for their registration. In the bulletin of the licensing commission, the handball players are licensed, and club representatives and officials, as well as licensing decisions and solutions the same. It is published in the bulletin of the commission for conducting competitions—the commissioner delegation—drawing of officials; matches are registered, pronounced suspensions, warnings, and fines in the first instance; appeals are resolved in the first instance; a table is published after each round played and the judges' scores are recorded. In the bulletin of the commission for the implementation of the cup competition, the delegation of officials, matches are registered, suspensions, warnings and penalties are imposed in the first degree, complaints are resolved in the first instance, results are announced, and teams continue to play in cup matches after each round played and the judges' scores are recorded. By decisions of the Board of RFM, other information bulletins are issued to the permanent and the temporary commissions of the Management Board of RFM.[242]

238. Article 58, SHFM.
239. Article 59, SHFM.
240. Article 60, SHFM.
241. Article 61, SHFM.
242. Article 62, SHFM.

## 9. Secretary-General and Administration

*306.* The Secretary-General is the head of the RFM administration, and in relation to her rights, the obligations of the employees in the administration perform the rights and duties of an employer.[243]

*307.* The Secretary-General of the RFM appoints and dismisses the Board of Directors; accordingly, the conditions are determined by a special decision for a period of four years. The candidate for Secretary-General should have completed higher education (7th degree) or higher (6th degree), at least five years of work experience, organizational and others qualities to successfully perform the work and speak at least one of the official languages of EHF. The Secretary-General is independent in performing the tasks within his scope. The Secretary-General is responsible for his work before the Board of Directors and the Assembly of RFM. The Secretary-General may be dismissed before the expiration of the term for which he has been elected only in case of serious violations of the provisions of this Statute and other acts of the RFM, as well as in cases determined by law.[244]

*308.* Secretary-General:

- takes care of the legal operation of RFM and its organs and bodies;
- executes the decisions and conclusions adopted by the Assembly and the Management Board, and other organs and bodies of RFM;
- proposes measures for implementation of the decisions and conclusions of the bodies of the RFM
- is responsible for the proper implementation of the adopted agreements and contracts.
- is responsible for the proper application of regulations and general acts;
- is the commander for the execution of the financial plan and the work program;
- performs the function of an executive body of the administration—the professional service, accordingly with legal provisions;
- Participates in the work of the Assembly of RFM, the meetings of the Board of RFM, the commissions and other bodies and organs in giving advice and interpretation. If not able to attend, determines replacement.
- represents RFM in legal transactions and takes measures and actions on behalf of and for the account of RFM in accordance with the Statute and the decisions of the Management Board;
- performs other activities determined by law, the Statute and other acts of the RFM.[245]

*309.* Professional, administrative-technical and other matters for the needs of RFM and its organs and bodies, performed by the administration of RFM. The

243. Article 63, SHFM.
244. Article 64, SHFM.
245. Article 65, SHFM.

employees in the administration exercise their rights and obligations in accordance with labor law and other laws and regulations, collective agreements, as well as acts adopted by the bodies of the RFM.[246]

*310.* The work of the administration is managed by the Secretary-General who organizes and coordinates the work process in it and takes care of the implementation of measures, decisions and conclusions of the bodies of the RFM in accordance with the law, the collective agreement, the Statute and general acts of RFM.[247]

### 10. Termination of Operation

*311.* RFM ceases to operate:

- with a decision of the Assembly of the RFM adopted by a two-thirds majority of the total number of representatives of the Assembly;
- if there are reasons determined by Article 63 of the LAF(Official Gazette of the Republic of Macedonia No. 52/2010).

*312.* In case of termination of the RFM, the property of the RFM is transferred by a decision of the Assembly of sports association to be determined by the Assembly.[248]

## *D. Basketball Federation of Macedonia*

### 1. General Features

*313.* Basketball Federation of North Macedonia is hereinafter referred to as the Federation. An association of citizens that, through the clubs, achieve and harmonize the individual with general and common interests of basketball in the Republic of North Macedonia. The federation is depoliticized and bans the activities of political parties in its own rows from achieving political goals and interests.[249]

*314.* The Federation is independent in organizing and achieving the goals and activities determined by the Statute and other normative acts, exercising the rights and respecting their responsibilities in accordance with the Constitution and the Laws of the Republic of North Macedonia.[250]

---

246. Article 66 SHFM.
247. Article 67, SHFM.
248. Article 68, SHFM.
249. Article 1, SKFM.
250. Article 2, SKFM.

*315.* The Federation carries out the activity on the territory of the Republic of North Macedonia. The name of the Citizens' Association is the Basketball Federation of North Macedonia. The abbreviated name for internal use only is Basketball Federation of North Macedonia (KFSM).[251]

*316.* The Federation has the capacity of a legal entity with rights, obligations and responsibilities determined by The Constitution of the Republic of North Macedonia, by Law and the Statute, shall be entered in the register of Citizens' Associations maintained in the Central Register of the Republic of North Macedonia.[252]

*317.* The Federation is represented by the president and in his absence by the Deputy Chairman of the Management Board.[253]

*318.* Article 8 of Statute of the Basketball Federation of North Macedonia (SKFM) defines the seal and the stamp. The text of the seal and the stamp of the Federation are written in Cyrillic. The members of the Federation have a stamp and a stamp, and next to the name of the Federation, there is also member's name.[254] The federation has a sign consisting of a red basketball, with the flag of the Republic of North Macedonia in the shape of a basketball; in the middle and in the lower right part is written KFSM. The flag of the Federation has a rectangular shape with dimensions 2×1 in the middle, which is the sign of the Federation. The base of the flag is white.[255]

*319.* The Federation is a member of the Olympic Committee of North Macedonia by its own decision. The Federation is a member of the International Basketball Federation—FIBA, with all the rights and obligations.[256]

*320.* Members of the Federation are all basketball clubs that are registered in the sole KFSM register. Members of the Assembly of the Federation, with all rights and obligations, are all clubs that actively and continuously, from at least two competitive seasons, participate in one of the senior leagues organized by KFSM, as well as by a representative of the Association of Youth Categories, basketball referees and delegates association, players association, association of basketball coaches, three on three competition association, statisticians association and veteran's association.[257]

251. Articles 3–4, SKFM.
252. Article 6, SKFM.
253. Article 7, SKFM.
254. Article 9, SKFM.
255. Article 10, SKFM.
256. Article 11, SKFM.
257. Article 12, SKFM.

2. Activities, Aims and Tasks

*321.* According to Article 13 of SKFM, in accomplishing the established tasks of common interest in the field of basketball, the Federation realizes its activity through the following activities:

- Realizes the program orientation in the basketball sport within the development of sports in the Republic of North Macedonia.
- Promotes the basketball sport in the Republic of North Macedonia and creates organizational, material, professional and personnel conditions for representation of basketball sport.
- Establishes a system of basketball competitions in the Republic of North Macedonia.
- Links and coordinates the activities of basketball clubs and professional forms of organization.
- Supporting the activities for popularization of the basketball sport.
- Encourages and facilitates activities and actions aimed at the promotion and popularization of basketball.
- Establishes cooperation with sports and other organizations in the Republic of North Macedonia.
- Realizes international sports cooperation.
- Organizes and implements a marketing service for material and financial means for financing the activities of the Federation.
- Organizes and finances leagues for youth and cadet categories and the Federation in interest in basketball determines the rules, sets the propositions and the manner of competition through its own expert appointed by the Board of KFSM.

*322.* Article 14 of SKFM describes the implementation of the determined activities the Federation will engage with:

- Creating material conditions for education and training of professional staff who directly perform professional work in basketball.
- Providing organizational and professional assistance to the members of the Federation.
- Ensuring uniform application of the rules and regulations of the basketball game.
- Publicity at work.
- Providing health supervision over athletes as well as for the application of the achievements of sports medicine in the advancement of basketball.[258]

*323.* The Federation provides, alone or together with other bodies, organizations or communities, conditions for the development of scientific research, professional, propaganda, informative and publishing activity in the field of basketball.[259]

258. Article 14, SKFM.
259. Article 15, SKFM.

*324*. The Federation for the popularization and development of basketball in all areas of the Republic of North Macedonia organizes team basketball matches or representations of domestic or international character.[260]

*325*. According to Article 17 of SKFM, in achieving the goals and objectives of the Federation, basketball clubs and professional forms of organization, directly or through their representatives in the bodies of the Federation, have the following rights and obligations:

- To participate freely and equally in all jointly defined goals and tasks.
- To be elected and to be elected in the bodies of the Federation.
- The Federation informs the clubs about the work of the bodies and working bodies.
- To take the initiative and submit proposals for consideration of certain issues, i.e., making decisions and conclusions on them.
- To be regularly and timely informed about the work of the bodies and working bodies of the Federation.
- To work directly and to implement the established legal and other statutory obligations and tasks.
- Consistently implement the conclusions and decisions of the bodies and working bodies of The Federation.
- To initiate and undertake obligations for the realization of the given initiatives and to use other rights determined by law, the Statute and other acts of the Federation.
- With regular presence and active participation in the work of the organs and bodies that contribute to the advancement of the work of the Federation.

## 3. Administration and Organization

*326*. The federation ensures equal rights, obligations and responsibilities of the members. The Federation has bodies and professional forms of organizations composed of representatives of the members of the Federation.[261]

*327*. The representatives of the members of the Federation in the organs and bodies are elected for four years, with the possibility of changing the members-representatives of the leagues (associations) each competition season. The mandate of the representatives of the members terminates with the expiration of the time for which they were selected. The mandate of the representative may end before the expiration of the term for which he/she has been elected by resignation or by revocation by the elected body.[262]

---

260. Article 16, SKFM.
261. Article 18, SKFM.
262. Article 19, SKFM.

*328.* According to Article 20 of SKFM, in exercising the function, the representative has the following rights and obligations:

- to attend the sessions of the bodies and bodies where he is elected, to participate in work and decide on all issues on the agenda;
- in a timely manner, together with the other members of the body or body, to be notified of maintenance and Agenda;
- to make proposals for improvement of the normative acts of the Federation;
- to receive answers to the questions asked about the work of the bodies of The Federation;
- to inform the club (Association) that represents him/her about the decisions made no later than the next meeting of the body or body of the Federation;
- to perform the tasks entrusted to him by the Federation or one of the bodies whose he is a member;
- to decide to respect the views and directions of the Federation, the acts of the Federation and the laws of the Republic of North Macedonia;
- is responsible for the work before the bodies of the Federation.

*329.* The members of the basketball organization are organized through clubs, professional forms of organizing and associations.[263]

*330.* Within the Federation, the clubs form Club Associations, First, Second and Third League in Men, First and Second League in Women's Competition and Youth Association categories of KFSM. The associations of the clubs in these leagues have a special sub-account on account of the Federation, to which the signatories are the Commissioner for Competition and the presidents of the respective Associations. The presidents of the associations are automatically members of the Board of Directors of The Federation, with the right to vote. Each competition season, the newly elected presidents of the associations automatically become members of the Board of Directors instead of the old members.[264]

*331.* Basketball clubs are associations in which citizens associate freely and voluntarily to meet the general needs and interests of basketball. Basketball clubs are established in accordance with the Law on Citizens' Associations and foundations, the Law on Sports and the Statute of the Federation. The work and relations in the clubs are determined by the Statute and other acts of the club based on the Statute, laws and other acts. All issues and activities of common interest are realized by the clubs within the Federation.[265]

*332.* In the realization of the activities, the basketball clubs have the following rights and obligations:

- independently determine the mutual relations;

263. Article 21, SKFM. .
264. Article 22, SKFM.
265. Articles 23–26, SKFM.

- propose consideration of issues of common interest in the bodies and organs of the Federation, receiving professional and organizational assistance;
- have insight into the work of the bodies of the Federation and the professional forms of organizing in basketball;
- raise questions of responsibility of the members of the bodies and organs of The Federation and other professional forms of organization;
- contribute to the achievement of the goals and tasks of the Federation;
- implement the Statute and the acts of the Federation, decisions and conclusions that arise from them;
- participate in the actions and manifestations of the Federation, in cooperation with other organizations to contribute to the reputation and promotion of basketball in the Republic of North Macedonia;
- participate in the performance of the financial obligations of the Federation and to it, where they themselves take part.[266]

*333.* In order to achieve the common goals and tasks and direct realization of the rights and professional obligations, professional forms of organization are organized (Article 28, SKFM). The professional forms of organization through the representatives are expressed and harmonize their special interests and influence the policymaking, the adoption of programs, plans, general acts and other decisions of the Federation and submit proposals to general acts and other decisions made by the bodies of the Federation.[267]

*334.* The position, rights and obligations of the professional forms of organization are closely determined with rules of work that specifically contain: rights, duties and responsibilities to members, how to organize them, decide and inform members and others issues, and in accordance with the goals and tasks set out in the Statute.[268]

## 4. Organs of the Federation

*335.* The bodies for the Federation are Assembly, Management Board and Supervisory Board.[269]

*336.* According to Article 32 of SKFM, the Assembly is the highest body of the Federation which consists of members-representatives from:

- Men's First League.
- First League Women.
- Men's Second League.
- Second League Women.

266. Article 27, SKFM.
267. Article 29, SKFM. .
268. Article 30, SKFM.
269. Article 31, SKFM.

- Men's Third League.
- One representative from the Association of Youth Categories of KFSM.
- A representative from the Association of Basketball Referees and Delegates.
- A representative from the Players' Association.
- A representative from the Basketball Coaches Association.
- A representative from Association 3na3.
- A representative from the Association of Statistics.
- A representative from the Veterans Association.

*337.* With a special statutory decision, the Assembly can change the number of members if there is a change in leagues or associations.

*338.* The manner of election, revocation and mandate of the members of the Assembly is determined by The Statute and the Rules of Procedure of the Assembly, in accordance with the provisions of the Law on Sports of the Republic of North Macedonia.[270]

*339.* The Assembly performs the work within its competence at sessions. The Assembly validly decides when more than half attend the session (50% +1) of the representatives. The Assembly makes decisions by a majority vote of the present members of the Assembly. The statute is adopted when it is voted for by two-thirds of the present members of the Assembly. The work of the Assembly is regulated by the Rules of Procedure.[271]

*340.* The Assembly adopts conclusions, recommendations, and decisions and adopts other acts relevant to the development and promotion of basketball.[272]

*341.* The sessions of the Assembly are held as needed and at least once a year. A session of the Assembly is convened by the President of the Federation. A session of the Assembly is convened on the proposal of the Board of Directors, the Supervisory Board or one-fifth of the total number of members of the Assembly. If the President of the Federation, within fourteen days from the date of the proposal of the proposer, does not convene a session, the session is convened by the proposer himself. The sessions of the Assembly are public.[273] The Assembly adopts Rules of Procedure which specify the manner of work and the decision-making of the Assembly.[274]

*342.* According to Article 38 of SKFM, the Assembly performs the following activities:

- adopts Statute and its amendments;

270. Article 33, SKFM.
271. Article 34, SKFM.
272. Article 35, SKFM.
273. Article 36, SKFM.
274. Article 37, SKFM.

- adopts medium-term, annual and semi-annual work programs and determines their guidelines for the development of basketball in the Republic of North Macedonia;
- reviews and adopts reports on the work of the Management Board;
- adopts the financial plan, determines the final accounts and reports for the financial operations provided by the laws of the Republic of North Macedonia;
- elects and dismisses the president of the Assembly, the president and the members of the Board of Directors and the members of the Supervisory Board;
- makes a decision for termination of the work of the Federation with a two-thirds majority of the members;
- makes a decision to establish a company for marketing needs, in accordance with legal provisions;
- adopts the Registration Rulebook and its amendments;
- performs other activities for which it is competent according to the Law on Sports of the North Republic Macedonia and the acts of the Federation.

*343.* The Assembly elects from its ranks a president of the Federation, responsible to the Board of Directors and the Assembly. The mandate of the president of the Federation lasts four years but a minimum of two years from the beginning; the President of the Federation is elected by a majority vote of those present authorized representatives of voting members.[275]

*344.* Article 40 of SKFM defines the tasks of the President of the Federation:

- represents the Federation in the country and abroad;
- convenes the sessions of the Assembly and the Management Board and manages them;
- proposes the composition of the Management Board;
- is a signatory of the acts adopted by the Assembly and the Management Board;
- vetoes the acts adopted by the Board of Directors and the bodies of The Federation, if they are in conflict with the provisions of the Statute;
- takes care of the execution of the decisions, programs, conclusions and views made by the Assembly and the Management Board;
- takes care of the realization of the Work Program;
- performs other activities provided by the Statute and other normative acts of The Federation.

*345.* The Board of Directors is an executive body of the Assembly, in which each member has equal rights and obligations and responsibilities for the operation and development of the Federation. Within the rights and duties, the Board of Directors is accountable for its work to the Assembly.[276]

---

275. Article 39, SKFM.
276. Article 41, SKFM.

*346.* The Board of Directors is composed of, automatically, the presidents of the Associations of the senior leagues in the current competition season and the presidents of the Association of Youth Leagues Management team that provides funds for national teams and other projects of The Federation in the interest of the development of basketball. The number and composition of the management team are at the proposal of the President of KFSM. Also, on the proposal of the president, the Board can replace and co-opt new members of the management team.[277]

*347.* The Board of Directors performs the following activities:

- Executes and implements the decisions, conclusions, and positions of the Assembly.
- Establishes normative acts, programs, plans and other materials.
- Adopts acts for execution of the regulations and general acts of the Assembly.
- Adopts a work plan for the execution of the work program of the Assembly.
- Within the framework of the policy established by the Assembly, it monitors and studies the situation and problems in basketball and proposes measures and activities for the promotion and popularization of basketball.
- Forms its auxiliary working bodies—commissions, appoints presidents and members of the same and directs their work.
- At the proposal of the Associations, appoints the Commissioner for Senior Competition.
- Adopts a calendar for each competition season.
- Establishes the system of league and cup matches in the Republic of North Macedonia.
- Makes a selection and proposes representatives in sports bodies and organizations.
- Selects an expert who will determine the propositions and the system of competition in youth categories.
- Decides on commendations, public recognitions and other awards of exceptional importance.
- Proposes an annual financial plan and final account and takes care of their execution.
- Names the executors of the financial plan and the signatories of the financial and other documents.
- Review and adopt work programs and work reports of its bodies and working bodies.
- Report to the Assembly on its work and on the work of its own working bodies.
- Organizes basketball matches of teams and national teams and other mass actions in order to popularize and promote basketball in the Republic of North Macedonia.
- At the proposal of the Judicial Commission, determines the list of judges for conducting the matches from its competence.
- Upon the proposal of the Competition Commissioner, establish a list of delegates for the system of competition.

277. Article 42, SKFM.

- Appoints the Secretary-General of the Federation.
- Provides conditions and bears responsibilities for the matches, for their regularity of level of the Republic of North Macedonia.
- Appoint coaches of the national teams.
- Adopts mandatory interpretations of all general acts of the Federation.
- Adopts Rules of Procedure.
- Proposes Registration Rulebook.
- Adopts a Rulebook for competition.
- Adopts Disciplinary Rulebook.
- Adopts a Rulebook for job systematization.
- Takes concrete measures in case of violation of interests and violation of the reputation of basketball.
- Performs other activities for which he/she is competent by the Statute or by other acts.[278]

*348.* The Board of Directors meets as needed, works in sessions and may have full authority decides if more than half of the members are present at the session. The Board of Directors decides by a majority vote of the members present.[279]

*349.* The sessions of the Management Board are convened by the president who manages them. In case of the absence of the president of the Federation, replaces the vice president. The sessions of the Management Board are public. In certain cases, to resolve urgent matters of interest for the regular operation of basketball, the Board of Directors can make full decisions at sessions held through video conference or by electronic voting. For the meetings of the Management Board held through video conference or voting conducted electronically, minutes are kept.[280]

*350.* In performing its rights and duties, the Board of Directors makes decisions, guidelines and conclusions.[281]

*351.* The mandate of the members of the Management Board is four years. The Board of Directors elects vice presidents from among its members for a term of four years, who, in the absence of the president, replace him. The mandate of the representatives of the associations—members of the Management Board—lasts one competition season, with the right of re-election by the respective association. Each member of the Management Board has the right to propose a search to the Management Board.[282]

278. Article 43, SKFM.
279. Article 44, SKFM.
280. Article 45, SKFM.
281. Article 46, SKFM.
282. Article 47, SKFM.

*352.* The Supervisory Board is composed of three members. The members of the Supervisory Board elect a president from among their members. The mandate of the members of the Supervisory Board lasts four years.[283]

*353.* The Supervisory Board controls the implementation of the provisions of the Statute and controls the intended use and disposal of the funds and revenues of the Federation. The Supervisory Board submits its findings and decisions to the Assembly and the Management Board of the Federation.[284]

## 5. Transparency in the Work

*354.* The work of the Federation is public. The publicity of the work of the Federation is realized through:

- Timely submission of materials for discussion to the representatives of the members of The Federation and other interested bodies, organizations and associations.
- Timely delivery of materials for discussion of the media, without the right to participate in the hearing, in case they are invited as guests at the session.
- Preparation of newsletters.[285]

*355.* The presidents of the bodies and organs of the Federation are obliged to the representatives of the media to present data and information about the work and to them enable uninterrupted monitoring of the work of the sessions.[286]

## 6. International Activities and National Teams

*356.* Due to the international affirmation of the basketball sport, the federation achieves international cooperation with national basketball federations, members of FIBA. The Federation makes decisions for the participation of teams and national teams in international competitions in accordance with the FIBA Calendar and launches an initiative to determine candidacy for the organization of Balkan, European and World Championships and other international competitions in all categories.[287]

*357.* The basketball national teams of the Republic of North Macedonia, in all selections, represent the basketball sport of Macedonia in the country and abroad at meetings with other national teams.[288]

---

283. Article 48, SKFM.
284. Article 49, SKFM.
285. Article 50, SKFM.
286. Article 51, SKFM.
287. Article 52, SKFM.
288. Article 53, SKFM.

*358.* The composition and preparation of basketball teams is a right and obligation of the professional council, the selector and the coaches of the national teams. The color of the equipment of the basketball teams should have national symbols. The obligation of the players determined by the coaches is to call and get involved in the work of national team selections. This obligation is also borne by the players who play abroad clubs. Failure to report the call entails an appropriate disciplinary measure within normative acts of the Federation.[289]

*359.* The national teams of the Federation can play in international matches only with the consent and organization of the Board of Directors of the Federation.[290]

*360.* For the achievements of the national team, the selectors and the players can receive awards, praise and sports trophies in accordance with the rules of the Federation for Public Recognitions and awards.[291]

## 7. Financial Issues

*361.* For the realization of the activities, goals and tasks, the Federation provides funds that are used under conditions and in a manner determined by law, the Statute and other general acts of the Federation. The funds for performing the activity are provided by the Federation from:

- The budget of the Republic of North Macedonia.
- Membership fees, contributions, donations, gifts, and other sources.
- Own revenue—marketing.
- Organizing basketball matches.
- Providing sponsorship of leagues.
- Fees and fines.
- Transfer of athletes and professionals.
- Profit income of companies established with the income of the Federation.

*362.* The funds from the fines, transfers and contracts are paid on a special subaccount of the Federation, whose purpose will be to finance the leagues in the junior categories and promote youth basketball.[292]

*363.* The federation approves the Financial Plan, the annual revenue and expenditure plan. The financial plan determines and allocates the funds for financing the activities of the Federation. The financial plan is adopted at the first meeting of the Board of Directors in each calendar year.[293]

---

289. Article 54, SKFM.
290. Article 55, SKFM.
291. Article 56, SKFM.
292. Article 57, SKFM.
293. Article 58, SKFM.

*364.* To reimburse the costs incurred in connection with the competition, the clubs included in the competition system pay monetary compensation to the Federation (registration fee).[294]

## 8. Administration, Acknowledgments and Normative Activities

*365.* The professional, operational, administrative and other tasks are performed by the General Secretary of the Federation, with a special rulebook determined by the Board of Directors, which at the same time organizes and manages the work of the professional service of the Federation. The Secretary-General is accountable for his work to the Board of Directors. He is not a member of bodies of the Federation. The Board of Directors appoints the Secretary-General of the Federation for a term of four years. The Secretary-General may be professionally employed with rights, responsibilities and responsibilities regulated by a separate agreement. The Secretary-General can be a volunteer without monetary compensation, whose rights and obligations and responsibilities are regulated by a Rulebook.[295]

*366.* For the achieved results in the development and promotion of basketball in The Republic of Macedonia, the Federation awards recognitions (thanks and plaques) to sports organizations, boards and individuals. More detailed provisions on the manner of awarding recognitions and prizes are determined by the rules of the Assembly of the Federation.[296]

*367.* The proposal for initiating a procedure for adoption, amendment or supplementation of the Statute or of the Federation may be submitted by the Board of Directors or any member of the bodies and working bodies and members of the Federation. The proposal is submitted in writing. The Board of Directors of the Federation, through the services of the office and its authorities' commissions, is obliged to review the submitted proposal within thirty days from the receipt of the proposal to make an appropriate decision.[297]

## 9. Termination of Work

*368.* The Federation ceases to operate if there are reasons set forth in Article 63 of the LAF. In case of termination of work of the Federation, its property is handed over for safekeeping to the Ministry, the relevant Agency for Youth and Sports within the Government of the Republic of North Macedonia, until a similar organization is formed with the same goals and objectives.[298]

---

294. Article 59, SKFM.
295. Article 60, SKFM.
296. Article 61, SKFM.
297. Article 62, SKFM.
298. Articles 63–64, SKFM.

## Chapter 2. Public Regulation

*369.* Today, most constitutions of modern states do not contain explicit provisions that define the right to sport as a human right.[299] In the Constitution, this issue is approached indirectly.

*370.* The Constitution only states that every citizen is guaranteed the right to healthcare. Citizens have the right and duty to protect and promote their own health and the health of others.[300] Regarding sports, the Constitution promulgates that the Republic of Macedonia stimulates and assists technical education and sport.[301]

*371.* In the context of Macedonian sport legislation, every person has the right to freely decide whether to engage in sports and physical activity, when to do so and in what way. Freedom of choice to play sports is allowed only within limits provided by the LS.[302]

*372.* In addition to the LS as the most important legal source in the field of sports, the Law on Prevention of Violence and Misconduct at Sport Competitions has been adopted in the Republic of Macedonia (LPVMSC).[303] It regulates the issues related to violence and inappropriate behavior in sports competitions, measures to prevent them for the safety of spectators, competitors and other participants in sports competitions, as well as the obligations of the organizers and the powers of the competent authorities to implement those measures.

*373.* The law consists of three parts: (1) basic provisions, (2) measures to prevent violence and misconduct at sports events, and (3) misdemeanor provisions.

*374.* LPVMSC provides the following basic notions:

- A sports competition, in the sense of the law, is any individual competition in an organized system of sports competitions, according to the provisions of the Law on Sports.
- An organizer of sports competitions are sports clubs and national sports federations, as well as other legal and natural persons who organize a sports competition in accordance with the provisions of the Law on Sports.
- A sports ground is the space on which the sports competition takes place, as well as the space between the audience and the space on which the sports competition takes place.[304]

---

299. *See*, Stefan Andonović, Pravo na sport kao ljudsko pravo, Strani pravni život, No. 61, Beograd, 2017, 136.
300. Constitution of the Republic of Macedonia, Art. 39.
301. Constitution of the Republic of Macedonia, Art. 47.
302. LS, Art. 5.
303. Official Journal of the Republic of Macedonia 89/2004, 142/2008, 135/2011, 27/2014, 154/2015.
304. LPVMSC, Art. 2.

*375.* The following acts are considered acts of violence and indecent behavior in sports competitions:[305]

- possession or consumption of alcoholic beverages or narcotic drugs, possession of pyrotechnics, weapons and other means suitable for causing damage or causing violence by persons coming to the sports competitions, during the entire period of arrival, during and after the holding of the sports competition;
- importation and use in sports facilities of alcoholic beverages, narcotic drugs, pyrotechnics, weapons and other means suitable for causing damage or causing violence;
- importing and displaying banners, flags and other objects with text, pictures, signs or other symbols, as well as singing songs or posting messages that cause and incite hatred or violence based on racial, national and religious bias or on the basis of other traits;
- throwing objects into the sports field or into the auditorium;
- lighting and throwing pyrotechnics;
- burning of cheering props, flags of other countries, club flags and other objects;
- calling, encouraging and participating in a fight or physical attack on athletes, caretakers, orderlies, officials, competition organizers and other participants in sports competitions;
- physical confrontation between the participants of sports competitions;
- unauthorized entry into the sports field by the caretakers;
- damage or destruction of the sports equipment and other business from the sports facility, as well as the vehicles during the entire time period upon arrival, during and during the sports competition;
- unauthorized entry into the spectator area of the sports facility intended for opposing fans;
- staying or keeping fans in the part of the audience for which they do not have an entrance ticket or a pass issued by the organizer of the match; and
- unauthorized entry of fans into facilities that are used for sports activities.

*376.* In addition to the Constitution and the LS, public regulations in the field of sports also include ratified international conventions. The MK Constitution contains a provision stating that ratified international agreements are part of the MK legal order, i.e., that the international agreements ratified in accordance with the Constitution are part of the internal legal order and cannot be changed by law.[306]

*377.* On the basis of ratified international conventions and documents important for the field of sports in the Republic of Macedonia is the Law on Ratification of the International Convention Against Doping in Sport.[307] Macedonia is also party to the European Convention against Doping in Sport[308] and the European Convention

305. LPVMSC, Art. 3.
306. Article 118.
307. Official Journal of the Republic of Macedonia, No. 103/2008.
308. Trough succession on Mar. 3, 1994. More info: https://www.coe.int/en/web/conventions/full-list?module=signatures-by-treaty&treatynum=135.

for the Prevention of Violence and Misconduct at Sports Events, especially Football Matches.[309] Macedonia has also ratified the Nairobi Treaty on the Protection of the Olympic Symbol.[310]

*378.* The Law on Ratification of the International Convention Against Doping in Sport ratifies the 2005 International Convention Against Doping in Sport adopted as part of the strategy and program of activities of UNESCO in the area of physical education and sport, having the aim to promote the prevention of and the fight against doping in sport, with a view to its elimination.

*379.* In addition to the Constitution, the LS and ratified international conventions, the field of sports in Macedonia is legally regulated by the following laws, regulations and by-laws:

(1) Criminal Code.[311]
(2) Law on Copyright and Related Rights.[312]
(3) Law on Games of Chance and Entertainment Games http://fsrim.org.mk/za-nas/[313]
(4) Law on Ski Resorts (LSRS) http://fsrim.org.mk/za-nas/[314]
(5) Law on Obligations (LO) http://fsrim.org.mk/za-nas/[315]
(6) Law on Industrial Property (LIP) http://fsrim.org.mk/za-nas/[316]
(7) Law on Misdemeanor (LM) http://fsrim.org.mk/za-nas/[317]
(8) Law on Audio and Audiovisual Media Services (LAV) http://fsrim.org.mk/za-nas/[318]
(9) Law on Labor Relations (LLR) http://fsrim.org.mk/za-nas/[319]
(10) Law on Free Access to Information of Public Character (LFI) http://fsrim.org.mk/za-nas/[320]

---

309. Trough succession on Mar. 3, 1994. More info: https://www.coe.int/en/web/conventions/full-list?module=signatures-by-treaty&treatynum=120.
310. Official Journal of the Republic of Macedonia, No. 165/2013.
311. Official Journal of the Republic of Macedonia, Nos. 37/96, 80/99, 48/01, 4/02, 16/02, 43/03, 19/04, 40/2004, 81/05, 50/06, 60/06, 373/06, 87/07, 7/08, 139/08, 114/09, 51/11-3, 51/11-79, 135/11, 185/11, 142/12, 143/12 166/12, 55/13, 82/13, 14/14, 27/14, 28/14, 41/14, 115/14, 132/14, 160/14, 199/14, број 196/15, 226/15, 7/17, 170/17, 248/18.
312. Official Journal of the Republic of Macedonia Nos. 115/2010, 140/2010, 51/2011, 147/2013, 154/2015 and 27/2016.
313. Official Journal of the Republic of Macedonia Nos. 24/2011, 51/2011, 148/2011, 74/2012, 171/2012, 27/2014, 139/2014, 61/2015, 154/2015, 23/2016 И 178/2016 Ч 132/2011; 90/2017.
314. Official Journal of the Republic of Macedonia, No. 37/2016.
315. Official Journal Nos. 8/01, 78/01, 04/02, 59/02, 05/03, 84/08, 81/09, 161/09, 23/13, 123/13, 215/21.
316. Official Journal Nos. 21/09, 24/11, 12/14, 41/14, 152/15, 53/16, 83/18, 31/20.
317. Official Journal No. 96/2019.
318. Official Journal Nos. 184/13, 13/14, 44/14, 101/14, 132/14, 142/16, 132/17, 168/18, 248/18, 27/19, 42/20, 77/21.
319. Official Journal Nos. 62/05, 106/08, 161/08, 114/09, 130/09, 50/10, 52/10, 124/10, 47/11, 11/12, 39/12, 13/13, 25/13, 170/13, 187/13, 113/14, 20/15, 33/15, 72/15, 129/15, 27/16.
320. Official Journal Nos. 13/06, 86/08, 6/10, 42/14, 148/15, 55/16, 64/18, 98/19.

(11) Law on Prevention and Protection from Discrimination (LPPD) http://fsrim.org.mk/za-nas/[321]
(12) Law on Associations and Foundations (LAF) http://fsrim.org.mk/za-nas/[322]
(13) Law on Employment and Insurance in the Case of Unemployment Insurance (LE).[323]
(14) Law on Health Insurance (LHE).[324]
(15) Code of Criminal Procedure (CC).[325]

*380.* A brief overview of the most important additional sources indicates the multidimensionality, heterogeneity, and importance of sports law in the legal system of the Republic of Macedonia.

*381.* This chapter will present the public regulations of the Republic of Macedonia important for engaging in sports activities with special reference to the basic rights and freedoms of citizens of the Republic of Macedonia in the field of sports: freedom of association, prohibition of discrimination in sports and sports for people with disabilities. In addition, government conditions and permits, public safety, tax treatment and dispute resolution in sports will be discussed.

## §1. Freedom of Association

*382.* Freedom of association in sports is guaranteed within the general freedom of association defined by the Constitution, in accordance with Article 20, which reads:

> Citizens are guaranteed freedom of association to exercise and protect their political, economic, social, cultural and other rights and convictions. Citizens may freely establish associations of citizens and political parties, join them or resign from them. The programs and activities of political parties and other associations of citizens may not be directed at the violent destruction of the constitutional order of the Republic, or at encouragement or incitement to military aggression or ethnic, racial or religious hatred or intolerance. Military or

321. Official Journal No. 258/20.
322. Official Journal of the Republic of Macedonia Nos. 52/2010, 135/2011 И 55/2016.
323. Official Journal of the Republic of Macedonia Nos. 37/1997; 25/2000; 101/2000; 50/2001; 25/2003; 37/2004; 4/2005; 50/2006; 29/2007; 102/2008; 161/2008; 50/2010; 88/2010; 51/2011; 11/2012; 80/2012; 114/2012; 39/2014; 44/2014; 113/2014; 56/2015; 129/2015; 147/2015; 154/2015; 27/2016 И 119/2016, 14/1999, 7/2002; 88/2007; 162/2008; 171/2010, 142/2008.
324. 25/00, 34/00, 96/00, 50/01, 11/02, 31/03, 84/05, 37/06, 18/07, 82/08, 98/08, 6/09, 67/09, 50/10, 156/10, 53/11, број 26/12, 145/12, 16/13, 91/13, 187/13, 44/14, 97/14, 112/14, 113/14), 188/14, 20/15, 61/15, 8/15, 129/15, 150/15, 154/15, 192/15, 217/15, 27/16, 37/16, 120/16, 142/16, Decisions of the Constitutional Court: Official Journals Nos. 104/00, 30/01, 48/01, 109/06, 88/07, 88/07, 106/07, 45/09, 14/10, 166/11.
325. Official Journal Nos. 150/2010, 100/12, 198/18.

paramilitary associations which do not belong to the Armed Forces of the Republic of Macedonia are prohibited.[326]

*383*. In this way, a solid legal framework has been created for the creation and operation of various sports associations and clubs in the Republic of Macedonia.

*384*. In accordance with the stated Constitutional provisions, there are the following forms of sports associations:

(1) Sports organizations (sports associations and sports economic associations);
(2) Sports associations.
(3) Branch sports federations.
(4) Association of Macedonian Sport Federations.
(5) Macedonian Olympic Committee.
(6) Macedonian Paralympic Committee.
(7) Professional and other associations and federations in the field of sports.
(8) Institute for Sports and Sports Medicine of the Republic of Macedonia.
(9) Institutions and companies for performing sports activities.
(10) Sports endowments of the foundation and funds.

*385*. The conditions for the establishment, operation and termination of each of the above forms of sports association are defined by the provisions of the relevant laws and by-laws (*see* Articles 5–11 of the LS), which were discussed in more detail in the previous chapter.

*386*. When it comes to freedom of association, we believe that due attention should be paid to sports for people with disabilities and their freedom of association.

## I. Freedom of Association of Persons with Disabilities and Nondiscrimination

*387*. According to the revised National Strategy for Equality of Rights of Disabled Persons (2010–2018),[327] the following issues are of particular importance for sport activities and their organization:

(1) Games, recreation and sports among children and young people with developmental problems and special educational needs, as well as in persons with disabilities, contribute towards improving their general state of the body, self-affirmation, socialization and active involvement in social and economic life.

326. Constitution of the Republic of Macedonia, Art. 20. Official Journal Nos. 1/92, 31/98, 91/01, 84/03, 107/05, 3/09, 49/11, 6/19.
327. Available at: https://mtsp.gov.mk/WBStorage/Files/FINALNA%20Revidirana%20Nacionalna%20Strategija.pdf.

(2) Of particular importance for the implementation of recreational and sports activities for children, young people, students and other persons with disability is the action of national disability sports federations, which sports associations have received a decision on sports activities from the Agency for Youth and Sports of the Republic of Macedonia, according to the Law on Sports and the Law on Disability Organizations.
(3) The Convention on the Rights of Persons with Disabilities, i.e., Article 30 point 5 provides appropriate measures that the signatory states undertake in relation to the participation of persons with disabilities in cultural life, recreation, entertainment and sports.
(4) Article 4 paragraph 2 of the European Charter for Sports adopted in 1992 reads, "Measures will be taken to provide all citizens with the opportunity to participate in sports, and when it comes to young gifted persons, as well as children with developmental disabilities and persons with disabilities, additional measures will be taken measures through which they will be provided with such opportunities to help them practice more effectively.&rdquohttp://fsrim.org.mk/za-nas/[328]

*388.* The Strategy furthermore notes that in the Republic of Macedonia, there is an obvious lack of sports and recreational facilities fully adapted to access and implement sports and recreational activities for children, young people and adults with disability in terms of spatial arrangement (external and internal), and the equipment with specific sports equipment. This refers to a lack of special training programs for physical exercise for children, pupils and students with disabilities in the education process, as well as in extracurricular activities.[329]

*389.* In order to achieve its special purpose, the realization of full participation in games and sports-recreational activities of children, students, students with disabilities, as well as enabling the same conditions for sports for the top athletes' disabilities in domestic and international competitions, the strategy foresees the following measures that should be implemented:

(1) to provide children with disabilities an equal opportunity to participate in games, entertainment, leisure and sports activities, including those activities;
(2) to enable persons with disabilities an equal opportunity to participate in recreational, sports games and entertainment;
(3) to enable the participation of persons with disabilities in regular sports activities in all degrees of sport;
(4) to ensure access of persons with disabilities to and in sports, recreational and tourist facilities;
(5) to ensure the possibility of organization, development and participation in sports and recreational activities intended for persons with disabilities and to provide spacious personnel and material conditions for organized action of

328. *Ibid.*
329. *Ibid.*

planning and implementation organizations of mass sport, sports recreation of persons with disabilities at local, regional and state level;

(6) to ensure the same conditions and opportunities for quality training process, preparations and participation in domestic and international championships of top athletes with disabilities under equal opportunities and conditions as for the top athletes without disabilities.

*390.* The key players in the realization of these measures are the Agency for Youth and Sports, the Ministry of Education and Science, the units of local self-government in development with the National Council of organizations of the disabled and other nongovernmental organizations.[330]

*391.* The National Strategy for Equality and Non-Discrimination (2016–2020) also refers to sports activities. The strategy contains three strategic objectives: advancing the legal framework for equal opportunities and nondiscrimination; capacity building, work advancement and coordination of the institutional mechanisms for prevention and protection against discrimination and promotion of equal opportunities; and raising public awareness to recognize forms of discrimination and promoting the concepts of nondiscrimination and equal opportunities. Of the strategic objectives, there are five specific objectives: work and labor relations; education, science, sports and culture; social security; judiciary and administration; and access to goods and services. The specific goals are achieved through the implementation of various specific activities.[331]

## §2. Government Conditions and Permits

*392.* As already stated, the freedom of association in sports is guaranteed within the general freedom of association defined by the Constitution, in accordance with Article 20 of the Constitution stipulates, *inter alia* that the Constitutional Court may prohibit only an association whose activities are aimed at violently overthrowing the constitutional order, violating guaranteed human or minority rights or inciting racial, national or religious hatred.

*393.* According to the provisions of the LS, a work ban is also envisaged if the sports association does not meet the conditions for performing sports activities and does not meet those conditions within the time limit set in the pronounced measure.

*394.* In order to fulfill the needs for dealing with activities and protection of rights and interests in the field of sports, citizens can freely join and establish sports associations voluntarily, under the conditions of manner established by law.

330. *Ibid.*
331. National Strategy for Equality and Non-Discrimination, Available at: https://www.mtsp.gov.mk/content/pdf/dokumenti/7.7_Strategija%20za%20ednakvost%20i%20nediskriminacija.pdf.

*395.* The sports clubs from different sports, for the purpose of realizing the public interest of the municipalities, the municipalities in the city of Skopje and the city of Skopje in the area of sports and for the purpose of planning and realization of program activities, can join together in municipal and city sports unions from different sports. The sports clubs from the same sport at the level of the municipality, i.e., the City of Skopje, for the purpose of realization and implementation of joint program activities, can join together in municipal, that is, city unions from the same sport.[332]

## I. Sports Clubs Permits

### *A. Issuing of Licenses*

*396.* A sports club, in the sense of LS, is a sports association, i.e., a commercial company engaged in sports (hereinafter "sports club"). The commercial company that carries out sports activity, in accordance with this LS, is obliged to implement the provisions of the Law on Commercial Companies. The company referred is also obliged to regularly deliver financial reports and on the basis of the report to carry out control by appropriate institution.

*397.* Sport clubs that compete at the highest level of competitions in senior competition, in sports in which there is a senior system of competitions at several levels in football, basketball, handball and volleyball, are registered as joint-stock companies in accordance with the Law on the trading companies. The name of the joint-stock company, in addition to the elements according to the Law on Commercial Companies, includes the type of sport for which the sports club was founded and registered as a joint-stock company, according to LS.

*398.* The sports club can organize a sports school in the sport for which it is available and receive a decision to perform sports activities in accordance with Article 11 paragraph 2 of LS. The sports club is issued a license to organize a sports school by the National Sports Federation.

*399.* A sports club registered as an association may cease to operate as an association of citizens and can be registered as a trading company for carrying out sport activity.[333]

*400.* A license for organizing a sports school is issued to the sports club by the National Sports Federation.

*401.* A sports club, registered as an association, may also operate as an association of citizens and register as a trading company for performing sport activity. Decision on the termination of a sports club, as an association, for the purpose of

332. Article 13, LS.
333. Articles 6–9, LS.

establishing a sports club as a commercial company, in accordance with LS, is enacted by the assembly of the sports club with a two-thirds majority of the total number of members of the Assembly.

*402.* The following must be attached to the decision:

- an act to regulate the rights and obligations of athletes who are members of the sports club;
- an act for regulating the rights and obligations of employees in the sports club;
- a report on the audit of the annual accounts by an authorized institution;
- report of an authorized appraiser on the estimated value of the club;
- data and evidence on the right of ownership, disposal, use and real estate management; and
- overview of interested legal and natural persons who will call for founders of the sports club as a trading company with a program proposal from interested founders.

*403.* In the procedure for registering the sports club from an association to a commercial company, the provisions of the Law on Commercial Companies are applied.

*404.* The decision to establish the joint-stock company adopted by the Assembly of the sports club is considered adopted if two-thirds of the members voted for it, the total number of members of the Assembly of the sports club.

*405.* The trading company, that is, the joint-stock company that was established with the registration of a sports association, assumes continuity of the rights and obligations of the sports association and continuity of the achieved results (achieved placement, rank and status in the competition system) within the National Sports Federation, of the sports club, regardless of whether the company keeps or changes the name of the sports club.

*406.* The National Sports Federation recognizes the continuity of the achieved result of the trading company, i.e., a joint-stock company which occurred by registering from a sports association to a trading company, i.e., a joint-stock company whose legal successor is the trading company.

*407.* Sports facilities and inventory owned by the state or local government units cannot be included in the property of the trading company by registering the sports association in trading company.[334]

334. Articles 7–9, LS.

*B. Professional Club Status*

*408.* Professional status, in the sense of LS, is assigned to a sports club that was founded for performing sports activities for participation in the system of sports competitions (hereinafter "professional sports club").

*409.* A professional sports club is a club that:

- participates in the highest level of competitions in the respective national sports federation; and
- has concluded contracts for professional performance, with at least 50% of the total number of competitors who compete in the highest system of competitions in senior competition in relation to the number of those registered for the competition year in the list corresponding sports list, managed by the federation.

*410.* The professional sports club in football, basketball, handball and volleyball in the highest level of competition has the status of a joint-stock company.[335]

*411.* Sports clubs and national sports federations of the Republic of Macedonia, due to the realization of common interest in the development of sports, can join together in an alliance of sports federations of the Republic of Macedonia.

*412.* Sports clubs can cooperate with appropriate sports clubs from other countries and with other foreign associations that implement programs in the field of sports in the manner and on the principles established in the statutes of national sports federations.[336]

*413.* The professional sports club is registered in the Register of Professional Sports Clubs (hereinafter "Register"), which leads the body of the state administration responsible for the affairs in the field of sports in electronic form.

*414.* For registration in the Register, the following evidence is required: proof of participation in the highest level of competitions in the respective national sports federation; proof that he has signed contracts for professional performance with at least 50% of the total number of competitors who perform in the highest system of competitions in senior competition in relation to the number of those registered for the competition year in the list that leads the corresponding sports federation; a decision for registration in the Central Registry and proof that the club keeps a register of members of a fan group.

*415.* The authorized official from the state administration body responsible for affairs in the field of sports, which leads the procedure within three days from the day of receipt of the request, is obliged to deal.

335. Article 9-a, LS.
336. Articles 15–16, LS.

*416.* For the purpose of registration in the Register, the state administration authority responsible for the affairs of the sports area issues a decision within thirty days from the day of submission of the enrollment application.

*417.* An appeal can be filed against the decision for registration. The appeal is submitted to the 2nd degree State Commission for decision-making in administrative and labor issues.[337]

### *C. Submission of Reports*

*418.* The professional sports club is required once a year, no later than March 31, to submit a report for the previous year to the authority responsible for affairs in the field of sports and the respective national sports federation. Reports are submitted regarding registered senior athletes, club members and members of club bodies and work plans for the coming year.

*419.* The national sports federation is obliged to notify the Agency of Sports regarding the report. Professional sports clubs in football, basketball, handball and volleyball registered as a joint-stock company are obliged once a year, and no later than March 31 of the current year, to submit a report on the operation, annual account and financial matters as well as work plans to the appropriate federation and the authority of the state administration competent in the area of sports.[338]

### *D. Management of Sport Clubs*

*420.* The members of the professional sports clubs and the members of the management bodies of professional sports clubs cannot be members in the management bodies, i.e., in the supervisory bodies of commercial companies in accordance with the provisions of the Law on Commercial Companies and the Law on Prevention of Conflict of Interest and members of the supervisory authorities and management authorities in accordance with the provisions of the LAF.

*421.* Members of professional sports clubs and members of governing bodies professional sports clubs cannot be persons who have been punished by a final decision for a crime with a prison sentence for at least six months; persons who are members of other sports clubs for a competition of the same sport; persons who are members of bodies in a sports club for a competition in the same sport or same system of matches; athletes who have a professional status; managers and trainers of sports clubs, as well as persons who during the period of at least one year before they performed that activity and—members of the legal entity who carry out

337. Article 9-a, LS.
338. Article 9-b, LS.

activity—organization of sports betting shops, as well as persons who performed that activity in the previous three years.[339]

*E. Sports Activities Performance Permit*

*422.* The sports club can perform sports activities if the following conditions are met:

- appropriate facilities are provided;
- the club has appropriate equipment;
- keeps a register in electronic form of members of a fan group;
- provided appropriate professional staff; and
- participates in an organized system of competitions, i.e., sports-recreational activities.

The professional sports club can perform sports activities if it:

- has signed contracts for professional performance with at least 50% of the total number of registered athletes in senior competitions;
- has concluded a contract for the professional work of one coach for the senior or two coaches for the youth competition;
- has concluded a contract for the professional work of a medical person;
- has employed at least one person for administrative and technical work;
- provides adequate facilities;
- has appropriate equipment; and
- participates in an organized system of competitions and sports and recreation activities.

*423.* The following evidence should be submitted for the issuance of a decision to carry out sports activity at a Sports Club:

- a decision for registration in the Central Registry;
- transcript from the register of members of a fan group;
- statute and other documentation.

*424.* Sports clubs from the same sport, as well as school sports, student sports and sports for the disabled organizations, can join together in an appropriate National Sports Federation of the Republic of Macedonia for the purpose of:

- encouragement and promotion of the respective sport;
- implementation of the established program for the development of sports;
- harmonizing and coordinating the program activities of the associated companies members;
- organizing and implementing the competition system;

339. Article 9-c, LS.

– advancement of professional work.

*425.* The National Sports Federation of the Republic of Macedonia (hereinafter "National Sports Federation") also compiles and takes care of the national teams.

*426.* Only one national sports federation can be established in one sport.

*427.* Decision on registration in the Register of Associations of the National Sports Federation is enacted by the Central Registry after previously obtaining a positive opinion from the Agency of Youth and Sport.

## II. Approval of National Sport Federations

*428.* A national sports federation is a federation in which more than half of the sports clubs are united in the Republic of Macedonia that has approval for performing activities of the same type of sport.

### *A. Licenses for National Sport Federations*

*429.* The National Sports Federation of the Republic of Macedonia can perform sports activities if:

– there is an organized system of competitions, and
– is organized in accordance with the provisions of Articles 13 and 14 of the LS.

*430.* A sports school can operate if the following conditions are met:

– the program for the implementation of the sports school is approved and accepted by the National Sports Federation;
– there are spatial conditions for its realization;
– basic equipment and requisites are provided.[340]

*431.* The fulfillment of the conditions for the work of the National Sports Federation of the Republic of Macedonia shall be determined by the authority of the state administration responsible for matters in the field of sports for which it issues an opinion. The sports club, that is, the National Sports Federation of the Republic of Macedonia, can start performing sports activities after the authority of the state administration responsible for the affairs of the field of sports determines that they have fulfilled the conditions for which he will make a decision.

*432.* For the issuance of a decision to perform sports activities for the National Sports Federation, the following evidence is required:

340. Article 10, LS.

– a decision for registration in the Central Registry;
– transcript from the register of members of a fan group;
– statute;
– evidence of provided appropriate facilities, equipment and professional staff;
– inventory of associated members; and
– description of the competition system.

*433.* For the issuance of a decision to perform sports activities, the Macedonian Olympic Games committee needs the following evidence:

– a decision for registration in the Central Registry;
– statute; and
– a list with an overview of the national sports federations of the Republic of Macedonia from Olympic sports that are united in it.

*434.* The authorized official from the AMC is obliged to decide on the above requests.[341]

*435.* The national sports federations can be members of the respective international associations only if the national sports federations of the respective sport have approval for performing sport activities.

## *B. Management of the Federations*

*436.* The Federation is represented by a person who is elected by a majority of votes from the total number of members of the Federation Assembly. A person representing the federation can be elected for a maximum of two four-year terms consecutively, and the same may be re-elected after the expiration of the time period of at least one full term.

*437.* The governing body of the national sports federation appoints a Secretary-General of the national sports federation, as previously announced public announcement.

*438.* The public article is published on the website of the national sports federation and in at least three daily newspapers, of which one of the newspapers is published in the language spoken by at least 20% of citizens who speak an official language other than the Macedonian language.

Furthermore, in addition to the general working conditions, the Secretary-General should possess a license to perform works on management in the field of sports and an internationally recognized certificate issued by an official European language tester, a member of the

Association of Language Testers in Europe (ALTE).

341. Article 11, LS.

*439.* For obtaining a license to perform management work in the area of sport, the body of the state administration responsible for matters in the field of the sport conducts an exam.

*440.* The secretary of the national sports federation may be appointed for a maximum of two consecutive terms with a term of four years. If at the time of the termination of the term of office of the person representing the federation, the federation's account has been blocked for at least thirty days, the person whose mandate ends cannot be re-elected.[342]

*441.* The assembly of national sports federations in team sports consists of the representatives from the first and second league clubs and the rest of the clubs united in federations, as well as representatives of sports coaches, veterans, referees and athletes of the respective sport proposed by their organizational forms.

*442.* The assembly of national sports federations in individual sports consists of the representatives from the clubs united in the federations, as well as representatives of sports coaches, veterans, judges and athletes from the respective sports suggested by their organizational forms.

*443.* In the national sports federations, the sports clubs that compete in the highest level of competitions in senior competition in sports in which a senior system of competitions is organized in several degrees, are organized in an organizational form in accordance with the Law on associations and foundations for the purpose of realizing their rights and interests.

*444.* The above organizational form of associations submit proposals to the National Sports Federation for determining the system of matches, the choice of the sponsor of the league, the broadcasting rights of competitions and other issues related to maintaining the highest level at competitions in senior competition in sports in which a senior system of competitions in several degrees. National sports federations provide spatial and other conditions for operation of the organizational form of the above associations.[343]

*445.* At least two lawyers and at least two economists have to be members of the governing body of the national sports federation. As previously noted, the members of the governing body of the national sports federation and the secretary must not be related by all lines up to the second degree with the president of the national sports federation. Other impediments to appointment of the above persons are the cases of companies that are capital or management related. The members of the governing body of the national sports federation should not be employees or members of management bodies in a company in which the president of the national sports federation has dominant ownership. The president of the governing body of the

342. Article 14, LS.
343. Articles 14 a, b, LS.

national sports federation may not have ownership shares or be part of the founding members of associations in the sports clubs for which they are responsible.[344]

### III. Revoking the Approvals

*446.* The Agency of Youth and Sport can ex officio revoke the approval for performing sports activity if it determines that the sports club, the National Sports Federation, or the Macedonian Olympic Committee does not meet the conditions with LS. An appeal can be filed against the decision to the second degree State Commission for decision-making in administrative and labor issues related to the second degree within fifteen days from the day of receipt of the decision.[345]

## §3. Public Safety

*447.* The safety of sports events is extremely important for the level of overall safety in a country. At sports events of various kinds, a large number of people gather, so any threat to their safety can have unforeseeable consequences. This is recognized by the legislator who paid special attention to the issue of safety of sports events.

*448.* According to LS, even during the design and construction of sports facilities, as well as when it comes to the existing sports facilities in addition to the application of standards, technical norms, and urban and other prescribed conditions, special conditions are also applied referring to the functionality, equipment and safety of the facilities. The official who manages the state administration authority responsible for affairs in the field of sports, in cooperation with the official who manages the authority of the state administration responsible for matters in the field of arrangement of the space, determines the special conditions that apply to functionality, equipment and safety of sports facilities.[346]

### I. Law for Prevention of Violence and Misconduct in Sports Competitions (LPVMSC)

*449.* The Law for the prevention of violence and misconduct in sports competitions (LPVMSC) regulates the issues related to violence and inappropriate behavior in sports competitions, the measures to prevent them for the safety of spectators, competitors and other participants in sports competitions, as well as the obligations of the organizers and the powers of the competent authorities to implement those measures.[347]

---

344. Article 14 c, LS.
345. Article 12, LS.
346. Article 52, LS.
347. LPVMSC, Article 1.

*450.* A sports competition, in the sense of the law, is any individual competition in an organized system of sports competitions in accordance with the provisions of the Law on Sports. Sports clubs and national sports federations, as well as other legal and natural persons who organize a sports competition in accordance with the provisions of the Law on Sports, are organizers of a sports competition in the sense of the law. Sports field, in the sense of the law, is the space on which the sports competition takes place, as well as the space between the auditorium and the space on which the sports competition takes place. A masked person, in the sense of the law, is a person who uses means of the body (face, head, etc.) for the purpose of creating difficulties in determining his identity, that is, for the purpose of concealing his identity. Wardens, in the sense of the law, are persons employed by the organizer, voluntarily registered persons or members of the club, fans and other persons, as well as private security workers from legal entities that provide private security in the form of providing services (hereinafter "the legal entities that perform private security").[348]

*451.* Violence and indecent behavior in sports competitions are considered:

- possession or consumption of alcoholic beverages or narcotic drugs, possession of pyrotechnics, weapons and other means suitable for inflicting injuries or causing violence by persons who come to the sports competitions, during the entire time period upon arrival, during and after the holding of the sports competition;
- introduction and use in sports facilities of alcoholic beverages, narcotic drugs, pyrotechnics, weapons and other means suitable for inflicting injuries or causing violence;
- entering and displaying banners, flags and other objects with text, image, sign or other features, as well as singing songs or posting messages that cause and incite hatred or violence on the basis of racial, national and religious affiliation or on the basis of other traits;
- throwing objects in the sports field or in the auditorium;
- lighting and throwing of pyrotechnics;
- burning fans' props, flags of other countries, club flags and other objects;
- calling, inciting and participating in a fight or physical attack on athletes, spectators, stewards, officials, competition organizers and other participants in sports competitions;
- physical confrontation between participants in sports competitions;
- unauthorized entry into the sports field by spectators;
- damage or destruction of sports inventory and other parts of the sports facility, as well as means of transportation during the entire time period upon arrival, during and after the sports competition;
- unauthorized entry into the part of the spectator area of the sports facility intended for opposing fans;
- staying or keeping fans in the section of the auditorium for which they do not have an entrance ticket or a pass issued by the organizer of the match; and
- unauthorized entry of fans into facilities that are used for sports activities.

348. LPVMSC, Art. 2.

*452.* All actions determined in paragraph 1 of the article represent a more serious form of violence and unworthy behavior if they are carried out by a masked person.[349]

*453.* The organizer of the sports competition is obliged to assess the possibility of the occurrence of violence and inappropriate behavior at the sports competition and to take appropriate measures for their suppression and prevention, prescribed by the or another law.

*454.* The organizer of the sports competition is obliged to cooperate with the police and other competent authorities in assessing the danger of violence and inappropriate behavior while taking the necessary measures for their suppression and prevention.[350]

*455.* The organizer of the sports competition, depending on the type of sport and the level of the sports competition, the type of sports facility, the expected number of spectators and the assessment of the risk of violence and inappropriate behavior, is obliged to provide a sufficient number of security guards at the sports competition.

*456.* Wardens from paragraph 1 of the article, except for hired private security workers, are obliged to wear a vest with light-reflecting stripes with the inscription "Warden," which is visibly different from the insignia of members of the Ministry of Internal Affairs.

*457.* The organizer of the sports match can agree with the visiting club that the stewards from the visiting club will perform the stewardship work between the spectators of the visiting club.[351]

*458.* In order to take preventive action and reduce the risk of violence and inappropriate behavior at sports competitions, the organizer is obliged to:

- ensure exemplary behavior of his club and its fans;
- properly informs its fans (through meetings, issuing newsletters, etc.);
- coordinates the activities of the clubs when going with their fans to sports matches, where those clubs and their fans are guests;
- determine which sports competitions are considered to be competitions with increased risk and which measures he is obliged to take in accordance with Articles 4, 8 and 10 of the law;
- prepared a plan for preventive action and organization of a sports competition and
- draw up an evacuation plan in case of emergency.[352]

---

349. LPVMSC, Art. 3.
350. LPVMSC, Art. 4
351. LPVMSC, Art. 5
352. LPVMSC, Art. 6.

*459.* The organizer of the sports competition is obliged to provide a sufficient number of stewards in order to:

- denying entry to a person who does not have an entrance ticket;
- banning access to the facility where the competition is held for persons under the influence of alcohol or other intoxicants;
- preventing the introduction or sale of alcoholic beverages in the sports facility;
- preventing the introduction of objects into the sports facility that can be thrown, that is, can be used for violent behavior in the sports field or the auditorium;
- disallowing the introduction of banners and symbols that encourage racial, national, religious or other intolerance;
- warning, i.e., keeping viewers away who can cause and incite hatred based on racial, national and religious affiliation by singing songs or posting offensive messages;
- admonishing, that is, moving away the spectators whose unworthy behavior can cause violence at the sports match;
- preventing the unauthorized entry of spectators into the sports field, as well as into the facilities that are used to perform sports activities;
- preventing damage or destruction of sports inventory and other parts of the sports facility;
- preventing unauthorized entry into the spectator area of the sports facility intended for opposing fans;
- admonition and removal of fans who stay or remain in the section of the auditorium, i.e., sit in a place for which they do not have an entrance ticket; and
- preventing any form of violent and inappropriate behavior.

*460.* Wardens perform the obligations from paragraph 1 of the article by verbally indicating, reporting and giving directions in a clear, comprehensible and unambiguous manner, except for private security workers, who perform their duties in accordance with a special law.

*461.* The organizer of the sports competition is obliged to prepare and submit a security plan to the Ministry of Internal Affairs no later than forty-eight hours before the start of the sports competition.[353]

*462.* The organizer is obliged to cooperate with the Ministry of Internal Affairs in order to implement the measures related to the maintenance of public order and peace.

*463.* The organizer is obliged during sports competitions to ensure the presence of a medical aid service and other competent authorities and organizations, and public services (firefighting units, communal services, etc.).[354]

353. LPVMSC, Art. 7.
354. LPVMSC, Art. 8.

*464.* The guest sports club participating in a sports competition is obliged to:

- inform the competent national sports federation about the organized arrival of his fans no later than seventy-two hours before the start of the sports match;
- keeps records of tickets given away by the organizer of the sports competition with data contained in the records established in Article 10 paragraphs 1 and 16 of the law; and
- take other necessary measures so that the club and its fans do not cause violence and behave inappropriately at the sports match.

*465.* Personal data from paragraphs 1 and 2 of this article are kept for three years from the day of entry into the records.[355]

*466.* Sports competitions with increased risk are:

- domestic and international sports competitions of greater competitive importance;
- sports competitions in which the presence of a large number of spectators is expected; and
- sports matches that fans of visiting clubs are expected to attend.

*467.* Which domestic and international sports competitions, in the sense of paragraph 1, paragraph 1 of this article, will be considered as competitions of greater competitive importance, is determined by a regulation of the competent national sports federation in the Republic.

*468.* Sports competitions with increased risk are determined by the competent national sports federations, and for their holding, they are obliged to notify the Ministry of Interior and the sports clubs participating in the competition no later than forty-eight hours before the start of the sports competition.[356]

*469.* For sports competitions with increased risk, the organizer of the sports competition, in addition to the obligations from Article 7 of the law, is obliged to:

- notify the competent authorities, sports organizations, as well as the athletes participating in the sports competition immediately, and at the latest within forty-eight hours before the start of the sports competition;
- designate a responsible person who will manage the implementation of measures to prevent violent and inappropriate behavior of spectators and for cooperation with the Ministry of Internal Affairs;
- submit to the Ministry of Internal Affairs a plan for preventive action and organization of the sports competition and an evacuation plan in case of emergency;
- cooperated with the representatives of the fan clubs in order to provide assistance in maintaining the order of the sports match;

355. LPVMSC, Art. 8-b.
356. LPVMSC, Art. 9.

- cooperated with the Ministry of Internal Affairs in order to act according to the guidelines related to ensuring public order and peace at the sports competition;
- ensure, in front of the sports facility, the separation and direction of opposing groups of fans to the separate entrances;
- ensure the separation of home and away fans in the auditorium;
- put tickets on sale depending on the capacity of the sports facility;
- ensure that on the day of the sports competition, ticket sales are carried out at separate points of sale outside the sports facility;
- provide technical equipment for monitoring and recording the behavior of viewers;
- provide a room for providing emergency medical assistance;
- provide space for safe accommodation of the guest club's means of transport;
- take all the necessary measures so that the home club and its fans do not cause violence and inappropriate behavior at the sports match;
- carried out coordination with the Ministry of Internal Affairs before putting the tickets on sale;
- ensure a controlled sale of tickets with an inspection of a personal identification document with the possibility for one person to buy up to five tickets;
- keeps records of tickets sold and given away, which in particular contains serial number, date of sale, first and last name, name of sports club, address of residence, i.e., residence, tribune, block, row and seat;
- did not allow the entry of fans from a visiting sports club for whom he was not previously notified, in accordance with Article 11 paragraph 1 of the law; and
- allowed the entry of fans from a visiting sports club for whom he had previously been properly notified in accordance with Article 11 paragraph 1 of the law and placed them in the part of the auditorium designated for visiting fans.

*470.* In sports competitions with increased risk, for entrance control, spectator screening, physical security and internal security of the sports facility, the organizer of the sports competition is obliged to use the services of legal entities that perform private security.

*471.* Personal data from paragraph 1, paragraph 16 of this article are kept for three years from the day of entry into the records.[357]

*472.* The guest sports club that participates in a sports competition with increased risk is obliged to:

- informed the organizer of the sports match about the organized arrival of its fans, as well as about all the elements important for the club and its fans, no later than seventy-two hours before the start of the sports match;
- determined the route of movement of his fans, about whom the organizer of the sports competition had previously informed in coordination with the Ministry of Internal Affairs;

357. LPVMSC, Art. 10.

- appoint stewards and a responsible person from the club who will travel together with its fans, who were previously notified by the organizer of the sports competition and oblige the responsible person to inform the Ministry of the Interior about the course of the organized travel and the arrival of the fans;
- keeps records of tickets given away by the organizer of the sports competition with data contained in the records established in Article 10 paragraphs 1 and 16 of the law; and
- take other necessary measures so that the club and its fans do not cause violence and behave unworthy of the sports match.

*473.* Personal data from paragraphs 1 and 4 of this article are kept for three years from the day of entry into the records.[358]

*474.* The Minister of the Interior prescribes the form and manner of keeping the records for persons who have been imposed a misdemeanor sanction banning entry and attendance at all or certain sports competitions and the records of initiated settlement procedures and their outcomes.

*475.* The official in charge of the state administration body responsible for matters in the field of sports prescribes the form and manner of keeping the records kept by the organizer of the sports competition for tickets sold and given away and the records kept by the visiting fan club for tickets given away by the organizer at the sports competition.[359]

*476.* The Ministry of Internal Affairs takes all necessary measures to prevent violence and inappropriate behavior of all participants during sports competitions with increased risk.

*477.* The Ministry of Internal Affairs, at least twenty-four hours before the start of the sports competition with increased risk, carries out an inspection in terms of whether the organizer has taken the necessary measures related to the prevention of violence and inappropriate behavior of the participants and if the minutes ascertain certain deficiencies, it gives instructions to the organizer for their removal.[360]

*478.* A fine in the amount of EUR 500 in denar equivalents will be imposed for an offense against a natural person if he acts in violation of the provisions of Article 3, paragraph 1, paragraphs 1 and 2 of the law.

*479.* A fine in the amount of EUR 550 to EUR 750 in denar equivalents will be imposed for an offense against a natural person if he acts contrary to the provisions of Article 3, paragraph 1, paragraphs 3, 4, 5, 6, 7, 8, 9, 10, 11, 12 and 13 of the law.

358. LPVMSC, Art. 11.
359. LPVMSC, Art. 11-a.
360. LPVMSC, Art. 12.

*480*. A fine in the amount of EUR 600 to 1,000 in Denar equivalents will be imposed for the violation of the natural person from Article 3 paragraph 2 of the law if he acts in violation of the provisions of Article 3 paragraph 1 of the law.

*481*. A fine in the amount of EUR 500 to EUR 1,000 in denars will be imposed for an offense against a natural person if he does not act in accordance with Article 13-c paragraph 1 of the law.[361]

*482*. For the offenses determined in Article 13 paragraphs 1 and 2, and in connection with Article 3 paragraphs 1, 2, 3, 4, 5, 6, 7, 8, 9 and 10, the competent court may impose a misdemeanor on the natural person; sanction ban on entry and participation in sports competitions for a maximum of three years.[362]

*483*. The competent court notifies the petitioner for the initiation of a misdemeanor procedure, as well as the national sports federations, of the final decision imposing a misdemeanor sanction and ban on entry and attendance at sports competitions.

*484*. The national sports federations, from paragraph 1 of this article, are obliged to inform the organizer of the sports competition about the persons who have been given a misdemeanor sanction banning entry and attendance at sports competitions, as well as the sports club if those persons are its registered fans.

*485*. The organizer of the sports match or the contractual distributor for the sale of tickets will refuse to sell or give away a ticket for a certain match to a person who has been imposed a misdemeanor sanction banning entry and attendance at sports matches.

*486*. The organizer of the sports competition is obliged to take all measures to deny access to the sports facility to a person who knows or is obliged to know that a criminal sanction has been imposed on him, banning him from entering and attending sports competitions.[363]

*487*. A person who has been given a misdemeanor sanction, a ban on entry and attendance at sports matches, is obliged to come and stay at the competent police station according to the place of residence or residence during the sports match and for one hour no later than two hours before the start of the sports match after the sports competition is over.

*488*. In the event that the person from paragraph 1 of this article is unable to come and stay at the competent police station due to health reasons, professional obligations or other justified reasons, which cannot be delayed, he is obliged to

361. LPVMSC, Art. 13.
362. LPVMSC, Art. 13-a.
363. LPVMSC, Art. 13-b.

notify the competent police station according to the place of residence or residence for the address at which he will be located during the time period from paragraph 1 of this article.

*489.* In the event that the person does not report to the competent police station, the Ministry of Internal Affairs, within its powers, will take all necessary measures and actions to find him in order to execute the imposed misdemeanor sanction.[364]

*490.* The Ministry of Internal Affairs keeps a record of persons who have been issued a misdemeanor sanction banning entry and attendance at all sports competitions.

*491.* The following personal data are collected, processed and stored: serial number, date of registration, first and last name of the offender, date and place of birth, place of residence, i.e., residence, type of offense, number and date of final decision by which the misdemeanor sanction was pronounced, which sports matches the ban applies to, duration of the ban on entry and attendance at sports matches and belonging to a fan group.

*492.* Personal data are kept for five years from the day of entry into the records.[365]

*493.* A fine in the amount of EUR 5,000 in denars will be imposed for an offense against the organizer of the sports competition, if:

- does not take measures to suppress and prevent violence and inappropriate behavior at the sports competition (Article 4 paragraph 1);
- does not cooperate with the competent authorities (Article 4 paragraph 2);
- did not provide a sufficient number of guards (Article 5 paragraph 1);
- did not act in accordance with Article 7 of the law;
- does not cooperate with the Ministry of Internal Affairs and does not ensure the presence of the medical aid service and other competent authorities and organizations and public services (Article 8);
- did not act in accordance with Article 10 of the law and
- did not act in accordance with Article 13-b paragraph 4 of the law.

*494.* A fine in the amount of 30% of the assessed fine for the legal entity will also be imposed on the responsible person of the organizer for the offense from paragraph 1 of this article.[366]

364. LPVMSC, Art. 13-c.
365. LPVMSC, Art. 13-d.
366. LPVMSC, Art. 14.

*495.* A fine in the amount of EUR 2,000 in denars will be imposed on the organizer of the sports competition if he does not act in accordance with the guidelines of the Ministry of Internal Affairs and does not remove the identified deficiencies (Article 12 paragraph 2).[367]

*496.* A fine in the amount of EUR 2,000 in denars will be imposed for a violation of the competent national sports federation if it does not act in accordance with Article 9, paragraph 3 of the law.

*497.* A fine in the amount of EUR 2,000 in denars will be imposed for a violation of the national sports federation if it does not notify the organizer of the sports competition and the sports club about the persons to whom the violation sanction was imposed (Article 13-b paragraph 2).

*498.* A fine in the amount of 30% of the assessed fine for the legal entity will also be imposed on the responsible person in the national sports federation for the offenses from paragraphs 1 and 2 of the article.[368]

*499.* A fine in the amount of EUR 3,000 in denar equivalents will be imposed for an offense against the visiting sports club if, within seventy-two hours, it does not notify the competent national sports federation and the organizer of the sports competition and does not take the necessary measures in accordance with Articles 8-b and 11 of the law.

*500.* A fine in the amount of 30% of the assessed fine for the legal entity will also be imposed on the responsible person of the sports club for the offense from paragraph 1 of the article.[369]

*501.* For the offenses determined in Articles 13, 14, 14-a, 14-b and 15 of the law, the uniformed police officer of the Ministry of Internal Affairs is obliged to issue the perpetrator of the offense a criminal payment order in accordance with the Law on Offenses.

*502.* Uniformed police officers are obliged to keep records of the issued misdemeanor payment orders from paragraph 1 of this article and of the outcome of the initiated procedures.

*503.* In the records from paragraph 2 of this article, the following data are collected, processed and stored: name and surname, i.e., title of the perpetrator of the offense; residence, i.e., residence, headquarters; type of offense, number of the offense payment order issued to him; and the outcome of the procedure.

---

367. LPVMSC, Art. 14-a.
368. LPVMSC, Art. 14-b.
369. LPVMSC, Art. 15.

*504.* Personal data from paragraph 3 of this article are kept for five years from the day of entry into the records.

*505.* The form and content of the delinquent payment order are prescribed by the Minister of the Interior.[370]

*506.* For all misdemeanors provided for by the law, the misdemeanor procedure is conducted, and a misdemeanor sanction is imposed by a competent court.[371]

*507.* The calculation of the amount of the fine for a legal entity is carried out in accordance with the Code of Offenses.[372]

## II. Other Criminal Acts Related to Sports

*508.* The safety of sports events is also protected by the provisions of criminal legislation, first of all, through the nature of the criminal offense of violent behavior at a sports event or public gathering under Article 386 (4) of the Criminal Code.

*509.* The act is committed by a person who maltreats, roughly insults, endangers the safety or performs rough violence upon another, and herewith causes a feeling of insecurity, threat or fear among the public, related to a sports competition and committed during, before or after the end of the competition. The punishment for this act is imprisonment of three months to three years. The organizer of the group that commits the crime, as well as the organizer of the sports competition that does not take measures for preventing the violence, shall be punished with punishment of six months to five years if the act has a consequence of death or heavy body injury.

*510.* All these criminal sanctions and measures are aimed at actively contributing to increasing the level of security of all participants in sports events (athletes, spectators, sports workers, etc.). Their consistent application is a condition for gaining confidence in sports and the safety of sports events, and at the same time, contributes to the free and fearless enjoyment of sports.

## §4. Tax

*511.* The tax system is a unique system of fiscal revenues of the state. When it comes to the fiscal obligations of sports associations, companies and athletes, the provisions of the relevant laws governing the tax area apply.

370. LPVMSC, Art. 15-a.
371. LPVMSC, Art. 15-b.
372. LPVMSC, Art. 15-c.

*512.* Sports entities are not exempted from the obligation to pay taxes on profit, property and other tax liabilities. At this point, the tax regime of sports organizations in the Republic of Macedonia will be briefly explained.

*513.* Sports associations have specific tax treatment in the Republic of Macedonia. They are subject to the obligation to pay the following income taxes: (1) Membership income; (2) Revenues from donations; (3) Revenues from sponsorships; (4) Rental income; (5) Revenue from ticket sales; (6) Revenues from the provision of services or sales of products on the market.

*514.* According to the Law on beneficiaries of the funds from the tax exemption (LBFTE) according to the Law on the tax on profit can be:

- national sports federations;
- sports clubs;
- active athletes who compete in individual sports; and
- other legal entities that have a decision to perform sports activities.

*515.* The beneficiaries from paragraph 1 of this article can use the funds from the tax exemption after fulfilling the following criteria:

(a) for the National Sports Federations:
  - number of active sports clubs and athletes in the National Sports Federation;
  - functioning of the National Sports Federation (assembly, organs and bodies, spatial conditions);
  - rank of the National Sports Federation on the official rankings of the international European and world sports associations in a certain sport;
  - organization and achieved sports results in the national system of competitions in men's and women's competition, in all age categories;
  - participation and achieved results in the international sports system of national sports teams in the last two years;
  - participation and achieved results in the international sports system of the sports clubs from the National Sports Federation in the last two years;
  - organization of European, regional and other international competitions in the country;
  - participation and achieved results in the international sports system of athletes in individual sports, in all-adult competitions categories in the last two years;
  - media coverage of the national sports system;
  - human resources in the National Sports Federation (professional administrative workers, coaches, judges, doctors, sports psychologists, nutritionists and others); and
  - material conditions for the functioning of the National Sports federation;

(b) for sports clubs:
  - number of active athletes in the sports club;

- functioning of the sports club (assembly, organs and bodies, spatial conditions);
- participation and placement of the sports club in the national system of competitions, for all categories and ages in the past two years;
- participation and achieved results of the sports club in international sports system of matches in the last two years;
- number of athletes from the sports club in the national teams of all ages (seniors, youths, children);
- participation and achieved results in the international sports system of the sports clubs from the National Sports Federation in the last two years;
- participation and achieved results in the international sports system of athletes in individual sports, in all-adult competitions categories in the last two years;
- media coverage of the national sports system;
- number of athletes from the sports club who have achieved sports category;
- human resources in the sports club (coaches, doctors, sports psychologists, nutritionists and others); and
- material conditions for the functioning of the sports club;

(c) for active athletes competing in individual sports:
- to be a member of a sports club and actively train and perform for the sports club and the national sports team;
- to be categorized as an athlete in accordance with the law;
- to have achieved top sports results in the past two years;
- to have participation and placement in the national system of competitions, organized by the National Sports Federation; and
- to participate and place in official international competitions, organized by the international sports associations, of which he is a member.

*516.* The National Sports Federation and international rankings sports associations.

*517.* Other legal entities that have a decision to perform sports activities should meet the criteria established for the National Sports Federations or sports clubs, and they are ranked according to their status determined in the solution for doing sports.

*518.* The funds are used on the basis of an issued voucher by the body of the state administration responsible for the affairs in the field of the sport.

*519.* The official who manages the state administration authority responsible for affairs in the field of sports prescribes the form, content and manner of issuing the voucher.

*520.* The body of the state administration responsible for matters in the field of sports prepares and establishes a proposal list with which to evaluate, verify and rank National Sports Federations that meet the criteria for using the funds from the tax exemption in accordance with paragraph 2 point of this article and the Law on profit tax.

*521.* Each National Sports Federation forms a commission that prepares a list of proposals for evaluating, verifying and ranking sports clubs and active athletes who meet the criteria for using the funds from the tax exemption this article and the law on profit tax.

*522.* The National Sports Federation is obliged by January 20 at the latest of the current year to submit to the state administration authority responsible for the affairs a request for the use of tax funds release and proposal list of sports clubs and active athletes who meet the criteria for using tax funds release in accordance with the law and the Law on profit tax.

*523.* The body of the state administration responsible for matters in the field of sports establishes a Central Commission for the evaluation of a proposal—the list (hereinafter "the Central Commission"), for a period of four years, consisting of a president and six members at the proposal of the Government of Macedonia.

*524.* The Central Commission, within ten days of receiving the request to use funds from the tax exemption with the proposal list of sports clubs and active athletes who meet the criteria for using the funds from the tax exemption in accordance with the law and the Law on the profit tax, performs evaluation and inspection and submits the proposal list to the Sports Council for adoption.

*525.* The Council for Sports, within five days of receiving the proposed list of sports clubs and active athletes who meet the criteria for using the funds from the tax exemption in accordance with the law and the Law on profit tax, determines and adopts the proposal list at a meeting.

*526.* The body of the state administration responsible for matters in the field of sports no later than February 10 in the current year, publishes on its website the official Lists of National sports federations, sports clubs and active athletes that compete in individual sports and of other legal entities that have a solution for performing sports activities that meet the criteria for using the funds from the tax exemption in accordance with the law and the law on profit tax.

*527.* The body of the state administration responsible for matters in the field of sports issues vouchers for the use of the funds from the tax exemption within the term of five days from the day of publication of the lists.

*528.* The national sports federations are obliged to complete the documentation at the request of the Central Commission.

*529.* If the request is not completed within the period of three days, the official of the state administration authority responsible for affairs in the field of sports adopts a decision rejecting how the unfounded request to use funds from the tax exemption.

*530.* The members of the Central Commission do not receive compensation for their work after a session is held.

*531.* The official who manages the state administration authority responsible for matters in the field of sports prescribes the closer quantitative and qualitative criteria that should be met by the users and the use of funds from the tax exemption, the method of scoring and ranking, as well as the form and content of the request for usage of the funds from the tax exemption and on the lists from paragraph 12 of this article.

*532.* The users of the funds from the tax exemption use the funds for:

- salaries, allowances and bonuses of athletes and professional staff based on the rules of the club which are submitted in written form to the national sports federation;
- organization of travel and stay of the club or the active athlete in the country and abroad for the purpose of competitions or preparations;
- rental or construction of halls or fields for competition;
- the payment for renting office space for the club's work, in the amount of no more than 10% of the received funds per year;
- repayment of a loan for the purchase of the club's own premises in the amount of no greater than 20% per year of the received funds. If premises are purchased for the club with these funds, they may not be mortgaged (except mortgage to the bank for the purchase or construction of the building itself) and must not be alienated at least fifteen years from the day of their purchase;
- trips for the purpose of participation in professional seminars, conferences and training and after a previous decision of the governing body of the national sports federation;
- subscriptions and membership fees in international bodies in which they are members;
- purchase of equipment;
- payment of utility costs for national sports federations and sports clubs;
- health care, pension and disability insurance and compensation for insurance against consequences of an accident and risks of active athletes;
- for the organization of international competitions in the Republic of Macedonia.

*533.* The funds with which the trading company participates in the financing of the entities are paid into a special dedicated account, and the money may not be transferred from them to the regular or other account of The National Sports Federation, the sports club, the active athlete or another legal entity that has the decision to carry out sports activity or else pay obligations under contracts from the regular account.

*534.* The funds with which the trading company participates in the financing of the entities are subject to control for the purpose of use at least once a year by the state administration body responsible for matters in the field of sports. The illegal use of funds is subject to the provisions of the Criminal Code.

*535.* National sports federations and legal entities that have a permit for performing sports activities as beneficiaries of funds from the tax exemption are obliged to submit a report to the authority no later than March 15 of the following year of the state administration in charge of affairs in the field of sports, in terms of how many funds have they received for the previous year, from whom they received funds on this basis and for which purposes are the funds spent.

*536.* The report is published on the website of The National Sports Federation and the legal entities that have a solution for practicing sports at least in the period from March 15 to the following June 15 year from when the funds were received.

*537.* The National Sports Federation is obliged to publish on its website the reports of all sports clubs and active athletes beneficiaries of funds from the tax exemption, and they are obliged to submit the reports by March 10 of the following year at the latest the previous year to the competent National Sports Federation.

*538.* The official who manages the state administration authority responsible for affairs in the field of sports prescribes the form and content of the reports.

*539.* It is quite clear that sports organizations have rights and obligations in the tax system of the Republic of Macedonia in accordance with the positive legal regulations in this area.

## §5. Sports Justice

*540.* Numerous disputes can arise in and about sports. Disputes may arise from nonperformance of contracts concluded between sports organizations and sports workers or between sports organizations.

*541.* Disputes in the field of sports can be resolved in court or out of court.

*542.* Judicial dispute resolution takes place before the bodies of the judicial system of the Republic of Macedonia. The courts of first instance are territorially located in the following cities in Macedonia (Veles, Gevgelija, Kavadarci, Kratovo, Kriva Palanka, Kumanovo, NegotinoBasic criminal court Skopje, Basic civil court Skopje, Bitola, Krusevo, Ohrid, Prilep, Resen, Struga, Berovo, Vinnytsia, Delcevo, Kocani, Radovi*sh*, Sveti Nikole, Strumica, Stip, Gostivar, Debar, Kicevo and Tetovo.) The courts of appeal are located in Skopje, Bitola Stip and Gostivar. The decisions of the appellate courts are, as a rule, final. Exceptionally, the Supreme Court of Cassation, the highest court in the Republic of Macedonia, with its seat in Skopje, decides on the submitted legal remedies.

*543.* In an out-of-court settlement of disputes, the dispute is decided either by out-of-court settlement or by bringing the dispute before one of the sports arbitrations. The advantage of this way of resolving disputes is that the parties to the dispute choose the arbitrator who will resolve the dispute. Decisions made in this way are final, and in that way, great savings are realized in the name of court costs. This leads to the conclusion that out-of-court dispute resolution has its advantages over judicial dispute resolution.

*544.* Members of a sports association and a sports association may agree to resolve disputes over their free rights, except for disputes for which the court has exclusive jurisdiction—entrust to an ad hoc sports arbitration court or a permanent sports arbitration court at the Macedonian Olympic Committee and when it comes to disputes related to termination, annulment or fulfillment of the contract between the athlete and the permanent sports arbitration court at the competent national branch sports federation.

*545.* The provisions on arbitration of the law governing the procedure before arbitration shall apply accordingly to sports arbitration.

*546.* The dispute may also be the subject of international sports arbitration in cases determined by sports rules of the competent international sports federation.

## I. Permanent Sports Arbitration of the Macedonian Olympic Committee

*547.* From the aspect of legal certainty, the authorization of the Permanent Sports Arbitration of the Macedonian Olympic Committee is especially important. Its role is of a principled nature and helps to harmonize legal practice in the field of sports.

*548.* Disputes in the field of sports can also be resolved through mediation. Unlike arbitration, where the parties independently choose an arbitrator for their case, who resolves the dispute, in the case of mediation in sports, the parties to the dispute themselves choose a mediator who will help them to jointly and amicably resolve the dispute. It is important to point out that a mediator never makes a decision that resolves a dispute. The advantages of such dispute resolution are numerous. The costs of mediation proceedings are incomparably lower than the costs of court proceedings. In this way, in addition to resolving a specific dispute, future disputes can be prevented because mutual trust between the parties is strengthened. This is especially important for the development of the sports system as a whole. Unfortunately, mediation, as a model for resolving disputes, is not sufficiently developed in the Republic of Macedonia, regardless of all its benefits. With the development of mediation in Macedonia, mediation related to disputes in sports will also develop.

*549.* The Rulebook of the Sports Arbitration Court at the Macedonian Olympic Committee regulates the organization of the Sports Arbitration Court at the Macedonian Olympic Committee (hereinafter "SAS"), the jurisdiction and composition of the Arbitral Tribunals, the rules of the Arbitral Tribunal procedure and costs in the proceedings before the SAS in disputes of national dimension.[373]

*550.* The jurisdiction of the SAS may be agreed upon for the arbitral settlement of disputes between athletes, natural and legal persons performing sports activity and sports associations and organizations for rights that the parties freely dispose of if the law does not provide exclusive jurisdiction for the resolution of certain types of disputes in the courts of the Republic of Macedonia.

*551.* The provisions of this Rulebook shall apply to all types of disputes which can provide for the competence of the SAS.

*552.* The parties may agree to deviate from the application of the provisions of Arbitration rules, except for the provision of Article 55 of this Rulebook, if their agreement is not contrary to the enforced regulations of the Republic of Macedonia.[374]

*553.* In this Rulebook:

(i) an Arbitral Tribunal shall mean an individual arbitrator or Arbitral Tribunal who acts and decides in a specific dispute;
(ii) the plaintiff designates the party initiating the arbitration proceedings and includes one or more plaintiffs;
(iii) the defendant designates the party against whom the arbitral proceedings are instituted and includes one or more defendants;
(iv) a party or parties designates plaintiff (s) and defendant (s);
(v) a lawsuit means a written submission by the plaintiff with whom they initiate the arbitration procedure;
(vi) decision means any kind of decision rendered by the Arbitral Tribunal.[375]

*554.* The SAS operates within the Macedonian Olympic Committee. The SAS is a permanent, independent and sovereign body. The headquarters of SAS is in Skopje. SAS has its own seal, which reads: “Macedonian Olympic Committee—“Sports Court Arbitration.”

*555.* The Macedonian Olympic Committee (hereinafter “the IOC”) provides spatial and administrative-technical conditions for the smooth performance of the activity of SAS.

*556.* SAS is an independent body of the Macedonian Olympic Committee to resolve disputes over the rights freely available to the parties unless exclusive jurisdiction is provided for that type of dispute in a court of the Republic of Macedonia.

373. SAS Rulebook, Art. 1.
374. SAS Rulebook, Art. 2.
375. SAS Rulebook, Art. 3.

*557.* Bodies of SAS are the president, vice president and Secretary-General of SAS. The bodies of the SAS are the Arbitral Tribunals that act in disputes before SAS.

*558.* The work of the SAS is managed by the president of the SAS. A person who has graduated may be appointed president of the SAS (a lawyer who has completed four years of legal studies or legal studies according to the study program of European Credit Transfer System (ECTS) with three-hundred credits won) with at least five years of work experience. The President of the IAS is appointed by the IOC Assembly on proposal of the IOC Board of Directors for a term of five years. One person can be appointed president of the SAS for a maximum of two times.

*559.* The president of the SAS performs the following activities:

- appoints the arbitrators and the presidents of the Arbitral Tribunals in the cases provided by the Rulebook;
- decides on the removal and replacement of an arbitrator;
- submits the annual work program of SAS to the IOC;
- submits an annual report on the work of SAS and an annual financial SAS report to IOC;
- performs other activities determined by the acts of the SAS.

*560.* The vice president of the SAS replaces the President of the SAS when he is prevented from performing his duties, as in cases where The President of the SAS will delegate his powers to The vice president of the SAS. A person who has graduated can be appointed vice president of SAS lawyer (has completed four years of legal studies or legal studies according to the study program according to ECTS with won three-hundred credits). The vice president of the IAS is appointed by the IOC Assembly on proposal of the IOC Board of Directors for a term of five years. One person can be appointed vice president of SAS for a maximum of two times.

*561.* For the president, vice president, Secretary-General of the SAS and arbitrator, a person who is employed in a sports club, player or coach, sports club member or sports club official, partner or shareholder of a sports club, employee, official or official of a sports federation, of its member, licensed person for the organization of competitions and sports agents cannot be named. A person cannot be elected on the list of arbitrators of SAS if he is employed in a sports club, player or coach, member of a sports club or sports club official, partner or shareholder of a sports club, employee, official or official of a sports federation, on its member, a licensed person for organizing competitions and sports agents (Article 11, R).

*562.* SAS has a Secretary-General. The IOC Secretary-General shall be the Secretary-General of the IAS.[376]

---

376. SAS Rulebook, Arts 9–12.

*563.* The Secretary-General of the SAS:

- performs administrative-technical work for SAS;
- undertakes administrative actions for the purpose of constituting an Arbitral Tribunal and preparation of the hearing in a particular case;
- takes care of the proper execution of the conclusions and other decisions of Arbitral Tribunals;
- prepares the annual work report, the annual financial report, and the work plan of SAS for the next year and the same submits it to the president of the SAS;
- performs other activities determined by the acts of the SAS.

*564.* In case of temporary impediment of the Secretary-General of the SAS, The President of the IOC will appoint a person to replace the Secretary-General of the SAS, as a rule, from the IOC staff (Article 13, R).

*565.* The president, the vice president and the Secretary-General of the SAS undertake necessary activities for development and promotion of SAS in the Republic of Macedonia. The president, the vice president and the Secretary-General of the SAS shall monitor the legislation in the Republic of Macedonia that refers to sports and arbitration, supervise the implementation of the acts of the SAS and propose to the IOC Board of Directors amendments to the one Rulebook. The president, the vice president and the Secretary-General of the SAS organize and conduct seminars, consultations, expert talks and other events for the purpose of acquainting the professional and general public with the operation of SAS, then participate in scientific and professional gatherings in the country and abroad, prepare and publish professional and scientific papers related to the arbitrary manner of resolving disputes in sport. The president, the vice president and the Secretary-General of the SAS maintain regular contact with the CAS in Lausanne, Switzerland (Article 14, R).

*566.* The president, the vice president and the Secretary-General of the SAS have the right to reimbursement of expenses related to the performance of its functions in accordance with a decision of the IOC Board of Directors. The orders for payment of the compensation of the costs and the reward for the persons from paragraph 1 of this article are issued by the president of SAS. Order for payment of the reimbursement of the expenses for the president of SAS issued by the vice president of the SAS. The award of the Secretary-General of the IOC for the performance of the function The Secretary-General of the SAS is determined in accordance with the valid acts of the IOC.

*567.* The SAS has a list of arbitrators from which the individual arbitrators are selected, members and chairmen of arbitration boards. The list of arbitrators shall be determined by the IOC Board of Directors.

*568.* The jurisdiction of the Arbitral Tribunal arises from an agreement concluded in writing between the parties. The parties may provide for the jurisdiction of the Arbitral Tribunal with a written agreement concluded before or after the occurrence of the dispute. The agreement is considered to have been concluded in writing, and when it is concluded:

- by exchanging letters, telexes, e-mails or other means of communication that provide written proof of the concluded agreement;
- by exchanging a lawsuit, in which the plaintiff states the existence of the settlement and response to a lawsuit, in which the defendant does not dispute her existence.

*569.* During the arbitration proceedings, the Arbitral Tribunal shall assist the parties in resolving their dispute amicably, i.e., to conclude an agreement or settle.

*570.* If before a court of R. Macedonia has been sued in the same legal matter between the same parties or a lawsuit was initiated before a court of R. Macedonia which requires the court to declare the SAS incompetent, the Arbitral Tribunal procedure will not be interrupted or stopped. If before a court of R. Macedonia has been sued in the same legal matter between the same parties and an arbitration procedure was initiated before the SAS, and The Arbitral Tribunal found that there were particularly important reasons, The Arbitral Tribunal may decide to terminate the proceedings until the end of the court (litigation) procedure.

*571.* Any objection to the existence and validity of the arbitration agreement or incompetence of the Arbitral Tribunal should be filed no later than the day of the first hearing, and if the procedure is conducted without holding an oral hearing, no later than the moment when the response to the lawsuit will be communicated to the plaintiff. The objection must be submitted in writing to the SAS. For the objection of incompetence, a decision can be made only by the Arbitration tribunal. If the party submits an objection before the Arbitration is established, the tribunal makes the decision on the objection of incompetence to the president of the SAS. The decision of the president of the SAS that there is competence of SAS does not bind the Arbitral Tribunal, and the same, if it finds that it is not competent, may change the decision of the president of the SAS for competence.

*572.* The composition of the Arbitral Tribunal must be odd. If the parties have not determined the number of arbitrators and if, after expiration of fifteen days from the day when the defendant received the lawsuit, the parties do not agree to act arbitrator-individual, the dispute will be resolved by arbitration advice from three arbitrators. If the parties to the arbitration agreement have determined an even number of arbitrators, the president of the SAS will call on the parties to appoint an additional arbitrator. If the parties do not appoint an additional arbitrator within fifteen days from the date of receipt of the notification, the additional arbitrator will be appointed in accordance with the rules for the appointment of the president of the arbitration council. The arbitrators shall be elected, as a rule, from the list of SAS arbitrators. Each party may elect an arbitrator outside the list of arbitrators. Any person who will be selected from the list or will be named for the arbitrator accepts the SAS Code of Ethics and will act in accordance with its regulation.

*573.* For an individual arbitrator and for the president of the Arbitral Tribunal may, only a person who has graduated in law (has graduated) four-year legal studies or legal studies according to the study program according to ECTS with three-hundred credits won).

*574.* An individual arbitrator may act only if the parties are for that agreed in accordance with Article 21 paragraph 2 of the Rulebook. In the cases referred to in paragraph 1 of the Article, the parties shall be obliged to the Secretary-General to submit the name of the individual arbitrator no later than eight days from the day of filing the response to the lawsuit. If the parties do not submit the name of the individual arbitrator within the deadline determined in paragraph 2 of the article, in which case the Secretary-General of SAS will submit to the parties a list of arbitrators by summons within five days for each of the parties to choose one arbitrator. If both parties choose the same person as an arbitrator, that person will be appointed as an individual arbitrator. The list submitted by the Secretary-General of the SAS consists of three arbitrators from the list of SAS arbitrators. If the parties do not elect the same person as an arbitrator from the proposed list in accordance with paragraph (3) of this article, the individual arbitrator shall be appointed by the president of the SAS.

*575.* The Arbitration Council is composed of three members. Unless the parties have agreed otherwise, the Arbitral Tribunal shall constitute in such a way that the plaintiff appoints an arbitrator in the lawsuit, the defendant appoints an arbitrator in response to the lawsuit, and the president of the Arbitral Tribunal shall be appointed by the two arbitrators together. If any of the parties fail to appoint an arbitrator, the Secretary-General of SAS will summon the party who missed the appointment of arbitrator within fifteen days from the date of receipt of the request for appointment of arbitrator to appoint an arbitrator. If the party does not appoint an arbitrator by the deadline, the arbitrator will be appointed by the president of SAS. When the arbitrators appointed by the parties should appoint a president of the Arbitral Tribunal, the appointment must be made within fifteen days of the day of the appointment of the second arbitrator. If the appointed arbitrators do not appoint the president of the Arbitral Tribunal council within fifteen days determined by paragraph 3 of this article, the president of the Arbitral Tribunal shall be appointed by the president of SAS. The president of the SAS may appoint an arbitrator, an individual arbitrator and a chairman of the Arbitral Tribunal only from the list of arbitrators of the SAS.[377]

*576.* If in a dispute several plaintiffs or defendants appear in the role of a party, they are obliged to reach a mutual agreement on appointment of a joint arbitrator. If the parties referred to in paragraph (1) of this Article do not appoint a joint arbitrator, The Secretary-General of the SAS will submit a list of three arbitrators from the list to SAS arbitrators by summoning each of the parties within five days of the day on receipt of the request for an appointment to declare for the persons on the list. If a person is chosen by all parties, that person will be appointed joint arbitrator

377. SAS Rulebook, Arts 15–24.

of the litigants. If the joint arbitrator cannot be appointed in accordance with paragraphs (1) and (2) of this Article, the arbitrator shall be appointed by the president of the SAS.

*577.* The Secretary-General of the SAS shall inform the persons appointed for arbitrators from the parties within three days from the day when their name is submitted to the Secretary-General. If within ten days from the day of receipt of the notification, the appointed arbitrator did not submit a statement accepting the appointment, a statement of impartiality and independence is considered to have rejected the appointment. If the arbitrator rejects the appointment by the parties, the Secretary-General of The SAS will summon the party who appointed the arbitrator within ten days to appoint another person as an arbitrator. If the person appointed as president of the Arbitration Council refuses to accept the appointment, the president will be appointed in accordance with article 24 (4) of the Rulebook. The Secretary-General shall notify the Parties of the acceptance of the appointment of an arbitrator within three days from the date of receipt of notification.

*578.* Every person who could become an arbitrator is obliged to all who will be his turn about the possibility of his appointment to tell them each a circumstance that could lead to a reasonable suspicion of his impartiality and independence. The arbitrator is obliged immediately if a circumstance arises that might give rise to reasonable suspicion in his impartiality and independence to inform the parties except if he has previously informed them and they have not requested his removal. By submitting the statement for acceptance of the appointment, the arbitrator is obliged to submit a statement of impartiality and independence. In the statement, the arbitrator must disclose those circumstances to the parties which a reasonable third party would consider to be circumstances affecting the impartiality and/or independence of the arbitrator, and in particular:

- any relationship with the parties, their representative or other person participating in arbitration proceedings;
- if there is a direct or indirect financial interest in connection with resolving the case;
- if there is confidential information relating to the subject matter of the dispute, which he learned from sources outside the arbitration proceedings.

*579.* The Secretary-General of the SAS Statement on Impartiality and Independence, together with the statement of acceptance of the appointment of the arbitrator, submits it to both parties within eight days from the date of submission of the statement.

*580.* The mandate of the arbitrator ends:

(a) by signing the arbitral award, additional judgment, with signing the interpretation and correction of the arbitral award, partial judgment and supplementary judgment;
(b) by exemption;

(c) by making a decision on termination of the mandate of the arbitrator due to non-performance or inability to perform the duty of arbitrator.

*581.* Exemption of an arbitrator may be requested if there are circumstances that call into question the impartiality and/or independence of the arbitrator. The party that appointed the arbitrator may request his removal if he finds out about the reason for the exemption after the appointment of the arbitrator.

*582.* The arbitrator shall be obligatorily excluded if:

- is himself a party, legal representative or proxy of a party, if with the party is in relation to a co-owner, solidary debtor or recourse debtor or if he has been heard as a witness or expert in the same case;
- the party or the legal representative or the proxy of the party blood relative in a straight line to any degree, and in a lateral line to the fourth degree, or is his spouse, extramarital partner or relative after marriage to the second degree, whether the marriage has ended or not;
- if he is a guardian, adoptive parent, adoptive parent, breadwinner or breadwinner of the party to its legal representative or proxy.

*583.* The party that intends to request the removal of an arbitrator is obliged to submit a written request for exemption to the Secretary-General of the SAS within fifteen days from the day of finding out the reason for the exemption of the arbitrator. The Secretary-General of the SAS shall submit the request to the arbitrator whose Exemption is requested, to the opposite party and to the president of the SAS. If the arbitrator whose exemption is requested is not withdrawn, i.e., if the party that appointed the arbitrator did not agree with the exclusion, the decision for the exemption will be adopted by the president of the SAS.

*584.* If the arbitrator, due to legal or factual reasons, is not able to perform his duty, or for other reasons does not perform by the exemplary deadline and damages the reputation of the parties and sports in R. Macedonia, his term ends if he resigns from that position or if the parties agree to terminate it. If the parties do not agree on termination of the duty of arbitrator, and there are reasons for paragraph (1) of the Article, each party may ask the president of the SAS to decide on the termination of the mandate of the arbitrator.

*585.* In cases when the arbitrator's mandate terminates on the basis of Articles 31 and 32 when the arbitrator himself withdraws from the duty of arbitrator when the parties themselves will jointly decide to terminate the mandate of the arbitrator as and in other cases of termination of the arbitrator's term, shall be appointed arbitrator in accordance with the rules and procedure for appointment that were applied in the appointment of the arbitrator to be replaced.

*586.* If during the procedure, there is a change in the composition of the Arbitral Tribunal advice, the hearing is repeated unless the parties agree otherwise. If an individual arbitrator and also a president of the arbitration council are replaced, the procedure must be repeated.

*587.* The parties are free to appoint a person who will represent them (proxy). Only a person who fulfills them can be appointed as a representative of the conditions for performing legal activity on the territory of R. Macedonia in accordance with the regulations of R. Macedonia that regulate the legal profession occupation. The parties are not limited to the number of persons they will represent, and they can be named at any stage of the procedure. The Secretary-General shall give the names and addresses of the persons referred to in paragraph (1) submitted to the opposing party within 3 days from the date of receipt of notification. The costs for representation are calculated in accordance with the Tariff for remuneration and reimbursement of lawyers' expenses incurred in The Bar Association of the Republic of Macedonia, which is valid at the time when the procedure is initiated.

*588.* The parties are free to appoint a person who will advise them during arbitration proceedings. The parties are not limited to the number of persons they will advise, and they can be named at any stage of the procedure.

*589.* The parties have the right to file objections in the procedure before the SAS and Arbitral Tribunal regarding the application of the Rules, the interpretation and more. The parties may not, by mutual agreement, waive the right to file an objection. The party that knows that some provision of this Rulebook or some condition arising from the arbitration agreement is not complied with, and in doing so, the party continues to participate in the procedure, or if in the foreseen deadline no objections will be deemed to have waived the right to object.

*590.* Unless otherwise determined by the Rulebook, the Arbitral Tribunal may conduct the arbitral proceedings in the manner it deems fit most appropriate, taking into account the circumstances and interests of the parties while taking into account each party at each stage of the procedure to and be given the opportunity to present their facts, legal allegations, claims and views. All submissions, documents and other information that one party will receive will be submitted to the Arbitral Tribunal, which will be submitted to the contrary party. The parties will be provided with any expert report, evidence a document on the basis of which the Arbitral Tribunal may decide.

*591.* Unless the parties have agreed otherwise, the place of the arbitration procedure will be in Skopje. The Arbitral Tribunal may decide to hold hearings and to take over a certain action in a place that he will determine having them in taking into account the circumstances and interests of the parties.

*592.* Unless the parties have agreed otherwise, the procedure shall be conducted in the Macedonian language and its Cyrillic alphabet. The Arbitral Tribunal may order the parties to any oral hearing to provide a translation of the language or languages for which the parties agreed. All evidence that is not in the language in which the procedure is conducted must be submitted in original and with an official translation into the language in which the procedure is spoken.

*593.* All written communications shall be submitted to the Secretary-General of the SAS, which further submits them to all parties and the Arbitral Tribunal. It is considered that the delivery of the written announcement has been done even then when the party or its proxy refuses to receive it; what they are for is compiled in a written note.

*594.* The arbitration procedure shall be initiated with a request which shall be submitted immediately to SAS. The request must contain the following elements:

- full name and data of the parties (addresses of the parties, telephone, fax, e-mail address)
- claim;
- facts on the basis of which the claim is based;
- evidence;
- name of the arbitrator;
- mark for the value of the dispute;
- signature of the submitter, i.e., electronic signature.

*595.* The lawsuit, the response to the lawsuit, the attachments with the lawsuit and the response to the lawsuit with the attachments that the party sends during the procedure to the Arbitral Tribunal shall be submitted in a sufficient number of copies for all opposing parties, for the arbitrators and one copy for the SAS.[378]

*596.* The Secretary-General of the SAS, after prior consideration of the lawsuit within the meaning of Article 42, submits it to the respondent for an answer and sets a deadline for response to a lawsuit that may not be shorter than fifteen days. If the lawsuit is not complete, i.e., if it does not contain all of the elements, the Secretary-General of the SAS shall return the claim to the plaintiff and will set an additional deadline for correction of deficiencies. If the plaintiff does not follow the instructions, the complaint will be submitted to the president of SAS for decision-making.

*597.* The provisions of Article 42(2), (3) and (4) shall also refer to the response to the lawsuit. The response to the complaint shall be submitted to the SAS, and the Secretary-General of the SAS will submit the answer together with the attachments to the plaintiff within three days.

*598.* Unless the parties have agreed otherwise, during the arbitration procedure, each party may amend or supplement its claim, that is, the response to the lawsuit unless the Arbitral Tribunal decides that the amendment is not expedient due to procrastination of the procedure or the damage the opposite party may suffer. In any

378. SAS Rulebook, Arts 24–42.

case, the Arbitral Tribunal shall not allow change and supplement the lawsuit, i.e., the answer to the lawsuit, for questions for which the Arbitral Tribunal is not competent.

*599.* The defendant may submit to the SAS until the conclusion of the hearing counterclaim or raise an objection due to netting in the form of counterclaim if the counterclaim, i.e., the objection, arises from the legal relationship covered by the arbitration agreement.

*600.* The Arbitral Tribunal shall determine the deadlines. When setting the deadlines, the Arbitral Tribunal shall take into account the nature of the action to be taken. The deadlines to be determined by the Arbitral Tribunal should not be longer than thirty days. The Arbitral Tribunal may, at its own motion, propose one of the parties or experts to extend the deadline. The deadlines determined by the Arbitral Tribunal shall be calculated in the following ways:

- start running the first next working day after receiving the decision, the notification and the proposal;
- if the following day falls on a non-working day, a public holiday in residence, i.e., the residence of the addressee or another holiday in accordance with the Law on Holidays of R. Macedonia, the deadline is extended to the first next working day. Public holidays, non-working days as well holidays in accordance with the Law on Holidays of R. Macedonia are calculated within the deadlines.[379]

*601.* Unless the parties have agreed otherwise, the Arbitral Tribunal, at the request of one of the parties, may, with a temporary security measure, instruct the opposing party to take a certain measure which the tribunal deems necessary according to the subject matter of the dispute. The temporary measure is a measure that is issued before the arbitral award is adopted, and it lasts as long as there are circumstances due to which it has been issued. The request for an interim measure addressed to a competent court by any party is not considered incompatible with the arbitration agreement and does not indicate withdrawal of the party from the arbitration agreement. If the party to whom the temporary measure refers does not agree with it to perform it voluntarily, then the party on whose proposal that measure is ordered may apply to the competent court for its implementation.

*602.* The Arbitral Tribunal shall make its decision on the basis of the evidence at its disposal. The Arbitral Tribunal, during the procedure, may request the parties to submit documents and other evidence for the purpose of establishing the disputed facts stated in the lawsuit, i.e., the response to the lawsuit. The Arbitral Tribunal may authorize the presentation of evidence executed by one of the members of the tribunal. The Arbitral Tribunal shall freely evaluate the evidence and shall not be bound by the expert report. For all evidence and documents submitted by one party, the Arbitral tribunal through the Secretary-General of the SAS must submit them to the opposing party and set a deadline within which the opposing party may

379. SAS Rulebook, Arts 43–47.

state in writing the submitted evidence and documents. Failure to submit a written response to the submitted evidence and documents by the opposing party does not mean that the party agrees with the probative value of the evidence, i.e., the content of the document.

*603.* The parties are free to appoint an expert who will prepare a report on a specific issue relating to the subject matter of the arbitral proceedings. At the request of the Arbitral Tribunal or the sports party, the expert appointed by the party will be called upon to explain its findings and opinion at the hearing. At the expert's hearing, questions set by the Arbitral Tribunal and the parties may arise. The Arbitral Tribunal shall compulsorily submit the report from the expert to the sports side. The report referred to in paragraph 1 of the article shall be submitted by the party as an attachment to the lawsuit, i.e., the response to the lawsuit.

*604.* Unless the parties have agreed otherwise, the Arbitral Tribunal may appoint one or more experts who will provide a finding of fact and opinion on certain issues to be determined by the Arbitral Tribunal. The Arbitral Tribunal shall immediately inform the parties about the appointment of the person appointed as an expert. The parties are obliged, at the request of the expert addressed through the Arbitration tribunal, to provide him with all necessary relevant documents and information or, for the purpose of examination, allow access of the expert to all relevant documents. After receiving the finding and the opinion of the expert, the Arbitral Tribunal shall be obliged to submit them to both parties. The parties must be given a deadline within which they can declare themselves in writing for the allegations and opinions of the expert. At the request of one of the parties, the Arbitral Tribunal shall schedule a hearing for the expert. The parties may ask him questions. The provisions for exemption and nonperformance of the duty of arbitrator from the rulebook also apply to the expert. The expert's fee is determined according to the rules applicable to the compensation of the experts in court litigation in the Republic of Macedonia.

*605.* Unless the parties have agreed otherwise, each party may request the Arbitral Tribunal to call a witness and the person to be at the oral hearing. The party that wants to call a witness is obliged at least fifteen days before the day of the hearing of the witness to submit the name, address, language of testimony and the subject of the testimony in writing to the Arbitral Tribunal. The Arbitral Tribunal shall be obliged to immediately inform the sports party for the witness to be heard and for the subject matter of the testimony. Each of the parties and the Arbitral Tribunal may decide questions of the witness. The hearing of witnesses shall be performed without taking an oath. The witness may not be forcibly brought or punished if he/she refuses to testify or leave the place of hearing. The witness may give his/her testimony in a written statement personally signed.

*606.* The Arbitral Tribunal shall hold hearings unless the parties have agreed otherwise. Before holding an oral hearing, the Arbitral Tribunal shall notify the parties, witnesses and experts of the day, hour and place of the event at the oral hearing. The Arbitral Tribunal when making an oral appointment of the hearing will take care to give the parties enough time for preparation for the oral hearing. Unless the parties agree otherwise, the arbitration procedure shall not be public. The Arbitral Tribunal may request the witness and witnesses to distance themselves during the testimonies of other witnesses. Unless the parties have agreed otherwise, the Arbitral Tribunal may conduct the hearing of witnesses and experts through the means of video communication that do not require the physical presence of a witness, that is, with the expert in the room where the arbitration procedure is conducted (video conferencing link).

*607.* Minutes shall be kept at the hearing. The minutes shall be kept by a person appointed by the Secretary-General of SAS. The minutes shall be kept in such a way that the president of the Arbitral Tribunal or the arbitrator-individual loudly tells the recorder what to enter in the minutes. The minutes shall be signed by the arbitrators, and the parties, i.e., their representatives or proxies. If one of the parties refuses to sign the minutes, the president of the Arbitral Tribunal or the arbitrator-individual shall state this in the minutes.

*608.* When the Arbitral Tribunal considers that the subject matter of the dispute is sufficiently debated and can make a decision, it will announce that the debate is locked. After concluding the hearing, the Arbitral Tribunal shall bring the decision according to the rules of this Rulebook for decision-making. If it is necessary to supplement the procedure or clarify important issues, the Arbitral Tribunal may, on its own initiative or at a reasoned proposal of one of the parties, decide to reopen the procedure.[380]

*609.* The Arbitral Tribunal shall render an arbitral award and other decisions by a majority vote. An arbitral award shall decide on the essence of the dispute. The procedural issues are decided by the individual arbitrator or the president of the Arbitral Tribunal. The arbitral award must be signed by the individual arbitrator or by members of the Arbitral Tribunal. In arbitration proceedings with multiple arbitrators, the signatures of the majority of the members of the Arbitral Tribunal shall suffice, which must state the reasons why someone is missing from the signatures of the arbitrators. The reasons for this must be stated in the arbitral award grounded unless the parties have agreed not to give an explanation or, in the case of an arbitral award on the basis of an agreement or settlement, in accordance with Article 63 of the Rulebook. The date and place of adoption shall be stated in the arbitral award. After the adoption of the arbitral award, each of the parties shall submit one transcript signed by the arbitrators in accordance with paragraph 3 of the article. Unless the parties have agreed otherwise, the submission of the arbitration Judgment shall be rendered in accordance with the provisions of Article 41 of the Rulebook.

*610.* The arbitral award shall be final and binding on the parties. The parties are obliged to execute the judgment without delay. The Arbitral Tribunal shall be obliged to explain the verdict, except that they agree that no explanation is required.

380. SAS Rulebook, Arts 47–56.

*611.* Before the arbitral award is rendered, the Arbitral Tribunal prepares a draft arbitral award which it submits to the president of the SAS, reviewing the formal side of the arbitral award. If the president of SAS, within ten days from the day of receipt of the draft judgment, did not identify any formal defect, the draft judgment is submitted to the Arbitral Tribunal for signing. For the formal shortcomings, the president of SAS issues an indication to the Arbitral Tribunal. The Arbitral Tribunal shall take into account the indications of the president of the SAS. The arbitral award shall be made in as many originals as there are parties and one original for SAS.

*612.* When submitting the arbitral award, the president of the SAS shall request written permission from the parties to publish the arbitration judgment in scientific and professional journals, as well as on the IOC website. When the judgment is published on the IOC website, it shall publish data on the parties. If the parties do not agree, the verdict shall not be published. The parties may, despite the disagreement for publication of the decision, allow it to be used in scientific research, but at the same time, it is forbidden to present the data of the parties and the facts of the dispute.

*613.* Apart from a final judgment, the Arbitral Tribunal may also issue a partial arbitral award if part of the claim is due. For claims for which the Arbitral Tribunal failed to decide, each party may, within thirty days from the day of receipt of the judgment, request the Arbitral Tribunal to issue an additional judgment. If the Arbitral Tribunal decides that it should bring additional judgment, it will make it within forty-five days from the date of receipt of the request for its adoption.

*614.* Within thirty days from the date of receipt of the judgment, each party may, after informing the opposing party about it, ask the Arbitral Tribunal for interpretation of a particular place or part of the judgment. If the Arbitral Tribunal deems that the request is justified, it shall give an interpretation in writing within thirty days from the date of submission of the request for interpretation of the judgment. Interpretation is an integral part of the arbitral award. Within thirty days from the day of receiving the verdict, each party may, after informing the sports party about it, ask the Arbitral Tribunal in the arbitral award to correct the settlement, writing or typographical error or any error of a similar nature. The Arbitral Tribunal may correct, on its own initiative, the error within thirty days from the date of the judgment. If the Arbitral Tribunal deems that the request is justified, the correction of the verdict will be prepared in writing within thirty days from the day of submission of the request for correction of the verdict. The sports arbitration will not calculate the costs for correction of the verdict. The provisions of this article refer to a judgment, a partial judgment and an additional judgment.

*615.* During the arbitration procedure, the parties may resolve the dispute with the agreement. If the agreement is reached during the procedure or the parties are settled, and if both parties so request, the Arbitral Tribunal shall render an arbitral award on the basis of the agreement, i.e., settlement. The Arbitral Tribunal shall not be obliged to explain the arbitral award.

*616.* The arbitration procedure ends with the adoption of an arbitral award. The arbitration procedure may end with the conclusion of the arbitration procedure:

- if the plaintiff withdraws the lawsuit unless the defendant objects to it, an Arbitral Tribunal considers that the defendant has a legitimate interest in making a final decision on the dispute;
- if the parties have agreed to complete the procedure;
- if the Arbitral Tribunal finds that the continuation of the proceedings, for any reason, became unnecessary or impossible.[381]

*617.* The parties participating in the proceedings before the SAS shall themselves cover the costs of the procedure, which consist of: (1)registration fee; (2) award of arbitrators; (3) administrative costs of SAS; and (4) material costs of the procedure (per diems, travel and expenses for accommodation of arbitrators, rent of premises, costs for translation and other costs).

*618.* The costs of the arbitration procedure shall be paid by the parties to the account which will be determined by the SAS and will be made public.

*619.* In the final decision made in an arbitration procedure, the Arbitral Tribunal will decide on the reimbursement of costs. The Arbitral Tribunal shall determine in the decision for reimbursement of the costs, which party and to what extent it is obliged to compensate the costs to the other party, taking it considering the success of the procedure. Unless the parties have agreed otherwise, the costs of the procedure shall be obliged to be compensated to the party who lost the dispute, and in case if the claim is partially accepted, the costs are paid by both parties in proportion to the adopted or rejected part of the lawsuit.

*620.* When filing the lawsuit, the plaintiff is obliged to pay a registration fee in an amount determined by the Rulebook and the proof of the paid registration fee to attach together with the complaint to the Secretary-General of the SAS. The same rules as in paragraph 1 of this article shall apply to a counterclaim. If more than two parties participate in the procedure, for each additional one, the registration fee increases by 10%. The registration fee is EUR 200 in denar counter value, calculated according to the selling rate of the National Bank of R. Macedonia on the day of the payment. The Secretary-General of the SAS shall submit the lawsuit, i.e., counterclaim in response, only after proof of payment has been attached registration fee. The paid registration fee is non-refundable.

*621.* The costs of the procedure referred to in Article 66, paragraph 1, items (2), (3) and (4) shall be paid to the plaintiff in advance (advance). The amount of the advance referred to in paragraph 1 of this article shall be determined by the president of the SAS after submitting the lawsuit to the defendant. The Secretary-General of the SAS shall perform the calculation of the costs and prepares a draft decision on advance payment of costs and submits it to the president of the SAS.

381. SAS Rulebook, Arts 59–65.

*622.* The Secretary-General of the SAS shall summon the plaintiff by a written summons to pay the advance, determined in accordance with Article 69 of the Rulebook, within thirty days from the day of delivery of the call. If the plaintiff does not pay the advance within the stipulated deadline, the president of the SAS will make a decision to delete the lawsuit from the records of SAS disputes. The deleted lawsuit can be resubmitted with a new payment of the registration fee. If during the procedure, there is an increase in the value of the subject matter of the dispute or the advance paid is not sufficient for covering material costs, the arbitrator-individual or the Arbitral Tribunal, on the proposal of the president of the SAS, may decide to pay an additional advance to the plaintiff. Until the additional advance is paid due to the increase in the value of the subject matter of the dispute, that increase will not be taken into account in the arbitration proceedings. The reduction of the value of the subject of the dispute will be taken into account when calculating administrative costs and costs for remuneration of the arbitrators only if it has been announced to the SAS at the submission of the files to the individual arbitrator, i.e., to the arbitrator's advice.

*623.* The costs related to the performance of the individual procedures' actions (costs of expertise, presentation of evidence, etc.) are a burden on the party proposing their takeover, which is obliged to deposit the appropriate amount in advance (advance). If the Arbitral Tribunal conducts on its own initiative certain procedural actions, the decision for their implementation will determine the party who should bear the costs for the actions. Decision on payment of advance payment of the costs referred to in paragraph (1) of this article adopted by the individual arbitrator, i.e., the president of the Arbitral Tribunal advice. If the advance payment of the costs referred to in paragraph (1) of this article is not paid, no procedural actions that should have been taken will be taken to cover that advance. If the costs of the arbitration procedure referred to in paragraph (1) of this article are at the request or with the consent of both parties, each of the parties pays half of the advance. If any of the parties miss paying half of the advance amount, the Secretary-General of the SAS shall, without delay, call upon the other Party to pay that amount within thirty days from the date of submission to the call.

*624.* If the plaintiff withdraws the lawsuit, the president of the SAS, in writing at the request of the plaintiff, will make a decision on the return of funds paid after the basis of Article 73 in the following amount:

(a) before appointing an individual arbitrator, i.e., constituting Arbitration Council .... 50%;
(b) before scheduling an oral hearing ... 40%.

*625.* After an oral hearing, the funds shall not be returned. The funds paid in the name of registration fee shall not be refunded.

*626.* The arbitrator is entitled to reimbursement of travel expenses, per diems and the cost of accommodation if he lives outside the place of arbitration. When the arbitrator travels outside the place of residence in his own car, travel costs increase by 50% of the regular fee of travel costs. The arbitrator shall refrain from incurring unreasonable costs, especially in the part of transportation and accommodation. Particularly unreasonable costs are travel by first class in air traffic. The placement of the arbitrator is considered to be reasonable if it uses a single room in a hotel with breakfast that is categorized with 4 stars. Unreasonable costs will not be reimbursed to arbitrators. The amount of allowances for travel expenses, per diems and the costs for accommodation of the arbitrators referred to in paragraph 1 of this article shall be determined by the decision of the president of the SAS which is published on the website of the Macedonian Olympic Committee and the national sports federations that recognize the competence of the SAS.

*627.* The administrative costs are 20% of the amount of the award of the individual arbitrator, i.e., of the arbitration council.

*628.* The party who is a natural person who has a domicile, i.e., usual residence in the Republic of Macedonia, i.e., a legal entity based in the Republic of Macedonia, pays the costs in denars at the selling rate of the euro set by the National Bank of the Republic of Macedonia on the day of payment.[382]

382. SAS Rulebook, Arts 72–77.

## Chapter 3. Private Regulation

*629.* Private regulations in the field of sports in the Republic of Macedonia include various agreements that regulate relations in the field of sports (agreements on the engagement of athletes, sports workers, sponsorship agreements, etc.). The rules of the law of obligations and sports law apply in principle to these contracts.

*630.* In addition to the above, private regulations may also include certain provisions of the LS relating to the internal legal acts of sports organizations. In this way, organizations are free to regulate their relations themselves within limits prescribed by law.

*631.* The general acts of a sports association are the statute, the rulebook and the decision which regulates certain issues in a general way.

*632.* The statute is the basic general act of a sports association.

*633.* It is obligatorily regulated by the statute:

(1) name and seat of the sports association;
(2) goals, content of activities and determination of sports branch and sports discipline, i.e., area of sports, in which sports goals are achieved;
(3) bodies, their powers, the manner of election and dismissal, the duration of the mandate and the manner of decision-making;
(4) the procedure of adoption, i.e., amendments to the statute and other general acts of the sports association;
(5) representation of a sports association;
(6) making the work public;
(7) conditions and manner of membership and termination of membership, determining the amount of membership fees, rights, obligations and responsibilities of members, especially minors;
(8) the manner of acquiring funds for achieving sports goals and disposing of funds;
(9) way of deciding on status changes;
(10) dealing with the property of the sports association in case of termination of the association;
(11) the procedure for adopting financial and other reports;
(12) the form and content of the seal;
(13) economic and other activities that the sports association directly performs;
(14) other issues of importance for the sports association, as well as other issues determined by law.

Every member of a sports association has the right to receive a copy of the statute of the sports association.

*634*. The statute and other general acts of the sports association must be in accordance with the sports rules, and the LS individual acts adopted by bodies and authorized persons in a sports association must be in accordance with the general acts of the sports association, sports rules and the law.

*635*. The provisions of the general act of the sports association are subject to the assessment of constitutionality and legality in accordance with the Constitution and the law.

*636*. In the Republic of Macedonia, public and private regulations in sports are part of a single legal system, which can be assessed as positive. Private initiatives in sports should be strengthened within limits set by law, which is a proposal *de lege ferenda*, which will contribute to the development of sports.

# Part II. Sport and Status

## Chapter 1. General Points

*637.* The issue of the legal status of athletes is one of the very important issues in the field of sports law. The significance of the issue is reflected in the fact that the legality of the work of all participants, subjects of sports law and the regularity of sports competitions depend on the precise definition and legal regulation of the rights, obligations and responsibilities of all participants in sports activities.

*638.* To better define the legal status of athletes in the Republic of Macedonia, the monograph will pay special attention to the qualification of athletes, their rights and obligations arising from the statutory qualification, the relationship between labor and sports law, the employment status of athletes, social, health and pension insurance and the tax treatment of athletes.

# Chapter 2. Public Regulation

*639.* In the Republic of Macedonia, the rights, obligations and responsibilities of athletes are regulated in detail by LS. In addition to LS, this issue is specifically regulated by the law on labor relations.

*640.* The law includes norms directly or indirectly regulating certain issues of importance for the legal status of an athlete, which is precisely regulated by sports rules, collective agreements in the field of professional sports and the agreement between the athlete and the sports organization regarding amateur athletes.

## §1. Qualification of the Legal Status

*641.* In order to discuss the legal status of an athlete and the rights and obligations arising from the appropriate legal status, the issue of defining the athlete necessarily arises as a preliminary issue.

*642.* Although this issue was discussed in the introductory part (athlete, amateur athlete, professional athlete, athlete competitor, top athlete, promising athlete, talented athlete, categorized athlete), as a reminder and for reasons of integrity or easier understanding of the rights and obligations arising from the appropriate legal status of the athlete, at this point, we will briefly look at only the most important categories of athletes.

*643.* According to LS, athletes are athletes of all ages participating in sports activities and all participants in sports-recreational activities.[383] Sports activities are performed professionally and amateur. The athlete who performs sports activities professionally exercises all rights and obligations from employment at the sports club-employer in a manner determined by law and collective agreement.[384]

*644.* A professional athlete is a person who participates in sports competitions and has concluded a professional contract and a contract for work in a sports club. To the professional athlete from paragraph 1 of this article, sport is his basic activity, and he realizes all the rights and obligations from employment in the sports club with which he has concluded a contract in accordance with law. The National Sports Federation maintains an electronic register of professional athletes participating in the competition system organized by the National Sports Federation. The form of the register of professional athletes is prescribed by the official who manages the body responsible for the affairs in the field of sports. Amateur athletes who have entered into professional contracts will lose their status as amateur athletes.[385]

383. LS, Art. 30.
384. LS, Art. 31.
385. LS, Art. 31-a.

*645.* Athletes who perform sports activities as amateurs can be provided with free use of facilities, equipment and props to be compensated for lost salary, travel and daily expenses during sports training and competitions, as well as to be created other necessary conditions for achieving top sports results. For athletes who perform sports activities professionally and participate in national team competitions, the national sports federation for which amateur athletes play should provide insurance based on disability and bodily injury caused by injury due to participation in sports activity. For athletes who perform sports activities as amateurs and participate in the system of competitions for sports clubs, the sports club for which they play should provide insurance based on disability and bodily injury caused by injury due to participation in sports activity. To the athletes who perform the sports activity as amateurs, the sports club can provide food up to the amount of the average monthly salary that is realized at the level of the Republic. Athletes from paragraph 1 of this article can also receive cash and other rewards for achieving sports results, i.e., for performing sports activity under conditions determined by an act of the club.[386]

*646.* An athlete competitor is equally understood as an amateur athlete and a professional athlete who participates in a sports competition. In doing so, they may participate in the competition as members of a sports organization or independently, in accordance with the law and sports rules. For an athlete to be able to compete independently, it is necessary that the sports rules allow it in accordance with Article 32 of LS.

*647.* The sports club in which an amateur athlete is a member concludes an agreement with the employer, with whom the athlete is employed, which determines the rights and obligations of the athlete and the sports club in relation to the performance of sports training and competitions. The rules also refer to the amateur coach of the athlete. The absence of a student-athlete, i.e., a student from classes for the purpose of performing sports training and competitions, is regulated in accordance with the relevant laws in the field of education.[387]

*648.* A foreign athlete exercises his rights and can participate in the highest level of competition if he meets the conditions set by this and another law.

*649.* The highest level of competition is:

- appearance in a system of matches from the first league; and
- performance at the state senior championship.

*650.* Athletes of the world and international categories have the status of professional athletes during the exercise of the right to categorization.[388]

---

386. LS, Art. 32.
387. LS, Art. 33.
388. LS, Art. 34.

*651.* Senior athletes, citizens of the Republic of Macedonia, based on the results achieved in a certain period of time, acquire the following sports categories:

– world-class athlete;
– athlete of international category; and
– athlete of state category.

*652.* Once acquired, the sports category has a lasting character and belongs to the athlete for life as a title.[389] Athletes acquire sports categories based on the results achieved in official competitions, national championships, European and world championships, world university championships and summer and winter Olympic Games.

*653.* When determining the sports category, only the results achieved at official international competitions that are in the calendar of European and world associations and national championships are evaluated.[390]

*654.* Athletes who have acquired a sports category (hereinafter "categorized athletes") are entitled to material compensation and other types of awards. The material compensation is in the form of:

(a) monetary compensation;
(b) compensation for lost salary; and
(c) accident insurance.[391]

*655.* The rights arising from the sports category of world-class athletes are used for four years, provided that the athlete is active in that period. The rights arising from the sports category of an international category athlete are used for two years, provided that the athlete is active in that period. The rights arising from the sports category of a state category athlete are used for one year. The rights arising from the acquired category of a world-class athlete and an athlete of international category, which refer to the monetary compensation, terminate if, during the exercised right, he achieved a higher category or confirmed the previously acquired category. For these categorized athletes, the temporary use of the right to monetary compensation is extended in accordance with the newly realized category.[392]

*656.* Athletes from the younger age categories can acquire a sports category in accordance with the achieved results that are provided for seniors. As an exception, if a team or individual meets the conditions provided in the categorization for

389. LS, Art. 35.
390. LS, Art. 36.
391. LS, Art. 38.
392. LS, Art. 39.

participation and achieves placement at the World or European Championships in the highest age category for youth, the category of athlete of international category is acquired.[393] (Article 37).

*657.* Young athletes, up to 20 years old, citizens of the Republic of Macedonia, based on the results achieved in a certain period of time, acquire a sports category athlete-sports hope. The category athlete—sports hope is awarded based on the results achieved in official national and international competitions for age categories up to 20 years in Olympic and non-Olympic sports. The athlete who has acquired the category of athlete-sports hope is awarded a diploma and monetary compensation. The rights arising from the category athlete-sports hope are used for one year, in which ten monthly cash benefits are paid in the amount of 20% of the average salary paid in the Republic of Macedonia in the previous year. The funds from paragraph 4 of this article are provided from the budget of the Republic of Macedonia and are paid through the body of the state administration responsible for the affairs in the field of sports.

*658.* The Government of the Republic of Macedonia, on the proposal of the body of the state administration responsible for the affairs in the field of sports, prescribes in more detail criteria and the manner of awarding the category athlete-sports hope.

*659.* The official who manages the body of the state administration responsible for the affairs in the field of sports, after previously obtaining an opinion from the national sports federation, and in accordance with the act from paragraph 1 of this article, determines the status of the athlete from the category athlete-sports hope.[394]

*660.* Professional staff in terms of LS are persons who have completed at least higher education in the field of sports or have obtained licenses obtained from an appropriate international sports association. Sports training and competitions of the national teams of the state sports federations can be conducted only by professionals who meet the conditions set out in paragraph 1 of this article.[395]

*661.* The professional staff in the field of sports, which leads sports training and competitions in sports clubs and national sports federations, are obliged to provide them with permanent professional development.

*662.* The professional development programs are determined and implemented by the national sports federations of the Republic from the respective sports branch (Article 28). Professional person-professional coach can lead sports training and competitions at all levels of competition if he meets the requirements set by law. Professional person—foreigner can lead sports training and competitions at the

393. LS, Art. 37-a.
394. LS, Art. 37-b.
395. LS, Art. 27.

highest level of competitions if he meets the conditions set by law and has concluded a professional contract with the club (Article 29).

## §2. Fundamental Rights and Obligations

*663.* According to LS, the athlete who performs sports activities professionally exercises all rights and obligations from employment at the sports club—employer in a manner determined by law and collective agreement.[396]

*664.* The sports club in which an amateur athlete is a member concludes an agreement with the employer, with whom the athlete is employed, which determines the rights and obligations of the athlete and the sports club in relation to the performance of sports training and competitions. The provision from paragraph 1 of this article also refers to the amateur coach of the athlete. The absence of a student-athlete, i.e., a student from classes for the purpose of performing sports training and competitions, is regulated in accordance with the relevant laws in the field of education.[397]

*665.* An athlete can earn money if he/she is:

- a world-class athlete who is not employed is paid monetary compensation in the amount of two average salaries paid at the level of the Republic in the previous year in gross amount; and
- an athlete of international category who is not employed is paid monetary compensation in the amount of 1.3 average salaries paid at the level of the Republic for the previous year in gross amount.

*666.* To a world-class athlete and to an international-class athlete who is employed, the monetary compensation shall be paid in the net amount of the monetary compensation referred to in paragraph 1 line 1, i.e., line 2 of this article.

*667.* The monetary compensation in the net amount referred to in paragraph 2 of this article shall also be paid to the athletes who perform their sports activity outside the Republic of Macedonia.[398] Athletes of state category are entitled to material compensation and other types of awards in accordance with the acts of the sports club where they are members, i.e., the national sports federations of the Republic.[399] The compensation for lost salary due to absence from work for preparation and participation in competitions of a world-class athlete and an international-class athlete is provided.

396. LS, Art. 31.
397. LS, Art. 33.
398. LS, Art. 40.
399. LS, Art. 41.

*668.* For state-class athletes, the lost salary allowance can be provided by the sports club of which the athlete is a member. The categorized athlete loses the rights to material compensation for the acquired category if:

– it has been convicted by a final court judgment of a criminal offense punishable by imprisonment of at least six months; or
– the citizenship of the Republic of Macedonia has ceased.

*669.* The National Sports Federation is obliged once a year in the period from December 1 to 31 in the current year to submit an opinion to the body of the state administration responsible for sports regarding the fulfillment of the obligations of the categorized athlete to the National Sports Federation. The salary compensation is provided by the categorized athlete through the employer where he is employed.[400]

*670.* A categorized athlete who, due to an injury acquired during training or competition, maternity leave or hospital treatment, has been forced to suspend sports training or competitions in the country or abroad is entitled to material compensation for a maximum period of one year from the day of suspension.[401]

*671.* The professional with whose professional work the athlete achieved a top sports result with which he obtained the category of a world-class athlete and international-class athlete is entitled to a one-time award of 40% of the total funds due to the categorized athlete for one year.

*672.* If in the realization of the top sports result of the athlete from paragraph 1 of this article participated, several professionals as a professional team, the prize provided for one person is distributed to the participants who participated in the work of the professional team, in accordance with the general act of the National Sports Federation.

*673.* The professionals who prepare the athletes (coaches in the clubs) are entitled to 20% of the amount determined in paragraph 1 of this article. A proposal for rewarding the expert or professionals who participated in achieving the sports result of the categorized athlete is given by the National Sports Federation when submitting a proposal to the list for categorization of athletes.

*674.* The body of the state administration responsible for the affairs in the field of sports when publishing the list of categorized athletes in the "Official Gazette of the Republic of Macedonia" publishes the list of their experts—coaches who participated in the work to achieve the sports result.[402]

400. LS, Art. 42.
401. LS, Art. 43.
402. LS, Art. 44.

*675.* The categorized athlete can, for the won ranking on the basis of which he acquired the sports category, receive a prize in the form of a one-time payment, sports equipment or other types of prizes. The categorized athlete can be rewarded by other legal entities and individuals.[403] The categorized athlete is obliged to comply with and fulfill the obligations arising from the acts of the club of which he is a member, the National Sports Federation, the IOC and the International Sports Federation.

*676.* If the categorized athlete does not fulfill the obligations from paragraph 1 of this article, a procedure is initiated for deprivation of the rights from the acquired category. The procedure for deprivation of the rights from the acquired category is initiated by the club of which it is a member, the National Sports Federation or the body of the state administration responsible for the affairs in the field of sports.[404] The official who manages the body of the state administration responsible for the affairs in the field of sports adopts a rulebook for the categorization of the athletes from the Republic of Macedonia, which will prescribe the criteria and criteria for determining the status and rank of the athletes in the Republic of Macedonia. The official who manages the body of the state administration responsible for the affairs in the field of sports after previously obtaining an opinion from the National Sports Federation and the IOC for the Olympic team, and in accordance with the act from paragraph 1 of this article, determine the status and rank of categorized athletes.[405] The body of the state administration responsible for the affairs in the field of sports, twice a year, until June 30 and until December 31, publishes a list of categorized athletes in the Republic of Macedonia for the sports achievements from the past period. The list of categorized athletes from paragraph 1 of this article is published in the "Official Gazette of the Republic of Macedonia." The body of the state administration responsible for the affairs in the field of sports awards the athletes of the world and international categories for recognition and presents a certificate for the acquired category, and the athletes of the state category presents a certificate for the acquired category.

*677.* The body of the state administration responsible for the affairs in the field of sports keeps records of the athletes who have acquired a sports category and keeps the documentation that was attached to the request for acquiring a sports category.[406]

*678.* The verification of a world-class athlete and an international-class athlete is performed by the body of the state administration responsible for the affairs in the field of sports.

*679.* The national sports federations are obliged to timely submit complete documentation for the proposed candidates for categorized athletes. The data should, in

403. LS, Art. 45.
404. LS, Art. 46.
405. LS, Art. 47.
406. LS, Art. 48.

particular, contain the international calendar of the world or European federation; bulletin from the international competition, and if a record and minutes have been achieved and a professional person—coach, led by the athlete or the team; address; e-mail, the website of the International Sports Federation and other data that are important for the achieved result. The verification of a state category athlete is performed by the National Sports Federation, which submits to the body of the state administration responsible for sports affairs a list with documentation of state category athletes.

*680.* Athlete citizens of the Republic of Macedonia can gain national sports recognition.

*681.* The National Sports Award is given for the top sports achievement of athletes, as a recognition for winning gold, silver and bronze medals, i.e., for winning first, second and third place at the Olympic Games, Paralympic Games, Chess Olympics, world and European senior championships in the Olympics and Paralympic sports.

*682.* The National Sports Recognition can be awarded to athletes for winning a gold medal, i.e., first place at the world and European senior championships in Olympic and non-Olympic sports that have a long tradition in the Republic of Macedonia.

*683.* The national sports award can also be awarded in cases where the sport achievement of an individual has a particular international significance and value or in cases of achievement of a result that is a world or European record in Olympic sports achieved in an official international competition.[407]

*684.* The athlete who has gained national sports recognition is awarded a plaque and a monthly allowance in the amount of half to one and a half average monthly salary paid in the Republic of Macedonia in the previous year.

*685.* The funds from paragraph 1 of this article are provided from the budget of the Republic of Macedonia and are paid through the body of the state administration responsible for the affairs in the field of sports.

*686.* The conditions and the manner of awarding the national sports recognition for top sports performance and the amount of the monetary compensation shall be regulated in more detail by the Government of the Republic of Macedonia with a decree (Article 50-b).

*687.* The persons who are actively engaged in sports, i.e., sports-recreational activity in the sports clubs, are obliged to undergo health control.

---

407. LS, Art. 50-a.

*688.* The health control includes a health examination before the start, as well as systematic control examinations during the participation in sports activities.

*689.* The number of systematic control examinations is determined by the National Sports Federation from the respective sports branch.[408]

*690.* The health control of the participants in the sports activities is performed by a doctor-specialist in sports medicine.

*691.* In the municipalities where there is no specialist in sports medicine, the health control of the athletes will be performed by a doctor or a specialist in general medicine or a specialist in internal diseases.[409]

*692.* The participants in the sports and sports-recreational activities perform the health examinations within the framework of regular health insurance.

*693.* Sports clubs provide funds for the health control of athletes if they are not covered by compulsory health insurance.

*694.* Sports clubs provide compulsory health insurance to athletes who perform sports activities professionally. It is prohibited for a professional to force an athlete to train or participate in sports competitions while he or she is medically incapable of doing so or when such activity could worsen his or her health.[410]

*695.* Athletes are prohibited from taking or giving athletes stimulants that are prohibited and harmful to their health.

*696.* Doping control is an integral part of athletes' health care measures.

*697.* For the implementation of the Convention on Anti-Doping Control in the Republic of Macedonia, a National Anti-Doping Commission (hereinafter "the Commission") is established within the body of the state administration responsible for the affairs of sports.

*698.* The members of the Commission are appointed by the official who manages the body of the state administration responsible for the affairs in the field of sports, from the ranks of professional, scientific and other prominent workers in the field of pharmacology, medical, chemical and biological sciences, sports, in the field of law and other areas.[411]

*699.* Closer regulations for health control, for the scope and manner of organizing emergency medical care and doping control, are adopted by the body of the state

408. LS, Art. 51.
409. LS, Art. 52.
410. LS, Arts 53–54.
411. LS, Art. 55.

administration responsible for the affairs in the field of sports, in accordance with the body responsible for the affairs in the field of health.[412]

## §3. Labor Market Regulation

*700.* Sports activities are performed professionally and amateur. The athlete who performs sports activities professionally exercises all rights and obligations from employment at the sports club—employer in a manner determined by law and collective agreement.[413]

*701.* LS refers to the application of the Law on Labor Relations (LL) for sports employees.

*702.* LL also regulates the labor relations of the employees employed in the state government bodies, the bodies of the local self-government units, institutions, public enterprises, institutes, funds, organizations and other legal and natural persons that employ workers, if by another law it is not determined otherwise.

*703.* The employment can be terminated only in a manner and under conditions determined by law and a collective agreement.

*704.* In the employment relationship, each of the parties is obliged to fulfill the prescribed and agreed rights, obligations and responsibilities.[414]

*705.* By signing the employment contract, an employment relationship is established between the employee and the employer.

*706.* The rights, obligations and responsibilities based on the performance of the work from the employment and inclusion in the obligatory social insurance on the basis of the employment begin to be exercised on the day of the employee's employment, agreed in the employment contract.

*707.* The employer is obliged to submit an application/deregistration (electronic form M1/M2 printed by the system of the Employment Agency of the Republic of North Macedonia) for the employee in the obligatory social insurance (pension and disability, health and insurance in case of unemployment), in accordance with the special regulations, in the Employment Agency of the Republic of North Macedonia, electronically or directly in the Agency, by enclosing a relevant form, authorization of an authorized person with a list of persons to register/deregister, in which the name, surname and Personal identification number, as well as the number of the employment contract and the date of concluding the employment contract one day before the employee starts working, and for urgent and urgent matters, at least one

412. LS, Art. 56.
413. LS, Art. 31.
414. LL, Art. 3.

hour before the employee starts working. A certified photocopy of the application or an excerpt from a computer record from the information system of the Agency shall be delivered to the employee within three days from the day of starting work.

*708.* The Employment Agency of the Republic of North Macedonia, the Pension and Disability Insurance Fund of Macedonia and the Health Insurance Fund of the Republic of North Macedonia are obliged to keep and permanently keep the records of applications and deregistrations in social insurance at the request of the person to issue data on the status and changes related to the social security of the employee.

*709.* The Employment Agency of the Republic of North Macedonia, the Pension and Disability Insurance Fund of Macedonia and the Health Insurance Fund of the Republic of North Macedonia shall exchange data related to social insurance.

*710.* If the date of employment is not determined in the employment contract, the date of commencement of employment shall be the next day from the date of signing the employment contract, and the employee shall report to the Employment Agency of the Republic of North Macedonia on the date at the signing of the employment contract.

*711.* The employee may not start work before concluding an employment contract and before the employer reports him/her in the obligatory social insurance.

*712.* The rights, obligations and responsibilities on the basis of performing the work from the employment and inclusion in the obligatory social insurance on the basis of the employment shall start to be exercised on the day of starting the work, also in case if on that day the employee will not start working for justified reasons.

*713.* Justified reasons due to which the employee does not start working on the day determined by the employment contract are the cases when the employee is absent for justified reasons determined by law, the collective agreement and the employment contract.

*714.* If the employee does not unjustifiably enter work on the first day of the day determined for starting work, in accordance with paragraph (6) of this article, it shall be considered that he/she has not established employment.

*715.* If the employer, after the termination of employment, within eight days from the day of termination of employment, does not deregister the employee from compulsory social insurance, deregistration of the employee can be done at the request of the employee based on previously submitted minutes from the labor inspector to the Employment Agency of the Republic of North Macedonia.[415]

---

415. LL, Art. 13.

*716.* An employment contract is concluded for a period whose duration is not predetermined (employment for an indefinite period of time).

*717.* An employment contract may be concluded for a period whose duration is predetermined (fixed-term employment).

*718.* An employment contract, in which the time for which the contract is concluded is not determined, shall be considered as an employment contract for an indefinite period of time.[416]

*719.* The employment contract is concluded in writing.

*720.* The employment contract is kept in the working premises in the headquarters of the employer.

*721.* A copy of the concluded employment contract shall be handed over to the employee on the day of signing the employment contract.[417]

*722.* The parties to the employment contract are the employer and the employee.[418]

*723.* If the employer is a legal entity, a unit of local self-government, a subsidiary of a foreign company or other organization, on behalf of the employer acts his representative, determined by law, the founding act or the statute or a person authorized by him in writing.

*724.* If the employer is a body of the state government, the official or a person authorized by him in writing shall act on behalf of the employer unless otherwise determined by law.

*725.* When an employment contract is concluded with persons with special authorizations and responsibilities, the body determined by the law, the founding act or the statute shall act on behalf of the employer.

*726.* When an employment contract is concluded with a manager during a procedure for establishment of the employer, the founder acts on behalf of the employer.[419]

*727.* An employment contract may be concluded by a young person under 18 years of age who has general health ability.

---

416. LL, Art. 14.
417. LL, Art. 15.
418. LL, Art. 16.
419. LL, Art. 17.

*728.* It is prohibited to work for a child under 15 years of age or a child who has not completed compulsory education, except for participation in activities that are determined by law to be performed, but not longer than two hours per day, i.e., not longer than twelve hours per week, and during the school holidays not longer than six hours per day, i.e., not longer than thirty hours per week, during which he must be provided with two uninterrupted working weeks of rest.

*729.* The employer is obliged to provide protection of the young persons from economic exploitation and from any work that may have a detrimental effect on their safety, health, physical, mental, moral or social development, or it may endanger their education.

*730.* A child under 15 years of age may, by paying a fee, exceptionally participate in activities that by their scope and character do not adversely affect health, safety, development and education, as follows: participation in cultural and artistic activities, sporting events and advertising activities.

*731.* Approval for performing the activities referred to in paragraph (3) of this article shall be issued by the body of the state administration responsible for labor inspection based on the request of the organizer of the activities referred to in paragraph (4) of this article, upon prior consent of the legal representative of the child and after a previous inspection of the place where the activities will be performed by the labor inspection.

*732.* A young person is any person who can conclude an employment contract, who is at least 15 years old and under 18 years of age and who is not included in compulsory education, for performing activities that are not harmful to his health and security.

*733.* The maximum number of working hours of a young person under the age of 16 is thirty hours per week, and in case the young person works for several employers at the same time.

*734.* The maximum number of working hours for a young person over the age of 16 is thirty-seven hours and forty-five minutes per week in case the young person works for more than one employer.

*735.* The working time of a young person must not exceed eight hours in a period of twenty-four hours.

*736.* The time that the young person spends in professional training within theoretical and practical teaching will be considered work.

*737.* Participation in training shall be considered work performed by the young person at the employer for which he/she receives paid compensation.

*738.* The employer must not use the reward method in order to increase the workload, which would endanger the safety and health of the young person.[420]

*739.* For the apprentice during the professional training with the employer, the provisions of this and other laws are applied, which regulate special protection of the workers who have not yet reached 18 years of age, the schedule of working hours, the leave during working hours, the weekly rest, for paid leave, absence from work due to celebration, absence from work due to inability to work due to illness, absence from work due to performing a function or obligations under special laws and liability for compensation.[421]

*740.* The employee who concludes an employment contract must meet the conditions for performing the work, determined by law, the act of the employer, i.e., the conditions required by the employer.

*741.* The employer is obliged by an act to determine the special conditions for performing the work at each individual job. This obligation does not apply to smaller employers.

*742.* The disabled person who is qualified for certain jobs is considered to have the health ability to conclude an employment contract for those jobs.[422]

*743.* Foreign citizens or stateless persons may conclude an employment contract if they meet the conditions determined by this and another special law which regulates the employment of foreigners.

*744.* If an employment contract is concluded contrary to paragraph (1) of this article, the contract shall be considered null and void.[423]

*745.* The employer has the right to freely decide with which candidate, who fulfills the prescribed agreements, i.e., conditions required by the employer to perform the work (hereinafter "conditions for performing the work"), respecting the legal prohibitions, will an employment contract be concluded.[424]

*746.* The employment contract contains:

(1) data on the contracting parties, their place of residence, i.e., seat;
(2) date of commencement of work;
(3) title of the job, i.e., data on the type of work for which the employee concludes an employment contract, with a short description of the work he will perform according to the employment contract;

420. LL, Art. 17.
421. LL, Art. 251.
422. LL, Art. 19.
423. LL, Art. 20.
424. LL, Art. 21.

(4) provisions on the obligation of the employer to inform the employee about the risky jobs and special professional qualifications or knowledge or necessary special medical supervision, in accordance with the law, stating the special risks that, according to the legal regulations, may be a consequence of the work;
(5) place of performance of the work. If the exact place is not specified, the employee is considered to be performing the work at the employer's headquarters;
(6) duration of the employment, when a fixed-term contract has been concluded;
(7) provision on whether it is full-time or part-time employment;
(8) provision for daily or weekly regular working hours and scheduling of working hours;
(9) provision for the amount of the basic salary, which is expressed in a monetary amount, which belongs to the employee for performing the work according to law, collective agreement and the employment contract;
(10) provision for other compensations that belong to the employee for performing the work according to law and collective agreement;
(11) provision for the annual leave, i.e., the manner for determining the annual leave; and
(12) Indication of the general acts of the employer in which the working conditions of the employee are determined.

*747.* The employment contract may contain other rights and obligations determined by this and other laws and collective agreements.

*748.* In the employment contract, in relation to certain issues, the parties should, where appropriate, refer to the laws, collective agreements and acts of the employer.[425]

*749.* Amendments to the employment contract may be proposed by the employer or by the employee.

*750.* The amendments to the employment contract shall be made with an annex to the employment contract.

*751.* The annex to the employment contract is concluded in the same form as the employment contract, in accordance with the law.

*752.* The amendments to the employment contract may be made if both parties agree on the same.[426]

*753.* The provision in the employment contract, which is contrary to the general provisions on the rights, obligations and responsibilities of the contracting parties,

425. LL, Art. 28.
426. LL, Art. 28-a.

determined by law, collective agreement, i.e., act of the employer, is null and void from the moment of concluding the contract.

*754.* The provisions of the law, the collective agreements, i.e., the general acts of the employer, which partially determined the content of the employment contract, are an integral part of this contract and supplement or directly apply it.[427]

*755.* The employee is obliged to conscientiously perform the work at the job for which he/she has concluded an employment contract at a time and place determined for performing the work, respecting the organization of work and the business activity of the employer.

*756.* In the cases determined by law and collective agreement, the employee is obliged to perform other work that is not provided by the employment contract if it is within the level of his/her professional training.[428]

*757.* The employee is obliged to comply with the requirements and instructions of the employer regarding the fulfillment of employment obligations from the employment relationship.[429]

*758.* The employee is obliged to respect and implement the regulations for protection at work, to protect his life and health, as well as the health and life of other persons. It is the right and obligation of every worker to take care of his own safety and the safety of other persons working with him, in accordance with the training and instructions given to him by the employer, to be acquainted with the measures for safety at work and to be trained for their application, in accordance with the regulations for safety and health at work.

*759.* The employee has the right to refuse to perform the work if he/she is exposed to imminent danger to health or life when the safety measures have not been implemented and to request their removal.[430]

*760.* The employer is obliged to provide the employee with a job for which the parties have agreed in the employment contract.

*761.* Unless otherwise agreed, the employer is obliged to provide the employee with all the necessary means and working material in order to be able to fulfill his obligations without hindrance and to provide him with free access to the business premises.

---

427. LL, Art. 29.
428. LL, Art. 30.
429. LL, Art. 31.
430. LL, Art. 32.

*762.* The employer is obliged to provide the employee with appropriate payment for performing the work.[431]

*763.* The employer must provide conditions for safety of life and health of workers in accordance with the special regulations for health and safety at work and take the necessary measures to ensure that each worker is given sufficient training appropriate to the special characteristics at work, taking into account his professional training and experience.

*764.* The employer should make a risk assessment in terms of a systematic review of all aspects of work in order to identify possible causes of injury or damage to the health of workers or safe working conditions.

*765.* After receiving a notification that a worker is pregnant, during the different stages of pregnancy, the employer is obliged to introduce multiple assessments of the risks that may affect the pregnant woman, her unborn or newborn child. Additional risk assessment is also applied when changing work catches, equipment or machinery.

*766.* After appropriate consultation and consent of the woman, and depending on the nature, intensity and duration of the risk, the employer should introduce measures to improve the health and safety at work of the pregnant worker, a worker who has recently given birth or breastfeeding, as well as removal or reducing the risk of:

- irreversible effects;
- causing cancer;
- hereditary genetic defects;
- causing harm to the unborn child; and
- causing harm to the child's diet.

*767.* If no risk is detected during the risk assessment, the employer should inform all employees about the potential risks. The employer should also explain what will be done to ensure that new pregnant workers are not exposed to risks that could cause harm to their health and safety.[432]

*768.* The employer is obliged to protect and respect the personality and dignity of the employee, as well as to take care of and protect the privacy of the employee.

*769.* The employer is obliged to ensure that no employee is a victim of harassment and sexual harassment. The personal data of the employees may be collected, processed, used and submitted to third parties only if it is determined by this or another law or if it is necessary for the realization of the rights and obligations from the employment or in relation to the employment.

---

431. LL, Art. 40.
432. LL, Art. 42.

*770.* The personal data of the employees can be collected, processed, used and submitted to third parties only by the employer or the employee, whom the employer has specially authorized for that.

*771.* The personal data of the workers, for the collection of which there is no longer a legal basis, must be immediately deleted and cease to be used.

*772.* The provisions of paragraphs (1) and (2) of this article shall also apply to the personal data of the candidates for employment.[433]

*773.* Fixed-term employment contract

*774.* An employment contract may be concluded for a definite period of time for performing the same activities, with interruption or without interruption, for up to five years.

*775.* A fixed-term employment contract for replacement of a temporarily absent employee may be concluded until the return of the temporarily absent employee.

*776.* The employment relationship established with a fixed-term employment contract, except for the employment contract for seasonal work, shall be transformed into an employment relationship for an indefinite period of time if the employee continues to work after the expiration of the deadline referred to in paragraph (1) of this article, under conditions and in a manner determined by law.

*777.* As an exception, the employment based on a fixed-term employment contract may be transformed into an employment relationship for an indefinite period of time before the expiration of the period referred to in paragraph (1) of this article if the employee works for more than two years in a job that is released on the basis of retirement or other grounds and for which financial resources are provided, if the employer determines that there is a permanent need for the employee, under conditions and in a manner determined by law.[434]

*778.* An employment contract may also be concluded for working hours shorter than full-time (part-time).

*779.* Part-time is considered the time that is shorter than full-time with the employer.

*780.* The employee who has concluded a part-time employment contract has contractual and other rights and obligations from the employment as a full-time employee and exercises them in proportion to the time for which he has concluded an employment contract, except for those for which it is determined differently by law.

---

433. LL, Arts 43–44.
434. LL, Art. 46.

*781*. The employee has the right to annual leave with a minimum duration of ten working days.

*782*. Unless otherwise specified in the employment contract, the employer of the employee who works part-time must not order the employee to work longer than the agreed working hours.

*783*. The employer is obliged to determine the beginning and the end of the part-time work of the employee in the part-time employment contract and to keep separate records for the part-time workers and for the concluded part-time contracts, the Employment Agency of the Republic of North Macedonia informs the State Labor Inspectorate once a month.[435]

*784*. When concluding the employment contract, the employee and the employer may agree on probation.

*785*. In the employment contract, in addition to all employment rights and obligations, the amount of the salary and the duration of the probationary period shall be determined, which may not be longer than four months. Probationary work can be resumed in case of justified absence from work (illness, etc.).

*786*. For performing seasonal work, the probationary work may last for three working days.

*787*. The employer may terminate the employment contract with probation for performing seasonal work within three days from the day of concluding the employment contract with probation.

*788*. During the probationary period, the employee may terminate the employment contract with a notice period of three working days.

*789*. Based on the assessment of the unsuccessfully completed probationary period, the employer may terminate the employment contract after the probationary period has elapsed.[436]

*790*. The employment contract expires:

(1) by the expiration of the time for which it was concluded;
(2) upon the death of the employee or the employer (natural person);
(3) due to termination of the employer in accordance with law;
(4) by amicable termination;
(5) by cancellation;
(6) by court judgment; and
(7) in other cases determined by law.

---

435. LL, Art. 48.
436. LL, Art. 60.

*791.* Upon termination of employment, the employer shall be obliged, within three days at the latest, to return to the employee all his/her original documents and to issue a certificate for the type of work performed.

*792.* The employer must not state in the certificate anything that would make it difficult for the employee to conclude a new employment contract.

*793.* The fixed-term employment contract ceases to be valid upon the expiration of the term for which it was concluded, i.e., when the agreed work is completed or upon the termination of the reason for which it was concluded.

*794.* The employment contract shall cease to be valid upon the death of the employee.

*795.* The employment contract shall cease to be valid upon the death of the employer (natural person).

*796.* In cases of opening a procedure for termination of the employer, the employment contract of the employee ceases to be valid in accordance with the law.

*797.* The employees to whom the employer has not paid the salary and has not paid the salary contributions for three consecutive months have the right to initiate before a competent court for termination of the employer.

*798.* The employees who, due to the opening of a procedure for termination of the employer, their employment is terminated in accordance with law, shall be provided with the right to payment of:

(1) net salaries, salary contributions for pension and disability insurance and allowances for the period from the last three months before the opening of the procedure for termination of the employer;
(2) compensation for injuries at work, which the employee has suffered at the employer, as well as for occupational diseases; and
(3) unpaid salary compensation for the duration of the unused annual leave for the current calendar year.[437]

*799.* All rights, obligations and responsibilities from the employment contract and employment relationship are transferred to the new employer in cases when status changes occur.

*800.* All rights, obligations and responsibilities of the employed workers referred to in paragraph (1) of this article; the new employer shall be obliged to provide for at least one year, i.e., until the expiration of the employment contract, i.e., the collective agreement binding the previous employer.

437. LL, Arts 62–67.

*801.* If due to a change of the employer for objective reasons the rights from the employment contract deteriorate and the employee therefore terminates the employment contract, the employee has equal rights, as if he/she has terminated the employment contract for business reasons. When determining the notice period and the right to severance pay, the work experience of both employers is taken into account.

*802.* If the employer temporarily transfers on the basis of a legal transaction (lease, rent) all or part of the activity of another employer, the employees transfer after the termination of the validity of the legal transaction back to the first employer or to the new employer undertaking the activity.[438]

*803.* Transfer of rights and obligations arising from employment may be performed only in the cases determined by Law or other regulations, in all cases, transfer of a company or parts of the company to another employer as a result of legal transfer or merger.

*804.* Transfer, in the sense of paragraph (1) of this article, means the transfer of an economic entity that retains its identity, i.e., an organized grouping of resources in order to perform a business activity, regardless of whether that activity is basic or secondary. Transfer refers to companies engaged in economic activities, whether or not they work for a profit.

*805.* It is not considered a transfer, in the sense of paragraph (1) of this Article, the administrative reorganization of the state bodies and the institutions of public service or transfer of the administrative functions between the state bodies and the institutions of public service.

*806.* In case of transfer of activities to a trading company or parts of the trading company or in case of transfer of tasks or part of them from the employer—transferor to another employer—acquirer, the rights and obligations arising from employment shall be fully transferred to the employer-—acquirer to whom the transfer is made. Tasks or activities of the employer are considered tasks and activities related to the production or provision of services or similar activities related to other statutory provisions by a legal or natural person in its own name and under its own responsibility in facilities or premises designated for their performance. Irrespective of the legal reason for such transfer and regardless of whether the property rights have been transferred, the acquirer is considered a legal or natural person competent to continue as an employer in the performance of the tasks or activities of the previous employer or in similar tasks or activities, for a period not shorter than one year.

*807.* The rights and obligations of the employer—transferor for his employees whose employment has been terminated remain unchanged until the day of transfer unless otherwise determined by other statutory provisions.

438. LL, Art. 68.

*808.* Transferee means any natural or legal person who, due to a transfer, in the sense of paragraph (1) of this article, ceases to be an employer of a trading company or parts of a trading company.

*809.* Acquirer means any natural or legal person who, due to transfer, in the sense of paragraph (1) of this article, becomes an employer that refers to a trading company or parts of a trading company.[439]

*810.* Before the transfer of the rights and obligations arising from the employment of the workers with the employer—transferor of the employer—acquirer, the transferor and the acquirer are obliged to inform the trade unions about this fact in advance and to consult them in order to achieve an agreement for:

(1) the determined or proposed transfer date;
(2) the reasons for such transfer;
(3) legal, economic and social implications for workers; and
(4) the envisaged measures regarding the workers.

*811.* The transferor is obliged to inform the representatives of the trade unions of its employees about the transfer in time before the transfer takes place.

*812.* The acquirer shall be obliged to inform the representatives of the trade unions of its employees regarding the transfer in any case before its employees are directly affected regarding their working and employment conditions.

*813.* When the transferor or the acquirer envisages measures related to their employees, the transferor or the acquirer shall be obliged to timely consult with the representatives of the trade unions of its employees regarding such measures in order to reach an agreement.

*814.* Where the law provides for the availability of workers' representatives to an arbitration board to decide on the measures to be taken in relation to workers, the obligations set forth in paragraphs (1) and (2) of this Regulation may be limited to members, in case the execution causes a change in the work for which there is a possibility to cause serious difficulties for a certain number of workers.

*815.* The information and consultation shall cover the measures envisaged in relation to the transfer of workers and must be implemented before the change in operation occurs, as stated in paragraph (1) of this article, regardless of whether the transfer decision has been taken by the employer or by the person controlling the employer.

---

439. LL, Art. 68-a.

*816.* The obligation for information referred to in paragraph (1) of this article shall also apply to the workers at an employer where the workers do not have a trade union organization.[440]

*817.* When the trading company ceases to exist due to the division of the trading company, the body that decides on the division of the trading company shall determine which of the newly established trade companies assumes the rights and obligations from the employment relations of the previous employer.

*818.* When the company ceases to exist, the body that decides on the termination of the company shall determine which company is obliged to fulfill the rights of the employees of such company or which company claims the rights on behalf of a company that has ceased to exist. . When the termination of a company is related to its liquidation, the liquidation procedure is conducted in accordance with the legal regulations and the statutory provisions.

*819.* When the transfer of the trading company occurs during the expiration of the period for which it is established or for the performance of the tasks for which it is established, the higher body designates another company to which the rights and obligations arising from the employment relationship are transferred.

*820.* The transfer of a trading company or parts of a trading company shall not in itself provide grounds for dismissal of workers, except for dismissals for economic, technological or organizational reasons that require personnel changes.

*821.* If a trading company or parts of a trading company retains its independence, status and function of the trade union representatives or the representatives of the workers affected by the transfer, it shall be kept under the same conditions that existed before the day of transfer, based on law, regulation, administrative provision or agreement, if the conditions necessary for the formation of trade unions of employed workers are met.[441].

*822.* Workers and trade union representatives who consider that they have been harmed by noncompliance with the obligations arising from the transfer may seek legal protection.[442]

*823.* The parties may terminate the employment contract at any time with a written agreement which must contain a provision on the consequences that occur for the employee due to the contract termination during the exercise of the rights based on unemployment insurance.

*824.* The agreement referred to in paragraph (1) of this article shall be signed on the day of termination of employment, and it should contain a handwritten name and

---

440. LL, Art. 68-b.
441. LL, Art. 68-d.
442. LL, Art. 68-e.

surname of the employee and the employer, a handwritten date of termination of employment by the employee and the employer and a personal signature of the employee and the employer.

*825.* If the agreement for termination of the employment contract is concluded contrary to paragraphs (1) and (2) of this article, it is null and void.

*826.* The contracting parties may terminate the employment contract with a notice period.

*827.* In the cases determined by law, the contracting parties may terminate the employment contract without a notice period.

*828.* Each of the parties can terminate the employment contract only in full.

*829.* The employee may terminate the employment contract if he/she states in writing that he/she wants to terminate the employment contract.

*830.* The employer may terminate the employment contract only if there is a valid reason for dismissal related to the employee's behavior (personal reason on the part of the employee), due to violation of the work order and discipline or work obligations (fault) or if the reason is based on the needs of the functioning of the employer (business reason).

*831.* The employee and the employer may terminate the employment contract in cases, i.e., for reasons determined by law, collective agreement, rules for work order and discipline and the employment contract.

*832.* The termination of the employment contract, which directly or indirectly puts the employee in a less favorable position on any of the grounds of Article 6 of LL, shall be null and void from the moment of dismissal.

*833.* If the employer terminates the employment contract, he is obliged to state the grounds for the dismissal, determined by law, collective agreement and act of the employer, to prove the justification of the reason justifying the dismissal and to state them in the explanation.[443]

*834.* Before terminating the employment contract for personal reasons by the employee, under the conditions of Article 80 of LL, the employer must warn the employee in writing about the non-fulfillment of obligations and the possibility of termination in case the employee does not improve his work.

*835.* The termination of the employment contract shall be obligatorily pronounced in writing.

---

443. LL, Arts 69–71.

*836.* The employer is obliged to explain in writing the termination of the contract, as well as to point out to the employee the legal protection and to acquaint him/her with his/her insurance rights in case of unemployment, in accordance with law.

*837.* The termination of the employment contract must be served on the contracting party to whom the employment contract is terminated.

*838.* The employer is obliged to deliver the termination of the employment contract personally to the employee, as a rule, in the premises of the employer, i.e., at the address of the domicile, i.e., the place of residence from which the employee comes to work daily.

*839.* If the employee cannot be found at the address of the place of residence from which he/she comes to work daily (except in cases of justified absence from work) or does not have permanent or temporary residence in the Republic of Northern Macedonia or refuses delivery, the employment contract shall be canceled and announced on the bulletin board at the employer's headquarters. After the expiration of eight working days from the announcement on the bulletin board, the delivery is considered completed.

*840.* The employer may terminate the employment contract of the employee when it is not possible to extend the employment, if:

(1) the employee, due to his/her behavior, lack of knowledge or opportunities or due to non-fulfillment of the special conditions determined by law, is not able to perform the contractual or other obligations from the employment relationship (personal reason); or
(2) the employee violates the contractual obligations or other obligations from the employment relationship (cause of guilt); and
(3) the need to perform certain work under the conditions specified in the employment contract ceases due to economic, organizational, technological, structural or similar reasons on the part of the employer (business reasons).

*841.* Termination of employment referred to in paragraph (1) item (3) of this article shall be performed on the basis of the need for efficient functioning of the employer's work, professional training and qualification of the employee, his work experience, work success, type and the importance of the job, work experience and other criteria determined by a collective agreement, as well as criteria for protection of disabled persons, single parents and parents of children with special needs whose employment is terminated on the same grounds.[444]

444. LL, Arts 73–76.

*842.* Unfounded reasons for termination of the employment contract are:

(1) membership of the employee in a trade union or participation in trade union activities in accordance with law and collective agreement;
(2) filing a lawsuit or participating in a procedure against the employer for the purpose of confirming the violation of the contractual and other obligations from the employment relationship before arbitral, judicial and administrative bodies;
(3) approved leave due to illness or injury, pregnancy, birth and parenthood, care of a family member and unpaid parental leave;
(4) use of approved leave from work and annual leave;
(5) service or completion of military service or military exercise; and
(6) other cases of suspension of the employment contract determined by LL.

*843.* The employer may terminate the employment contract for personal reasons on the part of the employee if the employee does not perform the work obligations determined by law, collective agreement, act of the employer and the employment contract.

*844.* The employer may terminate the employment contract of the employee for personal reasons on the part of the employee if the employee is provided with the necessary working conditions and is given appropriate instructions, directions and written warning by the employer regarding the work that the employer is not satisfied with the manner of performing the work obligations and if after the given warning within the deadline determined by the employer, which cannot be shorter than fifteen days, from the day of receiving the written warning the employee does not improve his work, in the cases determined by the collective agreement of branch level, department, or employer level.

*845.* The employer may terminate the employment contract of the employee due to violation of the work order and discipline or non-fulfillment of the obligations determined by law, collective agreement, act of the employer and the employment contract with notice period, especially if:

(1) he/she does not respect the work order and discipline according to the rules prescribed by the employer;
(2) he/she does not perform or negligently and untimely performs the work obligations;
(3) he/she does not comply with the regulations that apply to performing the work at the workplace;
(4) he/she does not adhere to the working hours, the schedule and the use of the working hours;
(5) he/she does not request a leave of absence or does not timely notify the employer in writing of the absence from work;
(6) he/she is absent from work due to illness or justified reasons and fails to notify the employer in writing within forty-eight hours;

(7) he/she does not act with the means of work conscientiously or in accordance with the technical instructions for work;
(8) there is damage, malfunction or loss, and the employer is not immediately notified;
(9) he/she does not comply with the regulations for protection at work or does not maintain the means and equipment for protection at work;
(10) he/she causes disorder and behaves violently during work; and
(11) he/she uses the funds of the employer illegally or unauthorized.

*846.* Other cases of violation of the working order and discipline may be determined by law, collective agreement and the rules of the employer for the work order and discipline.

*847.* The rules for the work order and discipline, the employer is obliged to display them in a visible place in the working premises of the employer and to submit them to the trade union.[445]

*848.* The employer may terminate the employment contract of the employee without a notice period in cases of violation of the work order and discipline or non-fulfillment of work obligations determined by this or another law, collective agreement, rules for work order and discipline and the contract for employment, especially if the employee:

(1) takes unjustified absence from work for three consecutive working days or five working days during a year;
(2) has abused the sick leave;
(3) does not comply with the regulations for health protection, protection at work, fire, explosion, harmful action of poisons and other dangerous substances and violates the regulations for protection of the environment;
(4) ingests, uses or is under the influence of alcohol and narcotics;
(5) commits theft or in connection with the work intentionally or through gross negligence causes damage to the employer; and
(6) discloses a business, official or state secret.

*849.* Other cases of violation of the work order and discipline and of the work obligations for which the employer terminates the employment contract without a notice period may be determined by law and collective agreement.

*850.* Depending on the degree of responsibility of the employee, the conditions under which the violation of work obligations and work order and discipline, previous work and behavior of the employee, the severity of the injury and its consequences, the employer may impose a fine on the employee, which may not exceed 15% of the last paid monthly net salary of the employee, lasting from one to six months.

---

445. LL, Arts 75–81.

*851.* The decision for termination of the employment contract, i.e., the decision for imposition of a fine, must be given in writing, with an explanation of the grounds and the reason for termination of the employment contract, i.e., the reason for imposition of the fine with legal advice.

*852.* The decision to terminate the employment contract and to impose a fine is made by the employer or the employee authorized by him.

*853.* The employee and the employer can terminate the employment contract within the legally or contractually determined notice period. When deciding, the parties must respect the minimum duration of the notice period, determined by LL, the collective agreement at the level of the activity, i.e., at the level of the employer.

*854.* If the employer terminates the employment contract of an individual employee or a smaller number of employees, the notice period is one month and two months in case of termination of employment of more than 150 employees or 5% of the total number of employees with the employer before the termination of employment.

*855.* If the employer terminates the employment contract of a seasonal worker, the notice period is seven working days.

*856.* The notice period starts the day after the delivery of the decision for termination of the employment contract.

*857.* The employer and the employee may agree on monetary compensation instead of a notice period.

*858.* If an agreement for monetary compensation is reached instead of a notice period, the employer shall be obliged to pay the monetary compensation to the employee for the entire notice period by submitting the dismissal on the day of termination of employment.[446]

*859.* In case of termination of the employment contract for business reasons, the employer shall be obliged to pay severance pay to the employee, as follows:

(1) up to five years spent in employment—in the amount of one net salary;
(2) from five to ten years spent in employment—in the amount of two and a half net salaries;
(3) from ten to fifteen years spent in employment—in the amount of three and a half net salaries;
(4) from fifteen to twenty years spent in employment—in the amount of four and a half net salaries;
(5) from twenty to twenty-five years spent in employment—in the amount of six net salaries; and

446. LL, Arts 82–90.

(6) over twenty-five years spent in employment—in the amount of seven net salaries.

*860.* The basis for calculating the severance pay is the average net salary of the employee in the last six months before the dismissal, but it should not be less than 50% of the average net salary paid per employee in the Republic in the last month before the dismissal.

*861.* Employment, in the sense of paragraph (1) of this article, is considered the time spent in employment with the same employer and the employment with the previous employer, where due to the status change, the last employer is the legal successor.

*862.* The severance pay shall be paid on the day of termination of employment.

*863.* The request, i.e., giving consent for waiving the right to severance pay by the employer to the employee, shall be null and void.

*864.* Remittance shall not be paid in case of termination of the employment contract for business reasons of an employee who performs seasonal work lasting up to three months (Article 97, LL).

*865.* The employer may terminate the employment contract of the employee, if:

(1) The employee is prohibited by a final decision to perform certain activities from the employment or if an educational, protective or safety measure has been imposed, due to which he cannot perform work for more than six months or will have to be imprisoned absent from work for more than six months; and
(2) The employee did not successfully perform the probationary work.

*866.* The employee may terminate the employment contract after the expiration of three days after previously warning the employer in writing of the fulfillment of the obligations, if:

(1) the employer does not provide him with a job for more than three months and thus does not pay him the determined salary;
(2) he/she is not allowed to perform the work due to a decision of the competent inspection for prohibition to perform the work process or prohibition to use the means of work for more than thirty days, and the employer does not pay the legally determined salary;
(3) the employer pays a reduced salary for the work for at least three months;
(4) the employer fails to pay the salary for the work three times in a row or in a period of six months within the legally determined contract period;
(5) the employer does not provide the protection of the employee at work, and the employee has previously requested the removal of the threatening immediate and inevitable danger to life and health;

(6) the employer insults him/her and treats him/her violently or, despite his/her warnings, does not prevent such behavior by other employees;
(7) the employer does not provide equal treatment with regard to gender; and
(8) the employer did nothing to prevent the employee from becoming a victim of sexual harassment.

*867.* The employee, in case of dismissal due to the behaviors referred to in paragraph (1) of this article, has the right to severance pay and compensation, at least in the amount of the lost salary during the notice period.

*868.* The employer must not cancel the employment contract of the employee during pregnancy, birth and parenthood, during the placement of a child with an adoptive parent, absence from parental work by a father or adoptive parent and part-time work due to care for a child with developmental problems and special educational needs and inability to care for a child up to three years of age.

*869.* The termination of the employment contract is null and void if on the day of the dismissal, the employer was acquainted with the circumstances referred to in paragraph (1) of this article or if the employee, within fifteen days of the dismissal, notifies the employer of the existence of the circumstances referred to in paragraph (1) of this article by submitting an appropriate certificate from an authorized doctor or competent authority.

*870.* The circumstances referred to in paragraph (1) of this article do not prevent the termination of the employment contract concluded for a certain period of time, with the expiration of the time for which that contract is concluded.

*871.* The prohibition for termination referred to in paragraph (1) of this article does not refer to termination of the employment contract due to serious violations of the contractual obligations, i.e., due to violation of the work order and discipline or work obligations for which dismissal is granted without notice in accordance with by law and collective agreement.

*872.* The employer may terminate the employment contract due to the grounds determined in paragraph (4) of this article, only with the prior consent of the trade union whose member is the employee who is protected from dismissal.

*873.* If the trade union within eight days does not declare for cancellation of the contract from paragraph (5) of this article by giving or not giving consent, it will be considered that it has agreed with the decision of the employer.

*874.* If the trade union does not give consent for termination of the employment contract of the employee referred to in paragraph (1) of this article, the employer may, within fifteen days from the day of submitting the statement for not giving consent, initiate a procedure for its review with the court or arbitral award.

*875.* The procedure for reviewing the consent referred to in paragraph (7) of this article shall be conducted by the competent court within 30 days from the day of filing a lawsuit by the employer.

*876.* If no trade union has been formed with the employer or the employee referred to in paragraph (1) of this article is not a member of a trade union, prior consent for the termination of the employment contract shall be given by the competent labor inspector.

*877.* During the procedure for prior consent in which the competent labor inspector participates, the deadlines and actions referred to in paragraphs (6), (7) and (8) of this article shall be applied.

*878.* If the court makes a decision stating that the employment of the employee has been terminated illegally, the employee has the right to return to work after the decision becomes final if he/she so requests.

*879.* In addition to returning to work, the employer is obliged to pay the employee the gross salary that he would receive if he were at work, in accordance with law, collective agreement and employment contract, reduced by the amount of income that the employee earned on the basis of work, after termination of employment.

*880.* The employee who disputes the dismissal may request the court, temporarily, until the end of the dispute, to order his return to work.

*881.* If the court determines with a decision that the employment of the employee has been terminated illegally, and it is not acceptable for the employee to remain in employment, the court, at the request of the employee, shall determine the day of termination of employment and shall award compensation.

*882.* The decision referred to in paragraph (1) of this article may be made by the court at the request of the employer if there are circumstances that justifiably indicate that the extension of the employment, respecting the interests of both contracting parties, is not possible.

*883.* The employer and the employee may submit the request for termination of the employment contract until the end of the main hearing before the first instance.

*884.* The employment contract shall cease to be valid if, under the conditions and in a manner prescribed by law, it is determined that the employee has lost his/her ability to work on the day of submitting a final decision for determining the lost ability to work.

*885.* The employment contract is terminated by the employer when the employee reaches 64 years of age and fifteen years of pensionable service unless otherwise regulated by another law.

*886.* The employee has the right to earnings—salary in accordance with the law, collective agreement and the employment contract.

*887.* The payment for the work under the employment contract must always be in monetary form. When paying, the employer must comply with the minimum amount determined by the collective agreement in accordance with the law, which is directly binding on the employer.

*888.* The salary is composed of the basic salary, part of the salary for work performed and the allowances unless otherwise determined by another law.

*889.* The employer may pay the employee the 13th salary if the employer has the opportunity to pay it.[447]

*890.* The basic salary is determined taking into account the requirements of the job for which the employee has concluded the employment contract.

*891.* The work success of the employee is determined by taking into account the domestic relationship, the quality and the scope of the performance of the work for which the employee has concluded the employment contract.

*892.* The allowances are determined for the special working conditions, which arise from the schedule of working hours, for work in shifts, work in divided working hours, night work, work on duty, according to law extended work, work in work on the day of weekly rest, work on holidays determined by law, work on Sunday and allowance for work experience.

*893.* The salary of a full-time employee may not be lower than the minimum wage set by law and collective agreement.

*894.* The employer is obliged to equal work with equal requirements at the workplace to pay equal salaries to the workers regardless of gender.

*895.* The provisions of the employment contract, the collective agreement, i.e., the general act of the employer, which is in contradiction with paragraph (1) of this article, are null and void.

*896.* The employee is entitled to reimbursement of work-related expenses for:

(1) business trip;
(2) field allowance;
(3) use of a private car for business trips;
(4) a separate life from the family; and
(5) death of the employee or a member of his family.

---

447. LL, Arts 90–105.

*897.* The employee is entitled to severance pay upon retirement, as well as jubilee awards.

*898.* The amount, the basis and the deadline for calculation and payment of the compensation of these costs shall be determined by law and collective agreement.

*899.* The employer may organize transportation to and from the workplace at its own expense, as well as food during work.

*900.* The food expenses referred to in paragraph 4 of this article may amount to a maximum of 20% of the average net salary per employee paid in the previous year, and the transportation costs in the amount of the actual costs in public transport.[448]

## §4. Social Security

*901.* If the employee considers that the employer does not provide him/her with the employment rights or violates any of his / her employment rights, he/she has the right to submit a written request to the employer to eliminate the violation, i.e., to fulfill his/her obligation.

*902.* If the employee considers that his / her right has been violated by a written decision of the employer, he/she has the right, within eight days from the delivery of the decision with which the right was violated, to request from the employer to remove it.

*903.* If the employer does not fulfill his / her obligations from the employment within the further period of eight days after the delivery of the written request to the employee, i.e., does not eliminate the violation of the right, the employee may request court protection before the competent court within fifteen days.

*904.* The employee has the right to object to the decision for termination of the employment contract to the management body, i.e., the employer, within eight days from the day of receiving the decision for termination of the employment contract.

*905.* When no decision has been made after the complaint, within eight days from the day of submitting the complaint or when the employee is not satisfied with the decision made after the complaint within fifteen days from the day of receiving the decision on the complaint, the employee has the right to initiate a dispute before the competent court.

*906.* Regardless of the deadlines referred to in paragraphs (2) and (3) of this article, the employee may realize the monetary claims from the employment directly before the competent court.

448. LL, Arts 106–113.

*907.* The unelected candidate for employment who considers that the prohibition of discrimination was violated during the selection, within fifteen days from the receipt of the notification by the employer, may request compensation for damages before the competent court.

*908.* In the event of an individual or collective labor dispute, the employer and the employee may agree to entrust the resolution of the dispute to a separate body determined by law.

*909.* Arbitration for resolving collective labor disputes may be determined by a collective agreement.

*910.* The collective agreement determines the composition, the procedure and other issues important for the work of the arbitration.

*911.* If the employer and the employee agree with the arbitral settlement of the labor dispute, the decision of the arbitration is final and obligatory for both parties.

*912.* A dispute before the competent court is not allowed against the decision of the arbitration.[449]

---

449. LL, Arts 181–183.

# Part III. Doping and Sports

## Chapter 1. General Issues

*913.* The essential value of sports is the sports spirit, which is the basis of Olympism, and it is characterized, above all, by ethics, honesty, respect for rules and laws, and respect for oneself and other participants in sports. Sport, as a sublime activity aimed at building the mind and the body, must be available to all under equal conditions. All participants in sports are expected to have a minimum of ethical behavior to preserve physical and mental health and the fair play relationship.

*914.* Unfortunately, abuses have been present since the beginning of sport. The use of doping is contrary to the stated basic values of modern sports and represents its gross abuse. Doping is harmful in many ways for athletes and sports in general. It destroys the health of athletes, leads to unrealistic results and irregularities of competition, and destroys the reputation of sports and sports organizations.

*915.* International organizations and all international and national sports federations put the fight against doping in the foreground and state it as a primary task. In the fight against doping, they see the basis for the protection of the health of athletes, preservation of the equality of chances (competition) and the maintenance of the credibility of the sports branch. The adoption of the World Anti-Doping Code and the European Convention against Doping in Sports clearly defines the role of all factors in the fight against doping.

*916.* In the Republic of Macedonia, where sport is defined as an activity of special importance (Articles 23, 55 and 56-2 LS of RM), a very restrictive anti-doping legislation is in force. In addition to LS, as the highest legal act regulating the field of sports, the European Convention against Doping in Sports was ratified. Its consistent application aims to ensure the protection of the health of athletes, regularity of sports competitions and results, as well as the preservation of the reputation of sports in society and the fight against doping in sports.

*917.* The abuse of substances and drugs, and their use for non-therapeutic purposes, is most often used in sports, which is directly related to doping, which is basically harmful to the health of the athlete, regardless of the improvement of his nervousness before and during the competition.

*918.* Most athletes use ergogenic and anabolic substances to improve their physical ability. However, the advantage gained by a substance must be seriously evaluated in terms of the ratio of the positive effect on performance versus the volume of damage to health. Athletes in doping use doses up to hundred times higher than the accepted therapeutic doses, which alone supports the thesis that they do not monitor the therapeutic effects of the substances they use but the secondary effects that occur with doses that are never given or achieved for therapeutic purposes. Health side effects depend on the type of substance, the amount and the time period of intake, as well as on the sensitivity of the organism itself to a certain substance.

*919.* In the Republic of Macedonia, from 2006 to 2014, a total of 630 tests were carried out for banned substances in sports, of which four had positive results. The frequency and severity of side effects are different and depend on the type of medicine, the dose, the duration of use and the personal sensitivity of the body.

*920.* In 2011–2014, eight athletes from all disciplines were confirmed to have used anabolic steroids (the figures are taken from the available literature).[450]

450. B. Georgievski, Misuse of Substances in Sports [In Macedonian: Злоупотреба на супстанции во спортот]. Thesis for Specialization, University Goce Delcev, Stip. 2016. Available at: https://eprints.ugd.edu.mk/16174/1/_specijalisticka.pdf.

## Chapter 2. Public Regulation

*921.* In the Republic of Macedonia, public regulations regarding doping in sports are based on both LS of RM. The constitutional framework for the enactment of this Law is contained in Article 46 of the Constitution, according to which the Republic of Macedonia regulates and provides the system in the field of sports.

*922.* Acording to LS, the persons who are actively involved in sports in sports clubs, i.e., sports—recreational activity, must undergo a health check control. Health control includes a health examination before starting how and systematic control examinations during participation in sports activities. The number of systematic control examinations is determined by the National sports federation from the relevant sports branch.[451]

*923.* In this sense, a sports organization, like all other participants in sports, is obliged to engage in the fight against doping in sports during the performance of sports activities. That the fight against doping in sports is one of the primary goals in the Republic of Macedonia is confirmed by Article 23 of the LS, in which the fight against doping is explicitly stated as a general interest in the field of sports.

*924.* The health control of the participants in sports activities is carried out by a doctor-specialist in sports medicine. In the municipalities where there is no sports medicine specialist, the health department's control of the athletes will be carried out by a doctor—a specialist in general medicine or a specialist in internal medicine.[452] Furthermore, for the participants in sports and sports-recreational activities, health examinations are carried out within the framework of regular health examination insurance.

*925.* Sports clubs provide means for health control of athletes if they are not covered by mandatory health insurance. The sports clubs of the athletes who perform the sports activity professionally provide them with mandatory health insurance.[453]

*926.* The Macedonian legislation forbids professionals to force an athlete to train or participate in sports competitions during the time when he is not physically able for that or when such activity could worsen his health condition.[454]

*927.* According to LS of RM, as a general act, it is prohibited that athletes be exposed to sports activities that may endanger or worsen their health condition. In terms of the prohibition of abuse in the field of sports, the Law explicitly states doping as a strictly prohibited activity. For the implementation of the Anti-Doping Control Convention in the Republic of Macedonia, the state administration body

451. Article 51, LS.
452. Article 52, LS.
453. Article 53, LS.
454. Article 54, LS.

responsible for the works in the area of sports, the National Anti-Doping Commission, was formed (hereinafter: "the Commission"). The members of the Commission are appointed by the official who manages the state administration responsible for works in the field of sports. The members are professionals, or scientists in the field of pharmacology, medical, chemical and biological sciences, sports, law and other areas.[455]

*928.* Detailed regulations on health control, the volume and method of organization of emergency medical aid and doping control are adopted by the body of the state administration responsible for the work in the field of sports, in agreement with the authority responsible for the work in the field of health.[456]

*929.* Doping in sports in the Republic of Macedonia is regulated by the following laws and regulations:

- Law on the Ratification of the International Convention against doping in sport.[457]
- LS Criminal code.

*930.* The Law on the Ratification of the International Convention against doping in sports acknowledges the International Convention against doping in sport, adopted on October 19, 2005, in Paris, in the Arabic, Chinese, English, French, Russian and Spanish languages.

*931.* The law envisages that organizations in the field of sports achieve their goals and perform sports activities and sports occupations in accordance with the Law, sports rules, ratified conventions in the field of sports and principles established in the documents of international organizations of which the Republic of Macedonia is a member.

*932.* To harmonize activities on the prevention of negative phenomena in sports, including doping, LS of RM envisages that the Government of the Republic of Macedonia establishes a National Anti-Doping Commission.

*933.* From the point of view of doping control, the athlete, under the World Anti-Doping Code, is any person who participates in sport at the international level (as defined by each international sports federation) or at the national level (as defined by each national anti-doping organization), and any other person who participates in sport at a lower level. At the national level, anti-doping rules are mandatory for all athletes in national teams and for all athletes who have the right to compete in any national championship in any sport. This does not mean that all these persons

---

455. Article 55, LS.
456. Article 56, LS.
457. Official Journal No. 103/2008.

must be included in the registered test group of the national anti-doping organization. The national anti-doping organization may include athletes in competitions at lower levels than the national ones in the anti-doping program.

*934.* According to LS, health protection and anti-doping control are regulated in Articles 51–56.

*935.* The persons who are actively involved in sports in the sports clubs, that is, sports—recreational activity, are obliged to undergo a health examination control. Health control includes a health examination before starting, such as systematic control examinations during participation in sports activities. The number of systematic control examinations is determined by the National sports federation from the respective sports branch.[458]

*936.* The health control of the participants in sports activities is performed by a doctor-specialist in sports medicine. In the municipalities where there is no sports medicine specialist, the health control of the athletes will be carried out by a doctor—specialist in general medicine or a specialist in internal medicine.[459]

*937.* For Participants in sports and sports-recreational activities, health examinations are carried out within the framework of the regular health examination insurance. Sports clubs provide means for health control of athletes if they are not covered by mandatory health insurance. The sports clubs of the athletes who perform the sports activity professionally provide them with mandatory health insurance.[460]

*938.* It is forbidden for the professional to force the athlete to train or he participates in sports competitions when he is not medically fit for that or when such activity could worsen his health condition.[461]

*939.* It is forbidden for athletes to take or to be given to athletes stimulants that are prohibited and harmful to health. Doping control is an integral part of healthcare measures for athletes. For the implementation of the Anti-Doping Control Convention in the Republic of Macedonia, the state administration authority responsible for the affairs of the area of sports is the National Anti-Doping Commission (hereinafter “the Commission”). The members of the Commission are appointed by the official who manages the authority of the state administration in charge of affairs in the field of sports, from the order of professional, scientific and other prominent workers in the field of pharmacology, medicine, chemical and biological sciences, sports, law and other areas.[462]

458. LS, Art. 51.
459. LS, Art. 52.
460. LS, Art. 53.
461. LS, Art. 54.
462. LS, Art. 55.

*940.* Closer regulations on health control, on the scope and method of organization of emergency medical aid and doping control, adopt the body of the state administration responsible for matters in the field of sports in agreement with the authority responsible for health matters.[463]

*941.* Macedonia is a signatory to all the official documents that are carried out with the aim of preventive action against not only doping but also doping controls and sanctions for offenders. In Macedonia, there is no accredited reference laboratory for testing prohibited substances in sports. The samples taken in Macedonia are tested in the reference laboratory in Vienna, Republic of Austria.

*942.* During 2004, all the necessary activities were carried out, including the selection of an accredited laboratory, programs and regulations of the anti-doping commission and conditions created for performing doping controls.

*943.* The first doping control was done on March 6, 2005, at the match between FC "Belasitsa" from Strumica and FC "Rabotnicki" from Skopje, at the stadium "Mladost" in Strumica. Two football players from both teams were tested. In the first case, the anti-doping control showed that one football player from FC "Rabotnički" tested positive for the substance salbutamol, which is in the group of stimulants on the list of prohibited substances, and that too in a relatively high value, above the permitted one. The player did not request to analyze sample B. After listening to the player's claims, it was established that he used nose drops without knowing it, which probably contained a prohibited substance, although it was not written on the declaration of the drug. The player was sanctioned with six months of non-play.

*944.* The second case is the case of FC "Prilepska Pobeda," which, after the competition, although selected and informed, does not appear at the doping control, which violates the anti-doping rules—refusal to provide samples for doping analysis after selection. The actual player was suspended for six months after the hearing (Stoilov, 2008, as cited in Georgievski, 2016).

*945.* In 2011, two football players of "Rabotnički" at a match with "Lazio" in Rome were tested for doping, and the substance 4 methyl-2-hexamine was detected, which is a stimulant and which is on the prohibited list of substances. After listening to the players, it was established that they used tablets called "Jeek 3d."

*946.* The football club "Rabotnicki" was fined EUR 30,000; the two players were suspended for two years; the physiotherapist was banned for three years, and the club's doctor was banned for two years.

*947.* The fourth case of doping was discovered in 2013 by a football player of "Vardar" from Skopje on illegal stimulants, who was punished with a disciplinary measure banning him from participating in the championship cup matches and a

463. LS, Art. 56.

two-year suspension from any function in football. In 2013—2015, the use of anabolic steroids was proven among eight athletes.

*948.* The National Anti-Doping Commission has adopted a Rulebook[464] which is, in fact, an operationalization of the Rules of the World Anti-Doping Code (hereinafter: "Code") as the essential document that harmonizes anti-doping policies, rules and regulations within sports organizations and among public authorities around the world.

## §3. Penalty Provisions

*949.* As per the CC, there is intention to fight against doping and prescribes misdemeanor measures for such criminal offenses. The LS and CC determine the liability of persons who have violated the anti-doping rules. Both Laws prescribe appropriate measures for violating the regulations on the prevention of doping in sports.

### I. Criminal Offences

*950.* It is important to emphasize that the CC of the Republic of Macedonia does not prescribe criminal offenses related to doping in sports and that there is no direct prescribed punishment for athletes who use doping. Athletes can be sanctioned by sports bodies for doping (national sports bodies, sports federations, clubs) but not a penalty or offense for athletes.

*951.* According to some authors, in connection to the use of doping, other crimes may appear that are not strictly targeted as crimes or offenses in sports. Such a criminal offense would be bodily injury[465] and serious bodily injury[466] with the potential death of the athlete, committing a crime of murder,[467] or murder by negligence,[468] with which the doctors, trainers or other athletes would be accused, and the doctors could also be accused of the crime of negligent treatment of patients[469] or failure to provide medical assistance (Article 208, CC).

*952.* Bodily injury is described in Article 130 on CC, such as he who physically injures another or impairs his health shall be punished with a fine or imprisonment for up to three years. Whoever commits the crime from paragraph 1 while committing domestic violence will be punished with imprisonment from six months to three years. With the penalty from paragraph (2) of this article, whoever commits the

464. Available at: http://madsf.mk/tsfm_documents/13%20-%20AMS%20PRAVILNIK%20ZA%20ANTI%20DOPING.pdf.
465. Article 130, CC.
466. Article 131, CC.
467. Article 123, CC.
468. Article 126, CC.
469. Article 207, CC.

crime out of hatred will be punished. The court may issue a court warning to the perpetrator of the crime from paragraph 1 if he was provoked by particularly offensive or rude behavior of the injured party. The prosecution for the crime from paragraph 1 is undertaken by private lawsuit and for paragraph 2 by motion.

*953.* Serious bodily injury is described in Article 131 on CC, such as anyone who seriously injures another person or seriously impairs their health will be punished with imprisonment from six months to five years. Whoever commits the crime from paragraph 1 while committing domestic violence or out of hatred will be punished with imprisonment from one to five years. He who seriously injures another person or seriously impairs his health, and because of this, the injured person's life is put in danger or an important part of the body or an important organ is destroyed or permanently and significantly weakened or permanent incapacity for work in general or for the work for which he is qualified will be caused, or his health will be permanently and severely impaired, or he will be disfigured, he will be punished with imprisonment from one to ten years. If the injured person dies due to serious bodily injury from paragraphs 1 to 3, the perpetrator will be punished with imprisonment for at least one year. Whoever commits the crime from paragraphs 1, 2 and 3 due to negligence will be punished with a fine or imprisonment for up to three years. Whoever commits the crime in an instant, brought to a state of strong irritation through no fault of his own by an attack or by serious insult or as a result of domestic violence by the injured party, will be punished for the crime from paragraphs 1 and 2 with a fine penalty or imprisonment of up to three years, and for the crime from paragraphs 3 and 4, imprisonment of one to five years.

*954.* Murder is described in Article 123 on CC, such as he who deprives another of his life shall be punished with imprisonment for at least five years. A punishment of imprisonment of at least ten years or life imprisonment shall be meted out to whoever:

(1) takes another's life in a cruel or insidious manner;
(2) takes another's life during domestic violence;
(3) deprives another person of life and will intentionally endanger the life of another person;
(4) deprives another of life out of selfishness, for the purpose of committing or concealing another criminal act, out of wanton revenge, out of hatred or out of other base motives;
(5) takes another's life by order;
(6) deprives another of life due to the extraction of an organ, tissue or cells for transplantation;
(7) takes the life of a female person whom he knows to be pregnant or a minor; and
(8) takes the life of a judge, public prosecutor or lawyer in the performance of his function, i.e., activity or official or military person in the performance of public or state security or the duty of maintaining public order, arresting a perpetrator of a crime or custody of a person deprived of liberty.

*955.* Anyone who intentionally takes the lives of two or more persons for whom he has not previously been tried will be punished with imprisonment of at least ten years or with life imprisonment unless it is a crime from Article 9 paragraph (3), Article 10 paragraph (3) and Articles 124, 125 and 127.

*956.* Manslaughter by negligence is described in Article 126 on CC, such as whoever deprives another of his life due to negligence shall be punished with imprisonment from six months to five years.

*957.* Negligence is described in Article 14 on CC, such as a criminal offense committed due to negligence when the perpetrator was aware that due to his action or omission, a harmful consequence could occur but thoughtlessly thought that he would be able to prevent it or that it would not occur or when he was not aware of the possibility of a harmful consequence occurring, although according to the circumstances and according to his personal characteristics, he was obliged and could have been aware of that possibility.

*958.* Negligent treatment of patients is described in Article 207 on CC, such as a doctor who, when providing medical assistance, applies an obviously unsuitable means or method of treatment or does not apply appropriate hygiene measures or acts negligently in general and thereby causes the health condition of a person to deteriorate, shall be punished with a fine or imprisonment for up to three years. The punishment from paragraph 1 shall also punish a midwife or other healthcare worker who acts negligently when providing medical assistance or care and thereby causes a deterioration in the health condition of a person. If the crime from paragraphs 1 and 2 is committed due to negligence, the perpetrator will be punished with a fine or imprisonment of up to one year.

*959.* Failure to provide medical assistance is described in Article 208 on CC, such as a doctor or other healthcare worker who, contrary to his duty, does not provide immediate medical aid to a person whose life is in danger or the crime was committed out of hatred, will be punished with a fine or imprisonment of up to one year. If, due to the crime from paragraph 1, the death of the person who was not provided with medical assistance occurs, the perpetrator will be punished with imprisonment from six months to five years.

## II. Offences

*960.* Offenses in the field of doping in sports, as illegal behavior of a lesser degree of social danger, are prescribed by other provisions of LS of RM (Articles 74 and 76).

*961.* A fine in the amount of EUR 5,000 in denar equivalent for an offense will be prescribed to the subject that performs sports activity if:

- the subject allows political and religious organization and action (Article 4);
- during the performance of the sport activity, the subject has not provided adequate facilities, equipment and appropriate professional staff (Article 10 paragraphs 1, 2 and 3);
- the subject has not received a decision by the state administration body responsible for sports activities (Article 11 paragraph 2) and
- the subject has not provided health control or systematic control examinations (Article 51 paragraphs 2 and 3).

*962.* A fine in the amount of 30% of the assessed fine for the subject performing the activity sport will be imposed on the person responsible for the offense from paragraph 1 of this article person in the subject.

*963.* For the offense from paragraph 1 of this article, the legal person may, in addition to the fine, impose a misdemeanor sanction banning him from performing sports activities duration from six months to two years.

*964.* For the offense from paragraph 1 of this article, the responsible person in the legal entity, in addition to the fine, may be imposed a misdemeanor sanction banning the performance of duty for up to one year (Article 74).

*965.* A fine in the amount of EUR 500 to EUR 1,000 in denar equivalent for a violation will be imposed on the person who gives or takes stimulants that are prohibited or harmful to health (Article 55 paragraph 1).

*966.* For the offense from paragraph 1 of this article, the professional person is subject to a fine determined in paragraph 1 of this article; a misdemeanor sanction may also be imposed on him, banning performing duty for up to one year (Article 76).

# Part IV. Sport and Commerce

## Chapter 1. General Issues

*967.* Sport is a primordial need, but sports has become a lucrative business today. Sports can bring huge profits not only to companies and sports clubs but also to individuals. Profit is an increasingly powerful driver, so athletes are transformed into modern gladiators in whom large multinational companies invest money. In the conditions of modern society, large international sports competitions are inconceivable without sponsors, and this trend is present, to a much lesser extent, in school sports competitions, as well as in the organization of recreational activities. The role of the media is immeasurable for the popularization of sports, but it is also immeasurable in terms of the promotion of sports products because sport is a synonym for health and the beauty of life.

*968.* In the conditions of modern society, sports clubs and other sports organizations independently earn income not only from their core business—participation in competitions and ticket sales to viewers—but also from advertising, sale of TV rights, transfers of top athletes and sponsorships. The influx of money in sports, on the other hand, increases the inequality between big and small clubs, between athletes from rich and athletes from poor countries. Making a difference between athletes and sports events of the 'first and second order' is not only out of alignment with the rules of fair play, but it is also the basis of discrimination because it is clear that, in this case, athletes do not have the same starting points.

*969.* Sport, as a special branch of the economy, especially top sports professionals, brings large revenues to the state through various fiscal and parafiscal revenues. On the other hand, earnings from TV rights in the Republic of Macedonia are still significantly lower in percentage than in developed countries, but a significant turnover of financial resources is achieved through sports transfers. Transfers are especially pronounced within the most popular sports, such as football and basketball.

# Chapter 2. Public Regulation

*970.* In the Republic of Macedonia, public regulations governing the field of sports within the commercial sector, especially media and television rights, sponsorship, trade and ownership in sports clubs, in addition to the LS, are prescribed, among others, by the following laws: Law on audio and audiovisual media services (LAAMS);[470] Law on electronic communications;[471] Law on the Ratification of the European Convention on Transfrontier Television;[472] Law on companies;[473] Law on trade, etc.[474]

## §1. Media and Television Rights

*971.* On this occasion, the specifics of the public regulations in the field of media and TV rights in the Republic of Macedonia will be presented.

*972.* According to LAAMS, sporting events represent an example of an audiovisual program, i.e., they are a type of complete unit of moving pictures with or without a sound, which represents a separate element within the chronological order of the programs (program scheme) or of the catalog of programs set by the provider of audiovisual media services on demand. In this sense, sporting events have audiovisual entertaining functions.[475]

*973.* Furthermore, sportive programs are defined as television or radio program services with a specialized format if they are comprised of at least 70% programs of sportive type.[476] Another important issue is the placement of products which is permitted in the sporting programs as an exception to the general rule for prohibition of placement of products.[477] LAAMS also provides a special rule regarding the annual fee for the license for television or radio broadcasting when it comes to sports programs, regulating that the amount of the license fee shall be calculated on the basis of the following formula: $((N \times GDP/200.000) \times Rt \times Kp) + A$, where the Kp is between 0.75 and 1. The Kp is between 1.15 and 1.5 for a broadcaster with program service of a specialized format, where all content is of the same type (in this case, sport.).[478]

470. Official Journal No. 184/13, 13/14, 44/14, 101/14, 132/14, 142/16, 132/17, 168/18, 248/18, 27/19, 77/21.
471. Official Journal No. 39/14, 188/14, 44/15, 193/15, 11/18 И 21/18, 98/19, 153/19, 92/2021.
472. Official Journal No. 18/2003.
473. Official Journal No. 28/2004; 84/2005; 25/2007; 87/2008; 42/2010; 48/2010; 24/2011; 166/2012; 70/2013; 119/2013; 120/2013; 187/2013; 38/2014; 41/2014; 138/2014; 88/2015; 192/2015; 6/2016; 61/2016.
474. Consolidated version of the Law on Trade is available at: https://www.economy.gov.mk/Upload/Documents.
475. LAAMS, Art. 3.
476. *Ibid.*
477. LAAMS, Art. 55.
478. LAAMS, Art. 80.

*974.* A specific is also promulgated with regard to the obligation of the public broadcasting service (Macedonian Radio and Television) to promote sporting and recreational activities and broadcast sporting events in the country and abroad where Macedonian national teams or athletes are participating, as well as less popular sports or sporting events.[479]

*975.* The basic document for the development of the media scene in the Republic of Macedonia is the 2019–2023 Regulatory Strategy for the Development of Audio and Audiovisual Business Activity. This Strategy outlines the directions of the activities in the period from 2019 to 2023, with the aim of improving a number of aspects in the media sphere in the forthcoming five-year period. The implementation of the activities envisaged by the Strategy is expected, among other things, to help improve the functioning of the self-regulation and co-regulation systems, the pluralism of media ownership and its full transparency, human rights protection and freedom concerning media contents. It is also expected to help provide a regulatory framework that will enable the development of the media and further development of media literacy.[480]

*976.* Institutions responsible for the implementation of laws and other legal regulations in the field of audio and audiovisual services are:

– The Agency of audio and audiovisual services.
– Regulatory Agency for Electronic Communications.
– Public Broadcasting Service (Macedonian Radio and Television).

*977.* According to the Article 6 of the Law on Audio and audio-visual media services, which entered into force on January 3, 2014, the Agency has the following duties and responsibilities:

– ensures transparency of the work of broadcasters;
– ensures the protection and development of pluralism of audio and audiovisual media services, encourages and supports the existence of diverse and independent audio and audiovisual media services;
– takes measures in accordance with the Law in cases where provisions of the Law on audio and audiovisual media services or where regulations adopted on the basis of the Law and conditions and obligations stipulated in the licenses are violated;
– ensures the protection of minors;
– adopts acts derived from the Law on audio and audiovisual media services;
– ensures protection of the interest of citizens in the area of audio and audiovisual media services; determines the existence of illicit media concentration;

479. LAAMS, Art. 110.
480. Available at: https://avmu.mk/en/strategy-for-development-of-the-broadcasting-activity-in-the-republic-of-macedonia/.

- decides on the assignment, extension or revocation of licenses for television or radio broadcasting; takes measures for temporary restriction on transmission and reception of audio and audiovisual media services from other countries on the territory of the Republic of Macedonia;
- adopts a list of events of major importance;
- encourages media literacy;
- maintains the registries established by the Law;
- conducts research and analysis on specific issues concerning audio and audiovisual media services; performs audience measurement in terms of viewership or listenership of programs, i.e., program services of broadcasters in the Republic of Macedonia;
- prescribes the manner of audience measurement in terms of viewership or listenership of programs, i.e., program services of broadcasters in the Republic of Macedonia;
- performs other duties determined by the Law on audio and audiovisual media services.

*978.* Advertising and sponsorship are of special importance for the realization of media and television rights.

## §2. Sponsorship

*979.* Sponsorship is connecting an organization with an individual or an event in order to promote the organization itself, its products or its services.

*980.* Sponsorship is a business relationship between organizations that provide funds or services, on the one hand, and individuals, events or organizations, on the other hand, who, in turn, for commercial purposes, put their image and resources at their disposal.

*981.* Athletes, sports organizations and sports events are most often sponsored due to high media visibility, allowing potential sponsors access to a wide audience to promote their products. The very thought of athletes is associated with the values that sport brings with it, and these are, above all, a healthy attitude toward life, a youthful spirit and competition. This is why sports activities attract a large number of spectators who identify with the sports role models or teams they support, which organizations know well and use well.

*982.* Potential sponsors are aware that a large number of consumers care about their health, and for this reason, they use sports as a model of health and healthy living in order to get closer to them. Consumers identify with successful athletes and sports clubs, and in this manner, the image of the winner from the consumer's point of view is transferred to the organization itself – the sponsor, and all this leads to the creation of profit. In addition, sponsorship has its advantages over traditional advertising. It is more favorable for the organization, and the media coverage is higher.

*983.* It is precisely the great media attention that is one of the most important preconditions for organizations to enter into sponsorship and create an image of a socially responsible company. The growing role of the media in creating public opinion also leads to an increase in investments in sponsorship.

*984.* In the context of this issue, the situation in the Republic of Macedonia is similar to that in the developed world, but there are some differences.

*985.* As in most legal systems of different countries, there is no special law in the Republic of Macedonia regulating the matter of sponsorship. This matter is partially regulated by-laws governing the area that may be the subject of sponsorship interest. The sponsorship agreement itself is not regulated by modern civil codes.

*986.* In the legal system of the Republic of Macedonia, the provisions related to sponsorship are contained in the LS, Law on the Ratification of the European Convention on Transfrontier Television, which ratified the 1989 European Convention on Transfrontier Television. Sponsorship is also regulated by certain provisions of other legal regulations which regulate the area that may be the subject of sponsorship interest.

*987.* LS recognizes sponsorship as a possible source of funds through the provisions that a sports association may acquire funds and generate income from contributions, membership fees, donations and gifts, subsidies, inheritances, interest on deposits, rents, dividends, services, sponsorships and other commercial, marketing businesses and economic activities in accordance with the Law. The funds acquired in this manner are the property of the sports association.

*988.* Financial assistance may be used to cover expenses that the athlete has personally incurred in preparing for or participating in competitions or for the treatment caused by an injury sustained in the competition, or to cover other particularly eligible costs, provided that these costs are not already covered by expenses of organizations in the field of sports, sponsors or donors, i.e., that the costs of treatment are not covered by health insurance, in accordance with the Law.

*989.* Sponsorship establishes a contractual relationship between two parties, the sponsor and the sponsored.

*990.* The sponsor can be a natural or legal person. Natural or legal persons can also be sponsored.

*991.* There are several types of sponsorship: sponsoring athletes, sponsoring a sports club/organization and sponsoring an event.

*992.* Legal persons can be legal persons of public and private law. Legal persons of public law are the state, autonomous province and local self-government, while legal persons of private law are companies, associations, institutions, endowments and foundations.

*993.* Regarding natural persons, athletes and trainers appear as sponsors, but it can be any other natural person for whom potential sponsors find interest in sponsoring it. An adult but also a minor natural person can be sponsored. On behalf of minor natural persons and athletes, contracts are concluded by their parents, i.e., guardians as legal representatives.

*994.* A legal person can also be sponsored. As shown in practice, companies, associations and institutions most often appear as sponsors. The sponsorship agreement is concluded on behalf and for the account of the association by the representative of the association, on behalf and for the account of the company by the representative of the company, and on behalf and for the account of the institution by the director of the institution.

*995.* A special type of sponsorship is event sponsorship, which refers to the sponsorship of sports events. In this case, the contract is concluded with the organizer of the sponsored event, which can again be both a natural person and a legal person. The organizer of the sponsored event concludes the sponsorship agreement in person or through a proxy if he/she is a natural person, and if it is a legal person, the sponsorship agreement is concluded by their representative in accordance with the law.

*996.* A sports competition is a sports event that takes place according to pre-established and known sports rules, which may be generally valid for a specific branch of sport, or only for a specific sports event and whose goal to which each participant strives is either winning the opponent or achieving a certain predetermined sports result. The organization of sports events must be in accordance with LS and the Law on the prevention of violence at sports events, as well as the rules established by the competent national branch sports federation.

*997.* In any case, the sponsor may not compromise the integrity of the sports content of the sponsored activity by sponsoring it and may not damage the reputation of the sponsored person. On the other hand, the sponsored person may not change the name, i.e., the name of the sponsor, its trademark or service mark, nor may it otherwise endanger the reputation or image of the sponsor. It can be concluded that this is a mutually beneficial relationship, which is regulated by the sponsorship agreement.

### §3. MERCHANDISING

*998.* The need for sports products is growing as awareness of healthy lifestyles increases. These needs are quite large, from the need for physical exercise and maintaining psychophysical condition to the desire to compete and affirm in sports and recreational activities, but also the need for achievement in terms of sports results. Market research identifies these needs, so manufacturers and merchants are directed in which direction they should design and market certain sports products.

*999.* The commercialization of sports and trade is playing an increasingly important role in the sports industry. The fact is that most of the income in sports, in addition to the sale of the right to broadcast and organize events, is generated through the trade of sports products.

*1000.* In the Republic of Macedonia, the same conditions and rules for conducting trade on the single market of the Republic of Macedonia, which are regulated by the Law on trade, apply to trade in sports products.

*1001.* The Law on trade applies to all persons who perform trade activities in the Republic of Macedonia, including those who trade in sports products.

*1002.* The basic concepts of commercial law are defined by the provisions of this Law in Article 2, which defines "trade" as the activities of buying and selling goods, as well as performing commercial services.[481]

*1003.* Trading for sports purposes is also considered a special way of trading at specially organized markets, sales by mail, at kiosks, sales by way of vending machines, television, internet sales, mobile street vendors, organized fairs, door-to-door sales, business exhibitions, exhibitions salons, fairs and sales organized for humanitarian and sports purposes.

*1004.* Electronic commerce is a type of remote commerce which is realized in a way that goods/services are offered, ordered and sold through the Internet.

*1005.* In the era of digitalization, remote and electronic commerce have become dominant.

*1006.* The legislative framework regulating intellectual property is of special importance for the trade of goods in sports. This legal framework is amended, especially in the areas of copyright, patents, and trademarks, and thus harmonized with the Agreement on trade-related aspects of intellectual property rights and European Union standards, as well as other international conventions in this field.

*1007.* With the Stabilization and Association Agreement with the EU, the Republic of Macedonia is obliged to the EU to apply the same standards of protection of intellectual property rights as those prescribed by the EU.

*1008.* Regarding sports brands and sports products, the most commonly used intellectual property[482] is certainly a trademark. Trademarks contribute to the brand value and identity and ultimately to the creation of revenues.

---

481. LT, Art. 2.
482. For analysis of intellectual property and sports, *see*: Naumovski G., Naumovski V. & Polenak Akimovska M., (2011). *Cybersquatting in the Social Networks: Additional Challenge for Sports Law, RIK, International Journal of Kinesiology and Other Related Sciences*; 39 (2), 159–163; Stojkov

*1009.* A trademark is defined as a right which protects a sign (mark) that in trade serves to distinguish goods, i.e., services of one natural or legal person, from the same or similar goods, i.e., services of another natural or legal person. The provisions of this law are in accordance with the Madrid Agreement on the International Registration of Trademarks and the Protocol to the Madrid Agreement.

*1010.* In respect of the protection of signs by trademarks in the Republic of Macedonia, foreign natural and legal persons enjoy the same rights as domestic natural and legal persons if this arises from international treaties or from the principle of reciprocity.

*1011.* More specifically, when it comes to sports trademarks, the following international conventions and agreements regarding trademarks are part of Macedonian legislation on trademarks: Madrid Agreement concerning the international registration of marks (1891);[483] Nice Agreement concerning the international classification of goods and services for the purposes of the registration of marks (1957);[484] the Convention Establishing the WIPO (1967);[485] the Vienna Agreement establishing an international classification of the figurative elements of marks (1973);[486] the Nairobi treaty on the protection of the Olympic symbol (1981);[487,488] the Protocol to the Madrid Agreement (1989);[489] Agreement on Trade-Related Aspects of Intellectual Property Rights (TRIPS Agreement) (1994);[490] and the Singapore Treaty on the law of trademarks (TLT) (2006).[491]

*1012.* The current Macedonian trademark legislation framework is mostly part of the LIP,[492] particularly its Chapter II, as well as the Rulebook on Trademarks, enacted by the Industrial Property Protection Office.[493] According to LIP, Article 3, "Trademark" (mark for goods, service mark, collective, and certification mark) is

---

A., Naumovski G. & Naumovski V., (2011). *Copyright and Related Rights Through Another Perspective: Interdisciplinarity of Economics, Law and Sports*, RIK, International Journal of Kinesiology and Other Related Sciences; 39 (2), 139–144; Polenak Akimovska M., Naumovski G. & Naumovski V. (2011). *Material Rights of the Trademark Holder and Analysis of Sports Trademark Cases*. RIK, International Journal of Kinesiology and Other Related Sciences; 39 (1), 53–59; Naumovski, G., Polenak-Akimovska M. & Stojkov A. (2011), Protection and Acquistion of Trademarks: Importance for Sport Products, RIK, International Journal of Kinesiology and Other Related Sciences; 39 (1), 85–90; Naumovski, G., Polenak Akimovska M. (2011). Basic Framework of Cybersquatting Disputes: Trademarks and Domain Names Interdependence, Law and Economy; (4–6), 845–857.

483. Notification of succession by the Republic of Macedonia: Jul. 23, 1993.
484. *Ibid.*
485. *Ibid.*
486. Notification of succession, Mar. 10, 1994. Official Journal of the Republic of Macedonia No. 19/2010.
487. Official Journal of the Republic of Macedonia, No. 165/2013.
488. Declaration/Notification of Succession: Jul. 23, 1993.
489. Official Journal of the Republic of Macedonia, No. 12/2002.
490. Official Journal of the Republic of Macedonia, No. 07/03.
491. Official Journal of the Republic of Macedonia, No. 19/10.
492. Official Journal No. 21/09, 24/11, 12/14, 41/14, 152/15, 53/16, 83/18, 31/20.
493. Official Journal of the Republic of Macedonia No. 92/2009.

defined as industrial property right acquired in a procedure in compliance with LIP and which protects the trade sign.[494] The Law on the Protection of Competition (LPC) is also relevant.[495]

## §4. Ownership of Clubs

*1013.* The LS regulates issues related to the legal status, organization and registration of entrepreneurs and legal persons in the sports system.

*1014.* For the purpose of performing sports activities and sports occupations, a sports organization may be established as an association or as a company.

*1015.* This part of the monograph will analyze the legal aspects of club ownership and potential problems related to the announced privatization of sports clubs.

*1016.* Sports clubs in the Republic of Macedonia are most often registered as sports associations, i.e., as voluntary nonprofit organizations based on the freedom of association of several individuals and/or legal persons, organized on the basis of the statute and established to achieve a common goal in sports.

*1017.* Although sports associations and sports companies have a similar organizational structure, since they are sports organizations, there are still differences. Namely, a sports company may be established by legal or natural persons with the status of a joint-stock company or a limited liability company, with the primary goal of gaining profit, while this is not the case with a sports association. In addition, sports companies must respect the regulations of commercial law.

*1018.* According to the Law on companies, the persons who establish the company and the persons who subsequently join it are the members with limited liability in the limited liability company and shareholders in the joint-stock company.

*1019.* Part I Organization of sport, Chapter 2 Public regulation explains in detail how sports associations and sports companies are organized; we will repeat certain specifics that are characteristic of ownership in sports clubs.

494. *See* LIP, Art. 175.
495. Official Journal of the Republic of Macedonia No. 80/99.

## Chapter 3. Private Regulation

*1020.* As noted in the previous chapters, private regulations in the field of sports in the Republic of Macedonia include various contracts which regulate relations and to which, in principle, the rules of the law of contracts and torts apply. The application of the rules of the law of contracts and torts for the regulation of contractual relations inter partes in the domain of sports law is framed by the provisions of LS. In other words, in the Republic of Macedonia, sports organizations and athletes themselves regulate relations between themselves and with third parties, but in accordance with the law. A unique and efficient legal system in the field of sports is created by the fact that private regulations must be in accordance with the laws and by-laws of the Republic of Macedonia. Indeed, this is one of the important preconditions because it is necessary to strengthen the private initiative for the development of sports in its entirety.

*1021.* In the Republic of Macedonia, freedom of agreement is guaranteed, so there are numerous agreements from the world of sports commercialization: Agreement on Television Rights, Trade Agreement, Sponsorship Agreement, Business Cooperation Agreement, but also other agreements in the field of media and copyright, as well as other forms such as direct agreements. In this Chapter, due to space constraints, we will mention only some of them.

*1022.* With the development of sports and their commercialization, sponsorship support is growing. However, the increasingly growing money in the sports market in the Republic of Macedonia has not been accompanied by appropriate regulations. The sponsorship agreement still falls into the category of unnamed agreements, which means that no rules have been defined that would regulate these agreements. The general rules of contract law apply to the conclusion and realization of the rights and obligations of the sponsorship agreement.

*1023.* The sponsor, on the one hand, and the sponsored, on the other hand, have complete autonomy of will in terms of regulating their relations. On the other hand, it also means that there is no unique type, i.e., form of the sponsorship agreement. Nevertheless, in practice, certain rights and obligations have been established arising from the sponsorship agreement, which are regularly contracted.

*1024.* The obligation of the sponsor always consists in paying a certain amount of money, providing certain services, transferring ownership or handing over the use of certain things, while the obligations of the sponsored differ from agreement to agreement.

*1025.* The Sponsorship Agreement is characterized by the fact that the support provided by the sponsor is equal to the value of the goods on which it acquires the right of use, and it is mostly the image of the sponsored athlete, sports organization or sports event, or the value of services provided by the sponsored.

*1026.* A potential problem can arise if a sponsor sponsors several sports organizations in the same competition rank, and in this case, it may jeopardize the very regularity of the competition. Also, the regularity of the competition can be called into question if the sponsor of the competition also sponsors one of the sports organizations or the athlete participating in this competition.

*1027.* From this aspect, the autonomy of the will of the contractor can thus lead to problems. These problems can be prevented by adopting special rules that would provide a framework for the effect of the Sponsorship Agreement. In any case, the validity of the agreement cannot be called into question due to noncompliance with sports regulations. For example, the exclusivity clause, when the sponsored person cannot conclude a sponsorship agreement with a third party, is something that may be contrary to the Law on the Protection of Competition.

*1028.* In addition, when an athlete, sports organization or event has more than one sponsor, the agreement must clearly define the rights, restrictions and corresponding obligations of each sponsor, as well as of the sponsored parties. Initially, the sponsored person is obliged to inform possible sponsors about what sponsors he/she is already in a contractual relationship with.

*1029.* On the other hand, the sponsor is obliged to refrain from all actions that may negatively affect the image of the sponsor during the term of the sponsorship agreement. If the athlete behaved differently, he/she would prevent the sponsor from making a business profit, which is why it entered the sponsorship.

*1030.* Agreements that sports organizations conclude with athletes who perform for them, as a rule, provide for certain restrictions for athletes in terms of concluding individual sponsorship agreements. Also, these agreements contain provisions on the right of the sports organization to use the name and image of the athlete.

# Conclusion

*1031.* This monograph is the outcome of numerous years of methodical and applied studies. It was written, on the one hand, with the desire to familiarize the scientific and professional public with the opportunities in the development of sports law in the Republic of Macedonia; on the other hand, it is part of a great project of the International Encyclopedia of Law within Kluwer Law International. Furthermore, this monograph can be a substantial textbook for students of faculties and colleges where sports law is studied. Even though the monograph is envisioned for the academic and professional public as well as students who show interest in studying sports law in Macedonia, it can also be the subject of interest of a broader audience concerned with sports law development.

*1032.* The objective of this monograph guided the content and the technique of elaboration of the text. Sports law in Macedonia is presented in four chapters: "Organization of sports," "Legal status of athletes," "Doping and sports" and "Sport and commerce."

*1033.* Given the low number of books on the same topic, this monograph is an effort to consolidate, in one place, and present all legal and statutory resolutions to these issues through the examination of laws and by-laws regulating them in the field of public and private law. In order to reach certain conclusions regarding the development of sports law, it was necessary to draw and present a number of statutory solutions, primarily contained in the LS, and then solutions of other regulations which are a subsidiary source of sports rights.

*1034.* Based on the detailed analysis conducted with the application of appropriate methods of scientific research (primarily normative, sociological, methods of induction and deduction, analysis and synthesis), the authors arrived at the following conclusions.

*1035.* In Macedonia, the sports system is very complex since it targets three areas: (1) the state institutions, (2) the sports associations, and (3) the business sector. In order to manage the system, competencies are divided between the governmental and nongovernmental sectors. This further points to the conclusion that in sports in the Republic of Macedonia, public and private regulations are part of a single legal system. Based on the showed research, an overall conclusion is presented, which is also a *de lege ferenda* proposal that it is compulsory to enhance the private initiative in sport within the framework provided by law, which is estimated to contribute to greater development and strengthening of sports law in Macedonia.

*1036.* The LS regulates in detail both the legal status of a professional athlete and an amateur athlete. In an effort to define the legal and employment status of the athlete, his/her rights and obligations, the social, health and pension insurance and the issue of tax treatment of the athlete were analyzed.

*1037.* Based on the attained research outcomes, it was concluded that in terms of regulating the legal status, public law regulations are dominant. Private regulation is present through the statutory possibility to regulate the rights and obligations of athletes. Differences between professional and nonprofessional athletes are reflected in both public and private regulation.

*1038.* Macedonian legislation is restrictive concerning the use of doping. The legislation on the illegal use of doping in the Republic of Macedonia is based on two main sources: (1) through the health protection provisions of the Law on Sports, and (2) indirectly through certain provisions. Criminal Code provisions, international conventions and agreements regarding doping are also implemented.

*1039.* From the aspect of commercial objectives, it is perceived that in contemporary society, this use is progressively visible, given the fact that sports in the modern marketplace are a more and more profitable business. In the Republic of Macedonia, there is an increasing necessity for the use of sports for commercial purposes, where the source of large incomes can be seen through the transfer of athletes, sale of TV broadcasting rights, sponsorship of athletes, etc.

*1040.* A general conclusion was reached that Macedonian sports law is a multidisciplinary field of law (sui generis) in which public and private law meet: sports law and civil law (issue of ownership of sports fields), sports and trade (management in sports clubs), sports and industrial property and copyright and related rights (trademarks, broadcasting rights), sports and labor (relationship between a professional athlete and a sports organization), sports and criminal law (existence of illicit and negative manifestations at sports competitions and fields, doping), sports and public international law (role of international sports organizations in the promotion of sports), sports and private international law (particularly regarding the status of foreign athletes).

# Selected Bibliography


Akimovska-Maletic, I., Naumovski, G., Chapkanov, D.: Analysis of the Regulation of Sport As Activity Of Public Interest In The European Union And In The Macedonian Legislation, Research in Kinesiology, 2017, Vol. 45, No. 1, pp. 72–77.

Amelotti, M., (1955). Laposizione degli atleti di fronte al diritto Romano, Studia et Documenta Historiae etluris, 32, pp. 123–156.

Ankum, H., (1995). Societas Omnium Bonorum and Dos in Classical Roman Law. Israel Law Review, 29(1–2), 105–129.

Begović, M. 2021. Sports Law in Montenegro: Origins and Contemporary Development. Entertainment and Sports Law Journal, 19: 1, pp. 1–8.

Buy, F., Marmayou, J., Poracchia, D., Rizzo, F. (2015). Droit du Sport, LGDJ, Lextenso edition.

Coakley J. (1994). Sport in Society: Issues and Controversies, Mosbey.

Dimova, K. (1978). Za tancot na Tetovskata Menada [On the Dance of the Maenad of Tetovo. In Macedonian]. Prilozi za istorijata na fizičkata kultura na Makedonija, Komitet za fizička kultura na SRM, 4, pp. 109–112.

Djurdjevic, N., Micovic, M., Vukovic, Z. (2014), Ugovori u Sportu, Pravni fakultet Univerziteta u Kragujevcu.

Du Cange, et al. (1883), Glossarium mediae et infimae latinitatis, éd. augm., Niort: L. Favre, 1883–1887, t. 3, col. 141a.

Encyclopaedia Macedonica, Macedonian Academy of Arts and Sciences, Skopje, 2009, p. 1772.

Forcellini,. Totius Latinitatis Lexicon, Tomus Secundus.

Galactic, M. (2015). Lex sportiva—Origin and Meaning of the Term, Themes, XXXIX, edition 2, Niš, pp. 559–577.

Gardiner, S., O'Leary, J., Welch, R., Boyers, S., Naidoo, U. (2012). Sports Law, Routledge.

Georgievski, B. (2016). Abuse of substances in sports. Shtip: University "Goce Delchev," Shtip, Faculty of medical sciences.

Godefroy, F. (1883) Dictionnaire de l'ancienne langue française et de tous ses dialectes du IXe au XVe siècle, Tome deuxième, Casteillon-Dyvis, F. Vieweg, Paris. p. 517, 634,

Huizinga, J. (2016). Homo Ludens: A Study of the Play-Eleent in Culture, Angelico Press.

Jorgić, B., Aleksandrović, M., Mirić, F., Čolović, H., Dimitrijević, L. (2020). Holistički pristup adaptiranoj fitičkoj aktivnostim, Fakultet sporta i fizičkog vaspitanja Univerziteta u Nišu, Niš.

Juvenal, 10.356.
Konstantinov D. (1978). Sport and Military Excersises of the Members of the Armed Forces of the Internal Macedonian Revolutionary Organization of the Ilinden Period (1903) [Sportski i voeni vezbi na pripadnicite na oruzenite sili od Vnatrešnata makedonska revolucionerna organizacija od ilindenskata epopeja (1903). In Macedonian]. Prilozi za istorijata na fizičkata kultura na Makedonija, Republički Komitet za Fizička Kultura Skopje, 4, pp. 67–79.
Kuševski V. (1983). The Existence of Folk-Forms of body Exercises and Competition among the Miacs according to Djurchin Cocale's Autobiography [Za prisustvoto I neguvanjeto na narodni formi na telesni vežbanja i natprevaruvanja srede Mijacite sportd Avtobiografijata na Gjurchin Kokale (1775–1863). In Macedonian]. Prilozi za istorijata na fizičkata kultura na Makedonija, Fakultet t za fizička kultura Skopje, 1, pp. 67–79.
Naumovski G. (2004).The Importance of Certain Roman Law Solutions for Contemporary Sports Law, 2nd FIEP Congress, Proceedings, Vrnjacka Banja, 2004, p. 482.
Naumovski G. (2004).The Importance of Certain Roman Law Solutions for Contemporary Sports Law, 2nd FIEP Congress, Proceedings, Vrnjacka Banja, 2004, p. 482.
Naumovski G., Naumovski V. & Polenak Akimovska M., (2011). Cybersquatting in the Social Networks: Additional Challenge for Sports Law, RIK, International Journal of Kinesiology and Other Related Sciences; 39 (2), 159–163.
Naumovski, G. (2004). The Concept of Societas in Justinina's Legislation, Proceedings of the International Symposium "Contemporary Law, Legal Science and Justinians Codification," Faculty of Law Skopje, Skopje and Ohrid, 2004, p. 515–523.
Naumovski, G., Polenak-Akimovska M. & Stojkov A. (2011), Protection and Acquistion of Trademarks: Importance for Sport Products, RIK, International Journal of Kinesiology and Other Related Sciences; 39 (1), 85–90
Naumovski, G. (2004). The Importance of Certain Roman Law Solutions for Contemporary Sports Law, 2nd FIEP Congress, Proceedings, Vrnjacka Banja, pp. 481–486.
Naumovski, G., Akimovska, P.M., Naumovski V. (2011). Roman Law and The Foundations of Contemporary Sports law: The Approach of Justinian's Legislation, Research in Kinesiology, 39(2), p. 197–200.
Nešić, B. (2020). Sportsko pravo, Sportska akademija, Beograd.
Panagiotopoulos, D. (2017). Sports Law, Lex Sportiva & Lex Olympica, Biblioedit, Athens, 2017.
Pharr, C. (1952): The Theodosian Code and Novels And The Sirmondian Constitutions A Translation with Commentary, Glossary and Bibliography By Clyde Pharr, Princeton University Press.
Pleket, H.W. (2001). Greek sport and Greek athletes. The International Sports Law Journal, (5/6), 4–5.
Polenak Akimovska M., Naumovski G. & Naumovski V. (2011). Material Rights of the Trademark Holder and Analysis of Sports Trademark Cases. RIK, International Journal of Kinesiology and Other Related Sciences; 39 (1), 53–59.

Pop-Gjorchev B. (1975). The Appearance and Development of Football in Macedonia until the First World War. [Pojava i razvitok na fudbalot vo Makedonija do Prvata svetska vojna. In Macedonian]. Komitet za Fizička Kultura Skopje, 1 pp. 83–86.

Povil, A.C, and Paloma, J.C.B. (1998). Origin of Sports Law. Fundamental Principles of Sports Law. Law in Sport. Tempus Joint European Project, Lectures and Summaries of the Intensive Course. Sofia: National Sports Academy.

Schriodt, B. (1981). Sports of the Byzantine Empire. Journal of Sport History, 8(3), p. 41.

Stanimirovic D. (1975). Elements and Appearance of Modern Sports in Macedonian untill World War I. [Elementi i pojavi na modernite sportovi vo Makedonija do Prvata svetska vojna. In Macedonian]. Komitet za Fizička Kultura Skopje, 1 pp. 73–82.

Stanimirovic D. (1975). Gimnazium vo antickiot grad Stibera [The Gymnasium in the Ancient City of Styberra. In Macedonian]. Prilozi za istorijata na fizičkata kultura na Makedonija, Komitet za fizička kultura na SRM, 1, pp. 93–112.

Stanimirovic D. (1976), Svedoštva za gladijatorski borbi vo antickiot grad Stobi [Testimonies for Gladiators' Fight in the Ancient City of Stobi. In Macedonian]. Prilozi za istorijata na fizičkata kultura na Makedonija, Komitet za fizička kultura na SRM, 2. pp. 107–114.

Stanimirovic D. (1977), Aktivnostite na fizičkata kultura vo rimskite termi so poseben osvrt na tie vo antičkiot grad Skupi [Activities of Physical Culture in Roman Thermae with special reference to those of the Ancient City of Scupi. In Macedonian]. Skopje, Prilozi za istorijata na fizičkata kultura na Makedonija, Komitet za fizička kultura na SRM, 3, pp. 103–114.

Stojkov A., Naumovski G. & Naumovski V., (2011). Copyright and Related Rights Through Another Perspective: Interdisciplinarity of Economics, Law and Sports, RIK, International Journal of Kinesiology and Other Related Sciences; 39 (2), pp. 139–144.

# Selected Bibliography

# Index

*The numbers here refer to paragraph numbers.*

## Index

www.ingramcontent.com/pod-product-compliance
Ingram Content Group UK Ltd.
Pitfield, Milton Keynes, MK11 3LW, UK
UKHW020140290926
15471UKWH00003B/615

9 789403 528465